DRUG POLITICS

DRUG POLITICS

Dirty Money
and Democracies

BY DAVID C. JORDAN

University of Oklahoma Press : Norman

Also by David C. Jordan

(With Arthur P. Whitaker) *Nationalism in Contemporary Latin America* (New York, 1966)

World Politics in Our Time (Lexington, 1970)

(Editor) *A Strategy for Latin America in the Nineties* (Washington, D.C., 1988)

Revolutionary Cuba and the End of the Cold War (Lanham, 1993)

(Coauthor) *Making Democracy Work in the Americas* (Washington, D.C., 1994)

Library of Congress Cataloging-in-Publication Data

Jordan, David C.
    Drug Politics : dirty money and democracy / by David C. Jordan.
        p.   cm.
    Includes bibliographical references and index.
    ISBN: 0–8061–3174–8 (cloth : alk. paper)
    1. Drug traffic.   2. Money laundering.   3. Political corruption.
    4. Organized crime.   I. Title.
    HV5801.J66   1999
    363.45—dc21   99–34614
                                                                 CIP

1   2   3   4   5   6   7   8   9   10

Dedicated to the memory of

Whittle Johnston

(1927–1996)

and

to Victoria Roberts,

my daughter

CONTENTS

ILLUSTRATIONS

FIGURES

TABLES

PREFACE

I began this book without knowing where it would lead me. My preliminary assumptions were that narcotics trafficking was best understood in a supply-and-demand context, that criminal elements were taking advantage of the addictive habit and profiting from it, and that traffickers assisted producers to meet demand with credit, transport, and distribution capabilities. According to this last assumption, traffickers actively corrupted police and judges in order to facilitate their illegal business. In more corrupt states, criminals bought off politicians who aided them in return for substantial payoffs. My understanding of the nature of narcotics trafficking evolved, however, as the book progressed.

In my new understanding I found governments and banks deeply involved in, dependent on, and even facilitating, if not promoting, the drug trade. True, both governments and banks cracked down on traffickers and money launderers, but the picture emerged that some had a greater interest in continuing the trade than in shutting it down. This finding had significant implications for other assumptions current in political science literature. If governments exercised only the forms of democracy and not the substance, did their claims to being accountable regimes remain valid? If democratic and authoritarian regimes promoted the drug trade, did this undermine claims of democratic peace? If the casualties from the drug trade exceeded those of many or most conventional wars, did the concept of war need to be broadened or transformed? Finally, if the diagnosis of the problem was essentially incomplete, were not the solutions likely to fail? These are some of the issues this book explores.

This book is not intended to be a historical investigation; rather it is intended to be an analysis that connects a maze of already existing information. The material included in this book was chosen because it focuses on a particular area, person, or event relevant to the analysis. I am deeply indebted to the many scholars past and present from whose excellent scholarship this book draws. It is my hope that the facts and information presented will permit a better understanding of the political, economic, and cultural issues shaping the new world. Political science uses history as a tool to help understand the present and project the future with coherence. The task of this book is to progress toward that understanding.

The drug problem is of worldwide concern. Three main regions in the world generate opium and heroin products: Southeast Asia, Southwest Asia, and Latin America. The principal producing areas of the Southeast Asia region—Laos, Burma, and China—manufacture over 50 percent of the world's total supply of opium and heroin. Thailand is the primary heroin refiner, and Thailand and China are the principal exporters for the region.

Southwest Asia produces 40 percent of the world's opium and over 40 percent of the world's heroin. Areas manufacturing heroin are Afghanistan, Pakistan, and parts of the former Soviet Union such as Turkmenistan, Uzbekistan, Tajikistan, and Kazakhstan. Much of the heroin in this region is refined and transported through Pakistan, but it is also refined and transported to the West through Russia.

By the mid-1990s Latin America produced approximately 3 percent of the world's opium and a similar amount of the world's heroin; in the 1980s it had produced almost none. This region is now the world's principal producer of cocaine, with Peru, Colombia, and Bolivia being the chief growers and Colombia the primary refiner and exporter.

While the growing and manufacturing of drugs in these regions is an important issue, there is much more to the drug problem than that. The problem extends to dirty money from drug trafficking and other illicit businesses, laundered through an intricate web of financial dealings that encircles the globe and protected both culturally and politically around the world. For many countries, criminal, financial, scientific, social, and political factors associated with this drug culture combine to threaten democratic stability and the international political environment.

This book analyzes how narcotics trafficking and corruption have deeply penetrated the international environment in the post–cold war era and the impact of this development on the theories of democracy and international relations. It explores the connections of the narcotics traffic to state policies, international finance, the globalization of organized crime, and culture wars. By exposing some of the depravity in the new world environment, this book points to the possibility of an international system that may enjoy the advantages of globalization without the scourge of corruption and unaccountable leadership.

ACKNOWLEDGMENTS

I am grateful to a number of people who helped in preparing this manuscript. Several students in my graduate seminars were particularly helpful. Michael Ard, Daniel Crocker, Stephen Holmes, Brian Menard, and Bill Prillaman provided insightful observations and participated in invaluable discussions. I am especially grateful for Joe Douglass's reading and commenting on several preliminary chapters. I also want to thank the many people who worked to edit and publish this book, especially Kimberly Wiar, Jo Ann Reece, and Ursula Smith, whose copyediting was outstanding. Of course, responsibility for the views expressed in this work is mine alone.

◆ ◆ ◆

I am indebted to my dear, admired, and remembered friend and colleague, Whittle Johnston, to whom this book is dedicated, for the many conversations we had over the years about the nature of democracy and many other issues raised here. This book is also dedicated to my daughter, Victoria Roberts, without whose hard work it could not have been completed. I am deeply grateful for her devoted efforts.

PART I

Drug Trafficking, State Corruption, and the Crisis of Democratic Theory

CHAPTER 1

INTRODUCTION

The growth and spread of narcotics trafficking accentuate the importance of the nation-state and the democratic republic in post–cold war world politics, even as the globalization of the market economy has led some to believe that the problems of the new world order were either too large for the nation state and therefore required supranational institutions or were too small and required substate or nongovernmental organizations (NGOs).[1]

The supranationalists can be either globalists or regionalists. The globalists seek a universal rule-making organization, the demise of state sovereignty, and global regulation of the economy. The regionalists, on the other hand, best typified by European integrationists, seek, under the Maastricht Treaty, a central bank that would set monetary policy no European parliament could hold accountable.

Proponents of a network of nongovernmental organizations find in computers and telecommunications the information systems that would allow NGOs to deliver services that governments cannot match. NGOs are credited, for example, with forcing the United States and Mexico to consider cross-border pollution problems, health and safety provisions, and other issues that were not initially on the North American Free Trade Agreement (NAFTA) agenda.

The claim that narcotics trafficking revitalizes the understanding of the importance of the nation-state and the democratic republic does not belittle the significant growth of supranational institutions or NGOs. But it does highlight the fact that states ruled by accountable governments cannot and must not yield their power to repress transnational criminal enterprises to either supranational or substate entities. If the democratic states were to fail in this struggle, then the state system, supranational institutions, and NGOs would all be part of a criminal international world. The degree to which the globalization process, coupled with narcotics trafficking, is facilitating this corruption of the state—a process called narcostatization—emphasizes the importance of maintaining healthy nation-states and democratic republics.

The amount of money created outside the control of the individual states is enormous. It is capable of forcing devaluations and making huge profits on bets against national currencies. This global capital should not be considered as just a wealth-creating phenomena but as power in itself, a power that can devalue currencies, discipline governments and companies, and shelter profits from state taxes. Among the most prominent examples are the seven funds created by George Soros. Born in Hungary, Soros became an American citizen in the 1950s. Backed now by great European wealth, he operates globally outside the U.S. regulatory system. All of the Soros funds are offshore—that is, outside the control of the federal govenment—and do not have U.S. citizens as investors. Soros himself is the prototype transnational capitalist. His speculative operations have created a vast amount of unregulated world money that flows in and out of national economies at the push of a computer key.[2] His Quota Fund wages huge bets on global currency, bond, equity, and commodity market trends.[3] The most famous Soros fund, the Quantum Fund N.V., has speculated against European and Asian currencies and made over $1 billion against the British pound in 1992.

Transnational, or "overworld," elites like George Soros not only make huge sums in their speculative bets, they also transfer money to pet projects worldwide that sometimes exceed the foreign aid that even the U.S. government provides. For instance, in October 1997, the Soros Foundation announced plans, in addition to its work in eastern Europe, to provide between $350 million and $500 million to Moscow for maternal and child health care and for the government's military reform plans. In comparison, the United States government gave Russia $95 million in all of 1996. In 1998 Soros acknowledged second thoughts about his activities in relation to Russia.[4]

One of the most interesting aspects of this overworld money has been its support for "alternatives" to the drug war, as they are euphemistically called. Transnational capitalist interests can operate locally and globally to weaken state resistance to drug trafficking. Because the supranational organizations and NGOs are too weak to deal with the narcotics problem, the state and its uncorrupted institutions are the principal means for combating trafficking. The new internationalism requires the state to forge relations with institutions of other states committed to controlling the drug trade. Thus the corruption of the state itself—and of its law enforcement agencies and judiciaries—can become a serious problem beyond its own borders, while within its borders, corruption undermines the accountability of the democratic republic.

CORRUPTION

Corruption can occur at every level of government and in all aspects of society, including the financial community. The very concept of democracy, arguably the most critical aspect of our culture, is under siege. Until now, experts have maintained that democracy is flourishing in the new global environment. However, new research shows that economic globalization, while in some ways helping democratization, is also hindering the consolidation of accountable government in many countries. Indeed, criminal, financial, scientific, social, and political factors are combining to threaten the international political environment.

Corruption generally is understood to be a discreet but illegitimate use of money by public officials or private citizens for illegal gain. Traditionally, corruption is considered to be an isolated event without a pervasive effect throughout a political system, even when it is chronic in police or other branches of a government's bureaucracy.[5]

Some political scientists maintain that corruption is a structural phenomenon of the political system.[6] In this view, the corrupt political system is far more powerful than civil society, and extortion and bribery become common practices. Official extortion takes place when public officials extract kickbacks or other payments from individuals for services, benefits, or permits the government normally offers free or with a minimal charge. Corruption within the political system also takes the shape of bribery, where strong forces in civil society buy favors from a weaker state.[7]

Extortion and bribery can reflect a corrupt civil society as well as a corrupt state. Contemporary circumstances in some countries indicate a merger between a corrupt political system and criminal elements of civil society.[8] Members of the ruling elite in both authoritarian and electoral governments find the merging of organized crime with the state useful, if not necessary, for maintaining power. Regimes with a tradition of elite domination, even where an electoral process exists, may find the temptation to work with organized crime particularly irresistible. When government and organized crime are allied, structural corruption is in place.

Of course, ruling elites are not always corrupt; they will, in fact, often use the forces of government to constrain corruption when it is in their interest. In this case, criminal mafias use their power within society against honest government officials. Sometimes the criminal mafias receive cooperation from government officials jockeying for influence within the ruling class. Officials in this kind of government ultimately manipulate drug trafficking as the most lucrative criminal activity. As one key aid to the leader of the Mexican Gulf cartel, Oscar Lopez Olivarez, reported, "Narco-trafficking is something that is completely managed by the government because from the protection of the marijuana plants . . . everything is completely controlled, first by the army, then by the federal judicial police, even including the crop eradication section of the Attorney General's Office, which even inspects the crops on the farms that are included within the approved system."[9]

A dynamic structural model stressing the merging of government and organized crime suggests that the political systems of certain countries are in a partial civil war. While elements within the government seek to control drug trafficking, other elements of the government form an alliance with the traffickers. The complex relation between elites and traffickers may corrupt both the democratic and the authoritarian state. Narcostatization does not respect political systems.

Since the end of the cold war, radical ethnic nationalisms and major cultural clashes have been portrayed as the most likely forms of conflict in the new international environment.[10] Although these clashes certainly demand attention, conflicts between and within states, in the context of massive criminal and illegal government behavior, should be of at least equal concern. The increasingly rapid spread of global capitalism creates expanded opportunities for the former regionally based underworld networks to operate globally. When spreading international crime combines with corrupt elements of government, the possibilities for domestic and international conflict increase remarkably.

THE POST–COLD WAR ERA

For some theorists, the end of the cold war has meant the triumph of liberal democracy and capitalism and an ongoing, generally positive trend in human development. This has come to be known as the "end of history" theory.[11] According to this theory, the basic positive trends of a cooperative international order lead to conditions whereby economies gradually combine and nondemocratic states, through a combination of internal pressure and external persuasion, gradually develop more enlightened governments. The consequences of this evolution are, quite naturally, the weakening of nationalist agendas and of the independence of states.[12] At the same time, international free trade expands under the World Trade Organization (WTO), regional and world currencies rise, and eventually there is generalized world cooperation.

The process of growing economic cooperation and the spread of democratic governments under the leadership and prodding of the United States is known as "neoliberalism" and is seen as an essentially benign development. However, the dark elements in this rosy scenario for the post–cold war era have been the growth of narcotics trafficking, the spread of organized crime, and the corruption of governments.

The three major developments of the neoliberal order that threaten the state-to-state institutional cooperation of post–cold war democracies are (1) the globalization of economic finance, (2) the growing dependence of states on drug profits to service debts,[13] and (3) the expanding dependence of a worldwide population on addictive drugs. Threats to democratic regimes are facilitated by the globalization of economic finance corrupted by organized crime. The main economic engine of organized crime is narcotics trafficking, which generates liquidity for states and profits for transnational financial institutions. The present increase in drug trafficking, in consumption of drugs, and in the widespread effects of drug trafficking, such as narcostatization, undermines domestic peace, strains international relations, weakens the democratic state, and seriously threatens fragile transitions to democracy.

David Held helps us understand that it is the globalized neoliberal system, more than a simple supply-and-demand, production-and-consumption concept, that explains what happens within political societies. The degree to which states are unable to control their own economic decision making alters the nature of democratic accountability. Held exposes the need to understand the problems of the democratic state in the context of the global economy.

> The underlying premises of democratic theory, in both its liberal and radical guises, have . . . been: that democracies can be treated as essentially self-contained units; that democracies are clearly demarcated one from another; that change within democracies can be understood largely with reference to the internal structures and dynamics of national democratic polities; and that democratic politics is itself ultimately an expression of the interplay between forces operating within the nation-state . . . [but] the global interconnectedness of political decisions and outcomes raise[s] questions which go to the heart of the categories of classical democratic theory and its contemporary variants.[14]

The implications of rivalry within the international system are that states will indulge in narcotics trafficking in order to defend themselves and to compete economically with other states. Even where a real interest in cooperation exists—or should exist—narcotics trafficking may be forced upon the states by the outside system. Domestic considerations may be subordinate to the international systemic pressures of competition. The structural implications of the neoliberal system make it in the interest of states to exploit that structure for their economic benefit.

NARCOTICS TRAFFICKING AND NEOLIBERALISM

The narcotics trafficking problem links governments in two ways to the international system. In the first, large powers use narcotics for economic and strategic purposes. The classic historical example of this is found in the nineteenth-century opium wars between the British and the Chinese. In the second way, small powers use the drug trade for defensive purposes—such as to reduce their economic vulnerability. In both ways, the states can be corrupted by the narcotics trade.

The first process is characterized in the use of narcotics trafficking by larger powers to control lesser states. Initially, this process was not seen as having a corrupting effect on the larger state's political system. It is quite evident that, as smaller states have become involved in the narcotics trade, clandestinely rather than openly, corruption within those states becomes a notorious given. But, corruption is increasingly detectable in the more developed and larger states as well. This has led to growing global concern of narcostatization—the corruption of the political regime as a result of narcotics trafficking.

Three interrelated phenomena work synergistically to produce the narcostate: organized crime, government policy, and transnational capitalism. The narcostate may develop in existing democratic regimes, in authoritarian regimes, or in regimes that are in transition to or from democracy. Narcostatization undermines weak democracies and transforms consolidated and transitional democratic regimes into pseudo-democracies, or anocracies. In the anocratizing process both consolidated and transitional democracies are in fact corrupted, and the political or ruling class maintains itself in power despite the apparent existence of contested elections and full public participation.

The term "anocracy" is sometimes used to describe a system where power is not concentrated in the hands of public authorities. However, for purposes of regime accountability, this book will use "anocracy" to mean a regime where democratic and autocratic features are mixed. The forms of democracy are in place, but the realities of power concentration in the executive preponderate over institutional and electoral constraints on the chief executive's power. The narcostate is one particular form of anocracy. Not all anocracies are narcostates, but narcostatization produces a form of anocracy. Some narcostatizations impact existing democracies and produce narcodemocracies; some impact autocracies and produce narcoauthoritarian regimes; some impact transition processes and produce narcoanocracies. For the public, there is little existential difference between narcoanocracies and narcodemocracies except that the latter are reversions from democracies and the former are incomplete democratic transitions.

The expectation for the evolving neoliberal world order was that cooperation would increase and economies would be combined, such as in the European Union. A consequence of this evolution was to be the weakening of individual states' policies and independence.[15] But unexpected problems for this new world order include the growth of government corruption, the globalization of organized crime, and international money laundering. The impacts of this process are seen in the loss of control over the domestic economy, a decrease in political accountability, and problems in social behavior. Another possible consequence of the globalization of the world economy is the growth of worker discontent. In fact, much of the criticism of the neoliberal order focuses on its threat to workers' interests. Indeed, in the late 1990s, the growth of unemployment in Europe undermined the movement toward a single monetary unit.

In the post–World War II economic settlement, the international system, as embodied in the Bretton Woods Agreement, protected the welfare state and organized workers from the pressures of capital markets that would destroy the protectionist policies of the states. This system has been called "embedded liberalism."[16] The belief was that states would protect their societies from the cost of global market fluctuations by maintaining an autonomy in domestic economic policy and implementing gradual trade liberalization.

The collapse of the Bretton Woods system in the 1970s made way for the neoliberal order. Capital flows were released from state control, and international cooperation among central banks became key to international financial stability. Central bankers of the Group of Ten (G-10)[17] created the Standing Committee on Banking Regulations and Supervisory Practices (the Basel Committee) in 1974 after the Franklin National Bank failed to share information about banks and regulatory systems. The Basel Committee laid down the principle that international banks should not escape supervision.[18] Nonetheless, regulation is difficult under the neoliberal system. It is vulnerable to attack because of drug trafficking and working-class discontent. And where the growth of unregulated trade and capital flows facilitate narcotics trafficking, the democratization process itself is threatened.

At certain levels of corruption, the democratic form can disguise the reality of dishonest elite control of the state. Such narco- or anocratic states are dangerous to their neighbors and vulnerable to intergovernmental conflict, civil war, and insurgency. Domestic and international low-level conflict become endemic among anocratic states, since these states are, by definition, unaccountable and subject to inconsistent policy pressures from below and from beyond their borders.

The economic transition of countries from statism to capitalism demonstrates the persistence of corruption. The euphoria in the United States over the alleged transitions of many governments from authoritarianism to democracy since the 1980s has been short-lived. Although Mexico's electoral system meets international standards, its transition from authoritarianism to democracy is more apparent than real. In the winter of 1995, the United States government took part in a multibillion dollar bailout of the Mexican government after a financial collapse of its economy. Despite many crises and political murders, Mexico is still considered to be in transition to democracy. However, its sensitivity to capital outflows in the neoliberal system have made the country vulnerable to dependence on drug revenues. Corrupt forces in the government and criminal cartels continue to take advantage of its vulnerability and dependence, furthering the criminalization of the state.

Nonetheless, the new internationalism stresses the need to see the state as made up of a variety of institutions rather than as a single unit. Consequently, part of the state can be corrupted while other parts, including the same institution, may remain healthy. This understanding of state-to-state relations is not part of the standard interpretation of how the states behave and of how the international system impacts the state.

THE STRUCTURAL AND THE INTENTIONAL PERSPECTIVES

Modern political theory explains social and international political developments as either systemic, that is, structural, or intentional. Through systemic explanations, political theorists attempt to rise above the viewpoints of the participants in a particular historical process. They stress that international results depend on structural analysis of the effects of the world setting and circumstances on the member states. Proponents of this perspective hold that the characteristics of international anarchy and the globalization of capitalism cause the corruption of the states. A structuralist interpretation of narcostatization would suggest that the logic of the post–cold war system in itself forces a state to become involved in narcotics trafficking.

The political perspective of Theda Skocpol, combined with the international relations perspective of Kenneth Waltz, explains the impact of narcotics trafficking on the international system. Skocpol claims that we can make sense of historical circumstantial patterns "only by focusing simultaneously on the interrelated situations of groups within specified societal institutional nexuses, and the interrelations of societies within dynamic international fields."[19] Waltz explains that the structure of the international system with its component parts determines the behavior of the states. It is the structure that determines the type of player likely to prosper in a given situation. For Waltz, if the structure determines that it is necessary for the units to help themselves, then all the units are compelled to behave according to the same standards: "The units of an anarchic system are functionally undifferentiated. The units of such an order are then distinguished primarily by their greater or lesser capabilities for performing similar tasks."[20] The implication of this structural theory is that, if drug trafficking enhances a state's relative power, other states will be compelled to participate in the trafficking of drugs in order to remain competitive.

The alternative to a structural interpretation is an agency, or intentional, one. The intentional interpretation sees an actor as choosing rationally from an available set of options. Rationality requires the actor to choose the course of action best suited to achieve the actor's goals. This "rational choice" explanation links the actors' intentions to the outcome. Many rational choice theorists use the "prisoner's dilemma" model to demonstrate how each of two actors, when following individual interests, ends up worse off than if he or she had acted to achieve a common goal.[21] Both intentional and structural explanations could lead to the conclusion that the narcostatization process cannot be prevented from spreading in the current international environment. However, if the state is made up of a variety of institutions, and the signals from the international environment are multiple rather than unitary, then some parts of the state's institutions may be corrupted while others are not.

The determinist structural implications for the narcotics problem may be challenged if the United States pursues a strategy of seeking arrangements with those institutions in other states that combat the criminalization of their system. By supporting nation-state regulation of finance and trade, the United States, as the preponderant actor in the post–cold war environment, has the capability to shape the international structure and support an accountable system of democratic regimes and transnational capitalism.

IMPLICATIONS FOR THE UNITED STATES

The implication of the state interest in narcotics trafficking is that the United States may have to reevaluate its commitment to the globalization of an unregulated international economic system. It is not necessary here to stipulate what these controls should be—other than the need for state institutions to network internationally—but it is important to see how the growth of the unregulated international financial and trade system facilitates narcotics trafficking.

It cannot be disputed that the United States has felt the impact of drug trafficking in undermining its society and in weakening the will to combat widespread drug use. The war on drugs in the United States is not being won. According to the director of the U.S. Office of National Drug Control Policy (ONDCP), 12 million Americans used illegal drugs in 1995 and teen tolerance for drugs increased in that same year 167 percent among eighth graders, 81 percent among tenth graders, and 46 percent among twelfth graders. Addiction experts predict that about 820,000 of this new group of marijuana smokers will eventually try cocaine. The cost of drug abuse and trafficking is enormous:

- 100,000 deaths were recorded and $300 billion spent in the 1990s alone.
- 500,000 new emergency room cases occur each year.
- 250,000 Americans currently serve time for drug law violations.
- Drug use is involved in at least a third of all homicides, assaults, and property crimes.[22]

The prevailing U.S. government model for conducting the war on drugs is based on the supply-and-demand approach. An entire school of policy analysts contends that drug trafficking is driven by consumption. Some of these analysts, such as Peter Andreas, present the consumption model as a public health issue: "Changing course in drug policy requires redefining the problem as fundamentally a public health rather than a law enforcement and national security concern," Andreas has said. "In other words, the surgeon general, rather than the attorney general and a retired military general, should direct our drug policy."[23] Although Andreas offers a different perspective, his approach is still based on the supply-and-demand model.

The war on drugs was crippled in the 1980s and 1990s because policy makers adopted the supply-and-demand approach, which disregarded the roles of global financial institutions, governments, and cultural change. The supply-and-demand model focused on the impact of producer and consumer countries and trade routes. It did not bring into the equation the emergence of a global financial system that was out of the control of any single state. This growth in the global financial system, coupled with the liberalization of international trade, meant that states not only lost control of trade but also of their capital markets.

There has been a shift in emphasis from the supply to the demand side in the war on drugs, and prevention and reduction of drug addiction has become a primary goal of the U.S. government. But attention has been focused on the 20 percent of drug users, the hard-core users, who account for 80 percent of total street sales of cocaine, and resources have not been allocated to prevention programs for casual and nonusers. Since 1995, the White House's national drug control strategy has identified its top priority as support for drug treatment "so that those who need treatment can receive it."[24] For this priority, requests for funds increased in FY95 ($2.647 billion), FY96 ($2.827 billion), and FY97 ($2.908 billion).

The shift in emphasis to reducing demand via treatment—if it is to succeed—requires that the removal of hard-core users from the treatment centers exceed the number of casual users who become hard-core users. However, treatment that provides hard drugs for addicts has actually caused an increase in the numbers in treatment centers. The U.S. experience suggests that, if more resources are directed at hard-core users than casual users, the number of casual users increases. If this relationship is not understood, the current treatment policy of the United States, in both its domestic and foreign applications, will lead to increases in both hard-core and casual use of drugs.

Legitimate efforts to reduce demand and to treat victims of drug abuse have been vulnerable to the influence of those who would bring about drug liberalization under the slogan "harm reduction." The ultimate objective of those who exploit the U.S. demand-reduction strategy is easily seen as the liberalization and then the regulation of drugs.

FIVE ASSUMPTIONS BEHIND THE WAR ON DRUGS

This book challenges the premises of the five current assumptions behind the war on drugs. The first assumption provides the model for understanding the problem; it sets the problem up as simply an economic issue of supply and demand. Within this model there is a debate between those who emphasize the supply side and those who stress the demand. The supply-side focus aims at disrupting the flow of drugs to consumers. All the stages in the process are targeted: cultivation, processing, transit, wholesale distribution, and street sales.

Based on U.S. government findings that two hundred hectares of coca produce a metric ton of retail cocaine, crop eradication campaigns became one of the most significant features of the "stop the supply" strategy in the 1980s. But the supply focus also deals with the production-distribution networks. As a result, a vast number of government agencies are involved in disrupting the flow of drugs to consumers. This complex of agencies includes the Departments of State, Defense, Treasury, and Agriculture; the Central Intelligence Agency (CIA); the Drug Enforcement Administration (DEA); the Federal Bureau of Investigation (FBI); the U.S. Customs Service; the U.S. Forest Service; the border patrol; the Bureau of Land Management; the Bureau of Alcohol, Tobacco and Firearms (ATF); the Coast Guard; the National Guard; and four major intelligence centers: the DEA's in El Paso, Texas; the CIA's at Langley, Virginia; the FBI's at Johnstown, Pennsylvania; and the Treasury's at Arlington, Virginia.[25]

The supply-side focus attempts to disrupt the flow of profits back to cartel bosses. The effort to disrupt the money-laundering side of the business falls primarily on the Department of the Treasury's Financial Crimes Enforcement Network (FinCEN). The Federal Reserve banks report their cash-flow data to FinCEN monthly, which helps FinCEN identify areas for investigation. A principal tool of the Federal Reserve is the cash transaction report (CTR). Since 1970, all banks are required to report all cash transactions of $10,000 or more.

The supply-side focus has been under sustained assault from those who argue that the war on drugs has failed. This argument comes from individuals representing a number of groups whose agenda ranges from legalizing drugs to treating the issue as a public health problem. These groups claim that treatment is a more cost-effective way to reduce consumption. They call for a shift from the punitive paradigm to the treatment-and-prevention paradigm.[26] They argue that there are three fatal flaws in the supply-side war on drugs. The first is that illegality raises the price for drugs, thereby making it more profitable and hence more attractive to criminal gangs. This is the so-called profit paradox. The second is that efforts to crush the producers actually only spread production to new areas, the "hydra effect." The third flaw is the "punish to deter fallacy." Those who see supply-side strategy as failing point to the statistics that show that more than two-thirds of arrested heroin addicts, for example, return to drug use and criminal behavior upon release from jail. These critics call for a shift to a public health paradigm, which they claim would promote "healing without harm."[27] The public health paradigm, however, is only one more version of the supply-and-demand paradigm. In fact, public health proponents claim the drug trade is a business "driven by the laws of supply and demand."[28]

The second assumption at the base of the current war on drugs is that the major culprits are ethnic or national gangs. The picture that is constantly held before us is of organized criminal elements—such as the Russian and Sicilian mafias, the Chinese triads, and the Japanese yakuza—victimizing governments, populations, and financial institutions. This assumption would make sense if the problem were exclusively one of a criminal economic group facilitating the production and distribution of narcotics and of obtaining the profits. However, a thorough under-standing of how the political and economic structure of neoliberalism facilitates and protects criminal activity forces a reexamination of the assumption that criminal gangs stand alone in promoting the drug problem.

The third assumption on which the war on drugs has thus far been based is that the financial system is essentially victimized by the criminal gangs because of their massive economic capability. In this view, banks and the financial systems of various governments are essentially opposed to allowing criminals to launder their profits and invest them in legiti-mate businesses but find that, under the globalizing financial system, it is too difficult for them to staunch such activity. This assumption claims the financial institutions are merely victims and not part of the problem.

On the other hand, if the model for approaching the problem of narcotics trafficking is the globalization of the neoliberal economic system and the unregulated activity of transnational capitalists, then it may well be that major components of the national and international financial system are not victims, but active participants in the money-laundering operations of the narcotics trade.[29]

The fourth assumption in the current war on drugs is that governments are essentially committed to combating the narcotics trade but in most cases are victimized by the criminal cartels through corruption and intimidation. Although it is clear that these elements are embedded in many governments, the problem must be understood as specific to the structural arrangements of the international system generally and of the post–cold war neoliberal order in particular. Governments may have a substantial interest in protecting the drug trade not only for economic reasons, such as earning foreign exchange and servicing national debts, but also for political motives—preventing a greater gap between the more and the less developed countries, for instance, and/or weakening a rival power.

A thorough understanding of this perspective will reveal deficiencies in the standard definition of war. An expanded definition of "war" would include forms of conflict in which the armed forces of one country are not necessarily directly involved against those of another nation. This expanded definition would force further revisions in political thinking about the democratization process and the "democratic peace" theory, the theory that holds that democratic states do not fight other democratic states. This kind of rethinking would necessarily reveal the vulnerabilities of the democratization and liberalization processes and would suggest the need for the uncorrupted institutions of states to cooperate with each other in order to avoid internal war and to lessen interstate conflict.

The final assumption in the current war on drugs is that the major societal forces in the United States and other countries oppose the consumption of narcotics and strive to maintain the criminalization of the production and distribution of addictive substances. However, major societal and institutional trends in the United States have led to a delegitimizing of the values and beliefs that are most predictive of resisting drug consumption. Indeed, these trends have promoted consumption and lifestyles that are conducive to consumption. Thus society itself becomes a factor in encouraging drug consumption.

If the conventional assumptions are inadequate, then an alternative set of premises will be required if there is to be a successful effort in the war against drugs. In addition, the model for understanding the war on drugs requires a post–cold war interpretation of the international political and economic systems. The war on drugs will not be won until appropriate assumptions are in place.

CHAPTER 2

DEFINING DEMOCRACY

PROCEDURAL DEMOCRACY AND CORRUPTION

The type of democracy that has emerged from authoritarianism since the 1980s is best defined as procedural. A procedural democracy is essentially a competition of parties in an electoral system. An electoral-based definition of democracy assumes that process is at the core of its legitimacy. The electoral definition emerged where the purpose of establishing representative institutions was taken for granted. Those using this definition did not deem it a problem that corrupt elites might use electoral procedures to maintain themselves in power against the best interests of the people.

The procedural definition of democracy does not therefore exclude the corrupt democratic regime. As long as a country is able to hold elections it is still considered a democracy, whether the government is corrupt or not. Advocates of the procedural definition do not necessarily believe that corruption can be avoided in an electoral system, nor do they address the issue that the electoral system can be used to maintain corrupt elites. Yet when corruption assists elites to manipulate the electoral system, then accountability, the very purpose of the electoral system, is nullified. In order to eliminate false claims of democracy, the understanding of the democratic regime needs to be extended beyond the procedural definition. It should take into account the potential symbiotic relationship between ruling elites, organized crime, and the globalized financial system.

The Concept of the Democratic Republic

Classic considerations of republican theory deal with the problems of holding power in check, with democracy as only one component of a limited, or constitutionalist, regime. The democratic republic has traditionally been the principal model of the mixed regime designed to deal with the corruption of rulers and ruled.

There have been two types of mixed regimes. One type, the classical mixed regime, is historically composed of monarchical, aristocratic, and popular elements. The Roman republic, according to Polybius's description, was a working model. The executive power was held by two consuls who administrated the state and had the power to declare war. The aristocratic senate held the purse strings, and the popular assemblies were the source of rewards and punishments. The other type, the modern mixed regime, is composed of executive, legislative, and judicial powers. Both types of mixed regimes seek to prevent corruption, tyranny, and abuse of power. They do not rely exclusively on the electoral process to maintain the regime's integrity and balance. The modern mixed regime adds interinstitutional accountability to electoral accountability.

The writings of Niccolo Machiavelli and Alexis de Tocqueville are particularly instructive regarding the institutional and cultural components necessary for an accountable republic. According to both Machiavelli and Tocqueville, the maintenance of the republican regime is the underlying purpose of the democratic process. In the classic Machiavellian formulation, the republic was designed to avoid tyranny at home and the loss of autonomy abroad. The republic, as a mixed regime in the Machiavellian sense, merges the principles of monarchy, aristocracy, and democracy in a form of checks and balances to prevent tyranny, degeneracy, and external domination. In its modern functional form, the republic separates the executive, legislative, and judicial functions of the state to accomplish the same purposes. Classically, the democratic processes served to promote domestic freedom and provide the popular loyalty the state needed to defend itself from its foreign enemies. It did not address the possible loss of state autonomy because of transnational economic interests.

Procedural democracy alone does not accomplish the objectives of true democratization, which requires additional institutional and civic cultural safeguards. A regime that includes constitutionally protected checks and balances and a moral civic culture deals most effectively with the challenges of narcostatization. Such a regime emphasizes the governmental and cultural components of an effective antidrug trafficking policy. The regime must also support mechanisms to control the transnational economic environment.

The democratic component of the republican regime both obliges and allows the people to agree on what is just and unjust in their culture and provides the common standards that hold the people's representatives accountable. It also provides the community principles whereby the people may accomplish much of their social, economic, spiritual, and governance needs without relying on an intrusive permanent state bureaucracy. An independent and self-reliant society, a mixed political structure, and mechanisms of transnational economic accountability are the essential ingredients of the modern democratization process. Yet a counter civic culture may subvert the process of democratization and assist the process of narcostatization by supporting the consumption of mind-altering substances.

NARCOSTATIZATION AND THE ANOCRATIZATION OF DEMOCRACY

The process of narcostatization may occur in stable or consolidated democracies, in transitional democracies, and in autocracies. Wherever it occurs, it undermines widespread democratic peace. If autocracy and democracy are at the opposite ends of a continuum, then the anocratic regime that possesses a mixture of democratic and autocratic features lies in the middle of that continuum. One definition of anocracy describes it as an uninstitutionalized state where the patterns of political competition cause the executive leaders to be constantly imperiled by rivals.[1] The anocratic state is an intermediate state where elites maintain themselves in power despite the existence of democratic procedures.

Anocratizing is the process whereby either an autocratic state or a democratic state becomes an anocratic state. An anocratic state has the procedural features of democracy while retaining the features of an autocracy, where the ruling elite face no accountability. Consequently, anocratizing may apply to an autocracy where electoral and competitive features are allegedly in place. It may also apply to a democracy where existing procedural democratic features are undermined. *Democratizing* takes place when an autocratic or anocratic system makes its ruling elements accountable. *Autocratizing* takes place when even the facades of democratic procedures are being eliminated.[2] As a state anocratizes, it is removed from inclusion in the democratic peace thesis, for conflict is likely to occur where democracies are in fact anocracies.

Currently, narcostatization appears to be the most common process facilitating the anocratization of a democracy, an autocracy, or an autocracy in transition to a democracy. Where there is narcostatization, what may appear to be a democratizing state producing peace will actually be an anocratizing state producing conflict.

LEGITIMACY AND CORRUPTION

The criminalization of the state, or narcostatization, allows the value-free definition of democracy to obscure the reality of who or what truly controls political power. Narcostatization insulates elected officials from accountability and thereby undermines the democratic checks on the abuses of power.

A political system's legitimacy is justified to the degree it prevents the abuse of power. When a political system abuses power, no matter what its institutional form, it loses legitimacy, or the right to be obeyed by the population. Where power is used to corrupt and abuse the citizens, no matter what the institutional label, that government is unaccountable. Thus does political corruption produce tyranny, the unaccountable use of power.[3]

If narcostatization distorts the concept of the public good and prevents accountability to the electorate, then the concept of the republican state, which is explicitly designed to check the abuses of power of those democratically elected, is subverted. The complex institutional nature of the republican regime stresses the purpose of the electoral component of selecting representatives and holding them accountable. Democracy, as well, calls for effective offsetting structures of government (checks and balances) that compel those elected to be responsible and honest while holding public trust. The democratic method is not the goal in and of itself. The accountability of leaders takes precedence over the method of choosing them. Procedures must neither disguise elitism nor substitute for genuine accountability.

Corruption and the criminalization of the state necessarily challenge a value-free, purposeless definition of democracy. Modern American political science focuses on a value-free, or scientistic, approach to democracy that attempts to exclude normative criteria. Dwight Waldo defines scientific political science as "an attempt to avoid all 'oughts,' care in the formulation of hypothesis, preoccupation with fashioning political models, meticulous attention to 'research design,' use of quantification where possible, concern for leaving a trail that can be followed— 'replication'—and caution in conclusions drawn from particular studies of an ever-growing establishment of generalizations."[4] This definition of a scientific political science undergirds the predominant perception of democracy in contemporary political science and is called the "procedural" definition of democracy. It stresses the *processes* of democracy in order to make the analysis independent of any value judgments about democracy. A majority of American political scientists probably agree with the procedural definition of democracy.

Joseph Schumpeter defines democracy as "that institutional arrangement for arriving at political decisions in which individuals acquire the power to decide by means of a competitive struggle for the people's vote."[5] Samuel P. Huntington supports Schumpeter's definition. Both men consider a minimal and procedural definition the basis for generalizing about democracy. Huntington writes that his study "defines a twentieth century political system as democratic to the extent that its most powerful collective decision-makers are selected through fair, honest and periodic elections in which candidates clearly compete for votes and in which virtually all the adult population is eligible to vote."[6]

The strictly procedural Schumpeter-Huntington definition is operationalized in Robert Dahl's books on democracy and polyarchy, which he defines as inclusive participatory regimes based on party alternation or contestation.[7] (The relationship between contestation and participation is depicted in figure 1.) According to Dahl's chart, the democratization process is exemplified by both the horizontal and vertical axes of figure 1. The vertical axis indicates the move toward contestation and the horizontal toward participation. The theory of democracy thus developed requires movement along both axes.

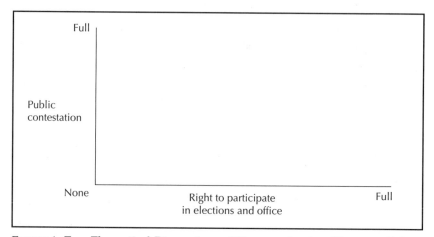

FIGURE 1. Two Theoretical Dimensions of Democratization (Courtesy Robert Dahl, *Polyarchy*, © 1971, Yale University Press.)

The procedural definition is defended on the grounds of its utility and the inadequacy of its alternatives. Dahl argues, "Even one who held the extreme position that a shift from hegemony to polyarchy is never desirable would want to understand, I should think, the conditions required to prevent such a change. In this sense, the analysis is intended to be independent of my commitments or biases in favor of polyarchy." Although Dahl admits to a bias in favor of polyarchy, he does not assume "that a shift from hegemony [a dominant power] towards polyarchy is invariably desirable."[8] Figure 2 suggests how regimes may fall into categories other than polyarchies. Anocracy embraces both competitive oligarchies and inclusive hegemonies that are democratizing. Competitive forms and participation may exist in anocracies, but the reality is of a preponderant executive power that is not fully accountable.

Samuel Huntington's concept of utility is similar but goes somewhat further. He recognizes that the procedural definition may require some refinements. Anticipating criticisms of his definition—such that governments may be "inefficient, corrupt, short-sighted, irresponsible, dominated by special interests, and incapable of adopting policies demanded by the public good"—he asserts that these "qualities may make such governments undesirable but they do not make them undemocratic."[9] He goes on to argue that democracy is just one public virtue and not the only one. For him, the relationship of democracy to other public virtues

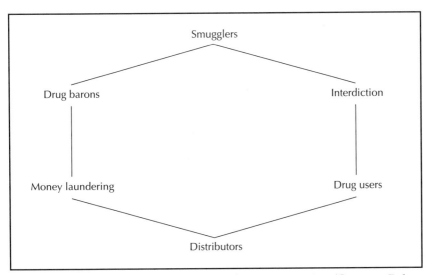

FIGURE 2. Liberalization, Inclusiveness, and Democratization (Courtesy Robert Dahl, *Polyarchy*, © 1971, Yale University Press.)

and vices "can only be understood if democracy is clearly distinguished from other characteristics of political systems."[10]

Besides the utility of this justification for the nonnormative definition of democracy, the Schumpeter approach is bolstered by the alleged inadequacy of the alternative classic definition. Schumpeter defines the classical theory as "that institutional arrangement for arriving at political decisions which realizes the common good by making the public itself decide issues through the elections of individuals who are to assemble in order to carry out its will." Schumpeter asserts that there is no such thing as "a uniquely determined common good that all people could agree on or be made to agree on by the force of rational argument." The justification for this assertion is (1) "that to different individuals and groups the common good is bound to mean different things" and (2) that even if a definite common good proved acceptable to all "this would not imply equally definite answers to individual issues." He concludes that the force of these two propositions means the concept of the will of the people vanishes.[11]

The stress on procedure in Schumpeter's debunking of classical theory transforms the democratic theory into an emphasis on the competition between elites. Democracy as a procedural system means that the people at regular intervals "have the opportunity of accepting or refusing the men who are to rule them."[12] This definition suggests a comparison with Gaetano Mosca's concept of the ruling class. The acceptance of proceduralism to establish a ruling-class definition of democracy requires that an elite be able to persist in government independently of the existence of contestation and inclusive participation. Mosca notes that "in all societies . . . two classes of people appear—a class that rules and a class that is ruled." He continues, "What happens in other forms of government—namely, that an organized minority imposes its will on the disorganized majority—happens also and to perfection, whatever the appearance to the contrary, under the representative system. When we say that the voters 'chose' their representative we are using a language that is very inexact. The truth is that the representative has himself elected by the voters."[13]

Antielitist theorists have charged that American political scientists accept an elitist theory of democracy. Giovanni Sartori has been identified by some as holding such a view, and his early writings on democratic theory have been cited as evidence. But in his later writings, Sartori explicitly denied having an elitist theory. He charged the so-called antielitist theorists with being the true elitists. His analysis of the antielitist critique makes clear that, in his view, the procedural definition depends on norms principally to avoid tyranny or unaccountability. He asserted that the procedural definition must not be seen as having an exclusively participatory function but also, and equally, a selective function. This function is critical because the purpose, as his discussion of America's founding pointed out, is to prevent tyranny.[14]

Despite the alleged moral neutrality of the procedural definition and its apparent bias toward elites, political scientists such as Sartori brought back into the discussion of democracy the purpose of elections. In actual circumstances, those who apply the procedural definition as an operationalizing device have had to modify their stance.

Authors attempting to deal with transitions and consolidations from authoritarian regimes (or in Dahl's terminology, "closed hegemonies") have had to come up with a number of variations for labeling regimes that include both contestation and inclusive participation. For example, scholars, particularly those dealing with Latin America who use the procedural definition of democracy, agree that democracy can "best be defined and applied in terms of the procedural criteria that Robert Dahl . . . has specified." They observe that "no real world regime fits the ideal type perfectly," and they are concerned that democracy may be "little more than a facade behind which a privileged economic elite dominates and exploits the popular classes."[15]

As a result, empirical scholars of Latin American politics do not espouse a simple distinction between democratic and undemocratic regimes. Instead, they introduce different stages in the democratic process and identify the possibilities for reversal. These modifications do not break completely with other procedural definitions, nor do they alter the elitist nature of the procedural approach: "A key to the stability and survival of democratic regimes is, in our view, the establishment of substantial consensus among the elites concerning rules of the democratic political game and the worth of democratic institutions."[16]

Other scholars of Latin America have also made the effort to distinguish between transitions from authoritarian rule to the consolidation of a democratic regime. They believe the minimal and procedural definition of democracy should only apply to the transition phase, from autocracy or authoritarianism to the installation of democratic procedures. They argue that the second transition, the transition to a consolidated democracy, "raises problems that are broader than those that pertain in a strict sense to the transformation of a political regime." They consider the second transition to the consolidation phase to be precarious.[17]

J. Samuel Valenzuela identifies four perverse institutions and deems a consolidated democracy one in which these elements are *absent*. The perverse institutions are

1. Tutelary powers, the principal example of which is the military.
2. Reserved domains, or areas of authority in policy that are excluded from the control of elected officials.
3. Discrimination in the electoral process, where significant sectors of the population are either grossly over- or underrepresented.
4. Noncentrality of elections, or the situation where elections are not the only means to constitute governments.[18]

Interestingly, the discussion of elites and democratic consolidations in the context of the procedural definition of democracy raises the problem that the electoral definition of democracy is not sufficient. For Michael Burton, Richard Gunther, and John Higley, elite unity is necessary, and for Valenzuela the absence of perverse institutionality is necessary.[19]

Although the market economy assists the transition and consolidation processes by strengthening the economic self-sufficiency of the society, the corruption or criminalization of the market economy may be exploited by elites. Funds supplied by corrupt elements allow corrupt elites to become independent of legitimate financial interests and to defeat the candidates those legitimate interests support. In these circumstances, democratic procedures disguise their unaccountability to the public. This unaccountability is furthered by the globalization of the financial capitalist economy. With the rise of corrupt political regimes, the transnational capitalist economy has become increasingly excluded from the control of legitimately elected officials.[20]

Even a cursory examination of the regimes that have been classified as "democratic" indicates a wide range of institutional framework. There is a growing literature discussing the impact of different constitutional frameworks (for example, parliamentarianism versus presidentialism) on democratic consolidations. Students of democracy search for the institutional form of democratic government that provides the most stability. This search presupposes that democracy is a good form of government, based on the principle of accountability.

Excluding the concept of corruption from their study of democracy, procedural democratic theorists ask the following questions about a supposed democracy:

1. What conditions increase or decrease the chances of democratizing a hegemonic regime?
2. What factors increase or decrease the chances of public contestation?
3. What factors support or retard participation?

In order to cope with narcostatization as the principal means for defeating accountability in a globalized economy, however, the normative implications of corruption must be incorporated in a theory of democracy. Schumpeter's description of classical theory fails to incorporate how corruption may defeat the essential accountability of democracy (its legitimacy), while maintaining democracy's external form. It becomes essential that the democratic procedures produce accountability and prevent tyranny. At the same time, the existence of the procedures themselves do not guarantee accountability if a certain degree of corruption exists.[21]

DEMOCRATIC REPUBLICANISM AS THE ALTERNATIVE TO PROCEDURAL DEMOCRACY

The alternative to procedural democracy is democratic republicanism, which explicitly grapples with the problem of corruption by seeking to prevent decay and politicians' abuse of power. Democratic republicanism provides an alternative foundation for democratic theory by focusing on how power may be abused and how the process of accountability may be corrupted. Democratic republicanism is historically based on the mixed regime that highlights the people's responsibility to maintain accountability.

The norms of the democratic republic were developed to address the problems of tyranny, to provide independence for the state vis-à-vis other states, and to promote liberty within the state. Democratic republicanism considers participation a phenomenon of a disciplined people, seeks to avoid electoral despotism, supports a mixed regime, and fears the corruption of the public and the public's servants. This book seeks to reach beyond the classical concerns of democratic republicanism, to add to those the challenges that arise from the globalization of the world economy and the threat of corruption.

POLITICAL AND PHILOSOPHICAL ANTHROPOLOGIES

Normative political science can be approached from two angles: political anthropology and philosophical anthropology. One establishes how a society understands itself and behaves and the other how all societies ought to be evaluated and conduct themselves.

Political anthropology approaches the understanding of a political society as it perceives itself. Human activities must be understood in terms of the meanings the actors in a society ascribe to them. The political order in which humans live is normative in the sense that people understand what they should or should not do in any given society. The rules from one society do not necessarily apply to another. Political anthropology provides a relative understanding of societies. The population's existence or its real situation in a society is guided by what is and is not permitted in that society. Members of a nation have no choice but to live in that nation's understood social order. Once the "rightness" of that order comes into question or is evaluated, the study of philosophical anthropology is being introduced.

The Greeks pioneered philosophical anthropology. They accepted the existence of a tribal order, *idios kosmos*, which were the rules of that particular order or city-state. There also existed a universal order, a *koinos kosmos*, which was a universal standard for judging all particular orders. Socrates, Plato, and Aristotle all believed in this universal order. The *koinos kosmos* was superior to the tribal orders and was the basis for evaluating each of them. The philosophical anthropology of the Greeks asserted that *koinos kosmos* was an ultimate truth, a Logos for all mankind.[22] For Heraclitus, the precursor thinker of the Logos concept, the Logos was the principle of order under which the universe exists. The Logos was the bridge between the Greek world and Christianity. Logos gave a person reason and knowledge of the truth, not only of the physical world, or the world of nature, but also of human events: "All things are controlled by the Logos of God. The Logos is the power which puts sense into the world, the power which makes the world an order instead of a chaos, the power which sets the world going and keeps it going in its perfect order. The Logos," said the Stoics, "pervades all things."[23]

The bridge between the Greek world and Christianity came with the identification of Christ's word with the Logos. Christianity spread the idea of the Logos, thereby rooting philosophical anthropology in Western culture. The practical application of philosophical anthropology confronts whether the universal standard could or should be applied in actual circumstances, and, if so, how.

MACHIAVELLI AND TOCQUEVILLE

Niccolo Machiavelli and Alexis de Tocqueville are two well-known classic theorists of democratic republicanism. Both use the methods of political and philosophical anthropology to determine how an existing political society can be reformed. Writing in different centuries, they each chose one state as a basis for describing how a good order works and how its lessons can be applied to other countries. In the 1500s, Machiavelli wrote about Rome to explain what made the republic work and to elucidate both the difficulties and prospects for reforming his native Florence and uniting Italy. Tocqueville wrote about the United States in the early 1800s in order to illustrate the success of American republicanism but also to suggest how his native France could avoid tyranny and deterioration while becoming democratic. Both of these perceptive thinkers are classic practitioners of the methods of political and philosophical anthropology.

Machiavelli and Tocqueville are not primarily concerned with establishing absolute normative standards. They are more preoccupied with what makes a system work and how another state's system may emulate it. Their views are similar to those of procedural democratic theorists in the sense they do not attempt to justify absolute normative standards. Machiavelli and Tocqueville enrich our concept of the purpose of democratic procedures and increase our understanding of how a freedom-sustaining democratic regime should operate. They argue that the values people need to sustain a democratic republic require a founding based on religion. In this sense, they are practical philosophical anthropologists—they use the idea of the "good" for reform purposes.

Machiavelli

Machiavelli's methodology starts with an assumption that human nature is constant and essentially bad. He wrote,

> All cities and all peoples are and ever have been animated by the same desires and the same passions; so that it is easy, by diligent study of the past, to foresee what is likely to happen in the future in any republic, and to apply those remedies that were used by the ancients, or, not finding any that were employed by them, to devise new ones from the similarity of the events. But, as such considerations are neglected or not understood by most of those who read, or if understood by these, are unknown by those who govern, it follows that the same troubles generally reoccur in all republics.[24]

Machiavelli assumed that the event critical to the solid foundation of a state is the establishment of good laws. Good laws are essential to the discipline of the people because, for Machiavelli, a well-disciplined people can master fate. He argued that the relationship of good laws and discipline is favorable to liberty. Paradoxically, he believed liberty to be derived from the quarrels of the two sides that exist in every state: the nobles and the people. He believed these agitations are necessary because, "every free state ought to afford the people with the opportunity of giving vent." In Machiavelli's analysis, the people have a normative role in fostering liberty, and he thought this to be particularly true if the republic is to be imperial. Machiavelli supported an imperial state because he believed a united Italy could defend itself against intervening neighbors.

Machiavelli studied how the Romans developed the discipline that permitted their people to protect both their internal liberty and the external autonomy of the Roman state. He argued that religion was the key to the Roman people's unity, freedom, and imperial grandeur. He noted that the founder of the republic, Numa, reduced the savage Romans to civil obedience through religion. Religion was the source of the discipline of the Roman citizens who "feared much more to break an oath than the laws." Machiavelli concluded that religion was the source of Roman discipline and that this source of discipline was a universal requirement for all free peoples, writing, "There never was any remarkable law giver amongst any people who did not resort to divine authority as otherwise his laws would not be accepted by the people."[25]

The generalization that Machiavelli extracted from his analysis of Rome is that religion is the critical element to sustain a democratic republic. He stated without any caveat, that "the observance of divine institutions is the cause of the greatness of republics, so the disregard of them produces their ruin, unless it be sustained by the fear of the prince which may temporarily supply the want of religion." This understanding of the fundamental importance of religion to the republic makes the problem of corruption the most critical one for the survival of the regime. Machiavelli was far more concerned with the corruption of the people than of the ruler. He believed that if the ruler or prince is corrupt but the people remain sound, liberty may be restored. "A corrupt people that lives under the government of a prince can never become free," he wrote. "Where corruption has penetrated the people, the best laws are of no avail, unless they are administered by a man of such supreme power that he may cause the laws to be observed until the mass has been restored to a healthy condition. And I know not whether such a case has ever occurred, or whether it possibly ever could occur."[26]

Machiavelli's study of the decay of Rome concluded that corruption was caused by the great inequalities of wealth that developed in the republic. Corruption caused the laws to change so that the most meritorious people in the country increasingly abstained from serving the republic and ultimately were wholly excluded from public affairs. Over the centuries, critics have questioned Machiavelli's argument that the restoration of good morals requires evil means. His reliance on evil means was based on his conclusion that it is nearly impossible to restore liberty "in a republic that has become corrupt, or to establish it there anew." A corrupt republic would inevitably be replaced by a monarchy, he felt, because the loss of moral discipline requires an "almost regal power" to maintain control.

Tocqueville

Tocqueville's methodology was similar to Machiavelli's. He studied how democracy functioned in the United States in order to understand how democracy could be prevented from threatening freedom in France. In December 1836 he wrote to his friend Louis de Kergorlay that his purpose was "to show people, so far as possible, what one must do to avoid tyranny and degeneration while becoming democratic."[27] Tocqueville believed that in the times he lived there was no alternative to democracy, but he feared that tyranny could also arise with the democratic system. He thought the Americans had avoided tyranny in their democratic republic, and he sought to understand how they had done this in order to help France avoid tyranny as well.

Tocqueville noted that geographical circumstances and American laws were all favorable to the country's freedom. However, he argued that the principal cause maintaining the democratic republic as a free polity was the manners and customs of the people. He saw religion (or the Logos) as the basis of the Americans' good customs, writing, "the greatest part of British America was peopled by men who . . . brought with them into the New World a form of Christianity which I cannot better describe than by styling it a democratic and republican religion."[28]

The similarity of Tocqueville's analysis of Christianity in America and of Machiavelli's analysis of religion in the Roman republic is remarkable. As Machiavelli wrote, "if the Christian religion had from the beginning been maintained according to the principles of its founder, the Christian states would have been much more united and happy than what they are. Nor can there be a greater proof of its decadence than to witness the fact that the nearer people are to the church of Rome, which is the head of our religion, the less religious are they."[29]

Like Machiavelli, Tocqueville focused on the political utility of religion, especially for a free republic: "I am at this moment considering religions in a purely human point of view," he wrote. "My object is to inquire by what means they may most easily retain their sway in the democratic ages upon which we are entering."[30] Tocqueville was aware that the directing classes of France had been deeply infected by the skepticism and rationalism of the Enlightenment and that Roman Catholicism in France had not developed as much of a republican consciousness as it had in the United States. Consequently, he addressed the most moral and intelligent elements of the directing class in France, urging them to copy the American founders by conscious decision.

Tocqueville's call for the conscious embrace of religion for practical purposes in France contrasts with America's experience. In America, the democratic republic arose where the people's belief in Christianity converged with a new territory and in new circumstances. Still, Tocqueville thought that if France imitated aspects of the American experience it would remedy the decay of public morals. He argued against political centralism in order to produce the practice of democratic accountability locally and regionally, against individualism in order to produce community cooperation, and against the elitist bureaucratic elements in the government that would destroy the people's consciousness. The essence of Tocqueville's effort to reform a corrupted polity was his belief that a country needed a moral leadership in order to fight the population's dependence on central government and to promote community cooperation through civic regeneration. He expected that the most meritorious people would want to serve an active, aware, and regenerated population.

◆ ◆ ◆

From a historical perspective, both Machiavelli and Tocqueville were prophets, advising against the corruption of a democratic republic.

Both sought political mechanisms that would reverse that corruption. Machiavelli despaired of achieving this without evil means, while Tocqueville relied on the ascendancy of a moral elite.

As practical philosophical anthropologists, both theorists sought to engineer the restoration of the moral state rather than to rely on the fortuitous development of a religious people. To this degree, they shared elements of the elitist theory of democracy. Because they believed that the moral nature of the people is critical to sustaining the democratic republic, they were fearful that corruption of the people is the most likely avenue from which tyranny might arise under the guise of democracy. They foreshadowed elements of the elitist theory of democracy but remained convinced that if corruption were to infect democracy, then the regime would be a disguise for tyranny.

Both Machiavelli and Tocqueville emphasized that to forestall the rise of tyranny, democracy in a large state required a focus on the people. Modern-day theorists who follow Machiavelli and Tocqueville ask different questions than do procedural theorists:

- What conditions permit political elites to remain unaccountable despite contestation and inclusiveness?
- Does privatization produce gross economic inequality and hence undermine civic virtue? (A capitalist oligarchy—that is, rule by the well-to-do few—concentrates economic power as much as a centralized bureaucratic oligarchy does.)
- What factors undermine the religious culture of the people?

When a government is corrupt, the elites are able to manipulate the electoral system to maintain themselves in power. This capability in itself indicates a lack of accountability. Democratic republicanism involves more than institutional checks on elected representatives. As Machiavelli and Tocqueville suggested, it requires a civic culture that leads people to value their own independence and the moral probity of their represen-tatives. Corruption is the most critical element in the decomposition of the republican regime. It attacks the moral core of the people and the people's representatives. If the democratic republic is to survive, it must protect itself from corruption-induced decay.

These two great thinkers concluded that a certain type of civic culture is basic to the health of the democratic republic. Unlike the procedural democratic theorists, who view the mechanism of participation as an end in itself, the democratic republican theorists argue that the purpose of an election is defined by its end: the protection of the public from arbitrary interference from the state. In order for liberty to be achieved, citizens must share a normative structure. As will be explained in subsequent chapters, narcotic consumption adversely impacts the normative basis of the civic culture.

CHAPTER 3

THE CORRUPTION OF ELITES

Corruption in politics enables elites to remain in power during and after democratic elections. In the democratic republic, governors are public servants who derive their legitimacy from representing the interests of society. The representative function requires both responsibility and responsiveness. The responsibility factor calls for a standard of resisting popular passions when the facts and circumstances honestly compel the representative to make a decision contrary to the wishes of the population.

The population must also have the moral capacity and ability to remove representatives from office when their decisions are unacceptable. In a democratic republic, accountability takes precedence over responsibility, thereby undermining the possibility of unaccountable elitism. A sense of responsibility may lead representatives to oppose popular wishes, but ultimately, they have to be accountable to the people.

Corrupt elites threaten accountable governments. Corrupt elitism can develop within an established democratic regime or persist after an apparent transition from authoritarian to electoral selection. The following three indicators are a means for identifying corrupt elitism:

1. Access to political office is limited to a relatively small group.
2. Officeholders are able to avoid accountability to the community despite pursuing interests the community repudiates. (Under a system of shared norms public officeholders would be responsible, have integrity, and not undermine these norms.)

3. Institutional checks on the self-perpetuating group are relatively unregularized and ineffective.

These three indicators recognize that where there is a system of corruption, irresponsibility, and self-perpetuation of elites, the normative purpose of elections has been frustrated. Where political elites in an electoral system can pursue policies the public essentially opposes, continue in or be returned to office with a record of corruption and irresponsibility, then one or more circumstances are occurring: The society is unable to enforce a shared normative judgment on its public servants, the society itself does not possess such a standard, or it is confused by the elites' ability to mold public opinion or prevent access of critical opinion.

Trends in accountability, which indicate whether concentration of power in the executive is more or less accountable to alternative institutions and the public, suggest three types of regime processes. These are outlined in table 1.

CIVIL SOCIETY AND POLITICAL PARTIES

Transitions from authoritarianism and consolidations of democracy raise the question of requirements for an accountable regime. The initiation of democratic procedures leads to the important issue of methods for holding elites accountable but does not confront the capabilities of the civil society to do so. If a democratization process is to become consolidated, then in addition to the government's accountability and mutually balancing institutions, the government and civil society must support a shared civic culture. What is a civic culture? One view has been to relate civic culture with liberalism. Liberalism, as the basis of a civic culture, has been defined as the effort "to restrict the powers of the state and to define a uniquely private sphere independent of state action. At the centre of this project was the goal of freeing civil society . . . from political interference and the simultaneous delimitation of the state's authority."[1]

Civic culture in the sense used here is not exclusively liberalism. In order for government to be accountable, the values of the society must compel the state's representatives to exercise power responsibly—which means the society's values must be expressed and disseminated. In short,

TABLE 1.

TRENDS IN ACCOUNTABILITY

Democratization Indicators (More Accountable Governments)	Anocratization Indicators (Partially Accountable Governments)	Autocratization Indicators (Less Accountable Governments)
1. There is competitive recruitment of presidential candidates.	1. Executive leadership moves toward more closed selection processes.	1. Executive leadership is decided by a ruling group.
2. Competitive outcomes in presidential elections are institutionalized; e.g., alternation in power by representatives of competing parties has occurred and is an expected outcome over time.	2. Popular ratification is less dependent on the population.	2. Outcomes of the ratification process by the population are preordained; any alternative to the ruling group is foreclosed.
3. Institutional constraints on executive power—checks and balances—actually exist.	3. Institutional checks on the executive are less regularized and effective.	3. Institutional checks on the executive power are few and not regularized.

in the democratic republic's civic culture, governors are public servants, not rulers.

Gabriel Almond and Sidney Verba give a standard account of civic culture. They argue that it "is not a modern culture, but one that combines modernity with tradition." For them, a civic culture is "neither traditional nor modern but partaking of both; a pluralistic culture based on communication and persuasion, a culture of consensus and diversity, a culture that permitted change but moderated it." The authors maintain that the civic culture they admire and seek for most countries "is present in the form of aspiration, and the democratic infrastructure is still far from being attained." These theorists infer the elements of the democratic culture by examining attitudes in a number of existing democratic states. Their account of a working democratic system stresses the need for congruence between the attitudes, affections, and cognitions of the populace with the system. They employ the concept of culture as the psychological orientation of people toward social objects, and they are concerned with the internalized feelings, values, and understandings of the population.[2]

The civic culture that produces public servants is a blend of three civic traditions, two of which are secular and one religious. Of the secular traditions one is the Aristotelian. This tradition sees political liberty as deriving from citizens imbued with public spirit or virtue who participate in politics and defend the state from external threats. Private property provides the public with the material preconditions to serve the state in peace and war.

The second secular tradition, the juristic, asserts the individual's right to be free from arbitrary authority. In this tradition, citizens have rights vis-à-vis the state. Since this tradition is commercial, property is also a fundamental right. Property and the market are critical both to the rights of the citizen and to the defense of the republic.

The third tradition is deeply linked to Judeo-Christianity. The strict observance of God's commandments is essential to this order, where the people are governed by religious elders distinguished for their wisdom and integrity. The republican principles were designed to prevent the polity from degenerating into oligarchy or tyranny. In this view, the only king of a godly people is God.

The Puritans in America followed this perspective. In this tradition, the welfare of the whole is dependent on the morality of the people, which in turn depends on a religious basis. On June 5, 1788, Samuel

Langdon gave a sermon promoting the ratification of the U.S. Constitution. It provided an important statement of the Puritan attitude about the religious basis to the republic.

> If you neglect or renounce that religion taught and commanded in the Holy Scriptures, think no more of freedom, peace, and happiness. . . . And if our religion is given up, all the liberty we boast of will soon be gone; a profane and wicked people cannot hope for divine blessings, but it may be easily foretold that "evil will befall them in the latter days."[3]

It is highly significant that in the United States the norms restraining both the civic culture and the elites have historically been religious. Tocqueville made a classic observation about the American polity: "Liberty," he said, "regards religion as its companion in all its battles and its triumphs, as the cradle of its infancy and the divine source of its claims. It considers religion as the safeguard of morality, and morality as the best security of law and the surest pledge of the duration of freedom."[4]

The two secular traditions also have a strong presence in the mix of values undergirding America's civic culture. The Aristotelian tradition was often expressed by people representing landed interests in the United States, and the juristic tradition was represented by commercial interests.

This view of the civic culture as it developed in the United States sees it as (1) epiphenomenal, or emanating from the economic base of society, and (2) metaphysical, or emanating from the people's religious beliefs and feelings. If accountability of the public's servants in this conception of the role of civic culture is to be maintained, then the shared normative political understandings must remain embedded in civil society.

John Dewey was one of the first to openly challenge the metaphysical basis to the classical civic culture of the United States. Dewey attempted to replace supernatural religion with the natural "religious." He argued that humanism had all the elements of a religious faith and that it needed to be made explicit and militant.[5] He may be perceived as having prepared America's intellectual culture for the elitist theory of democracy, because by his thinking, man is the ultimate or supreme authority, and those who understood this were the natural rulers of those who did not.

Dewey wrote, "To say emphatically of a particular person that he has soul or a great soul is not to utter a platitude, applicable equally to all human beings. It expresses the conviction that the man or woman in question has in marked degree qualities of sensitivity, rich and coordinated participation in all situations of life."[6]

Modern proponents of Dewey's perspective, such as Richard Rorty, attempt to retain the nation's religious tradition of sympathy with other cultures and human beings without making that tradition's religious orientation foundational for either public or private life. The objective is to continue the American culture's commitment to tolerance without restraining the private efforts of self-creation, play, and erotic exploration. Ideological pragmatists cannot be philosophical anthropologists. They have no convincing way of resolving the conflict between apparently legitimate preferences of differing cultures. They separate public from private morality, with the former based on human solidarity and the latter on the "irony" that one's beliefs are based on time and chance. A private aesthetic morality is Rorty's solution to public liberalism and private libertarianism because he believes it underscores "the ability of each of us to tailor a coherent self-image for ourselves and use it to tinker with our behavior."[7]

These views erode America's metaphysical component to its civic culture.[8] Certainly, the private aesthetic provides no basis to resist—and conceivably could even provide an intellectual incentive to experiment with—the use of narcotics.

Finally, the metaphysical perspective is critical to an understanding of how the party system works to maintain the accountability of public servants and the shared normative structure of the people. The system is necessary to support the normative relationship between the principles embedded in civil society about permissible human behavior and the limits on power of the public's servants.

Political parties and the party system were instituted to restrain the country's public servants and reflect the civic culture. The parties in a competitive system foster the people's sense of shared norms and the leaders' sense of accountability. Parties reinforce the concept of account-ability, respect for the temporary minority, and openness of opinion formation because they mediate the normative interaction between accountable leaders and restrained publics. While the epiphenomenal and metaphysical traditions are important for America's civic culture, the rise of the pragmatist challenge and the growing dominance of unrestrained economic interests indicate that the metaphysical component is in decline. Yet it would be pertinent to remember that Tocqueville held the religious tradition to be the most important for the maintenance of accountability. He wrote,

> When the religion of a people is destroyed, doubt gets hold of the higher powers of the intellect and half paralyzes all the others. . . . Such a condition can not but enervate the soul, relax the springs of the will, and prepare a people for servitude. Not only does it happen in such a case that they allow their freedom to be taken from them; they frequently surrender it themselves. . . . For my own part, I doubt whether man can ever support at the same time complete religious independence and entire political freedom. And I am inclined to think that if faith be wanting in him, he must be subject; and if he be free, he must believe.[9]

ELITE DOMINATION

The characteristic feature of the authoritarian regime is elite domination. How is it, then, that in alleged democratic transitions elites persist and maintain themselves in power even after the democratic regime has supposedly been consolidated?

In authoritarian regimes, elites are often considered critical to a successful democratic transition. They facilitate transitions through pacts or settlements among the ruling class. John Higley and Richard Gunther argue that elite settlements have two main consequences: "They create patterns of open but peaceful competition among major league factions, and . . . they can facilitate the eventual emergence of a consolidated democracy."[10] They argue that elite consensus is the essential precondition for consolidated democracy. For example, they submit that Colombia had an elite settlement in 1957–58 and Mexico had a similar elite settlement in 1929. Both case studies in the Higley and Gunther work, however, problematized the elite settlement. As John A. Peeler has written about Colombia, "The course of politics in Colombia since the end of the National Front in 1974 cannot be characterized as democratic consolidation. If anything, we are witnessing a process of deconsolidation, of gradual breakdown."[11] And, with regard to Mexico, Alan Knight has written, "It is impossible to avoid the conclusion that the 1928–29 elite settlement, though fostering consensual unity within the revolutionary elite, encouraged—or at the very least permitted—a deepening of divisions within the country as a whole, pitting revolutionary elites against their non- or antirevolutionary rivals."[12]

If the characteristic feature of the authoritarian regime is elite domination, then the key objective of a ruling elite facing democratic transitions and consolidations is to maintain its ruling status. The former authoritarian elite must seek to insulate itself from accountability to the population through elections.

For the democratic procedural definition to be normatively acceptable, the elite must be accountable to the people. It must not be able to either frustrate a community's desire for accountability or destroy a people's faith in the concept that the measure of good government is based on a shared norm that is binding on the public as well as the public's servants. Such an understanding of norms means that in the state neither the people nor the government are absolutely sovereign.

This understanding of procedural democracy denies the superior knowledge of the few as having authority over the collective judgment of the many. It asserts that representation means that the few are restrained by the interests, characteristics, symbols, authorizations, and judgments of the community all of which are guided by shared norms. On the other hand, elitism develops an ideology or political myth by which it justifies its rule to the rest of the population. When that ideology or myth loses its credibility with the population as a whole, the ruling elite needs to find a new legitimizing formula. The stunning discovery by elements of the authoritarian elites in a number of countries is that the electoral system may be used to both perpetuate and legitimize their rule.[13]

NARCOSTATIZATION AND REDEFINING DEMOCRACY

In the stage of advanced narcostatization, elitist unaccountable governments prevail within the structure of procedural or formal democracy. Governments interpenetrated with narcotics power depend on the monetary surpluses provided by narcotics trafficking to service debts, limit taxes, subsidize constituencies, buy off power contenders, and project state power into other states and societies.

These developments force a reconsideration of the definition of democracy, particularly of a "good regime," based solely on procedural norms. They also require a reconsideration of the democratic peace thesis and compel an exploration into the relations of drug cartels with the interests of certain government ministries, for narcostatization cannot be ruled out when considering the spread of insurgency and the alignment of public opinion with the interests of the insurgents.

The capacity of the democratic state to control narcotics trafficking is hidden by the procedural definition, which focuses primarily on contestation and participation. The weakness of that definition, with regard to the component of narcotics trafficking, is not only what it does not include, but also its failure to clearly indicate the logical conditions necessary for a democratic regime to work. The following description of democracy directs one toward understanding both the substantive and procedural problems and the logical and empirical conditions that permit a distinction between an actual democracy and a pseudodemocracy.

A democracy is a political system or regime in which the people with a civic culture, or Logos, constitutionally decide who will determine the decisions for the state. Those elected cannot decide or act independently of constraints, checks, and balances. It is the intention or purpose of the democratic regime to avoid tyranny and to produce and enforce good laws and policies. A democratic republic has plural institutional powers that clearly indicate that the regime has both procedural and institutional components capable of managing its vulnerability to global financial movements and oligarchical transnational interests.[14]

The key components of this definition need to be understood. "The people" means "a whole" and refers to the adult voting population. Over the years, the concept of the voting population has expanded from males with property to all males and finally to women. It may exclude, for example, criminals and the insane and represents a concept of the people as possessing moral and judgmental characteristics. There may be additional empirical characteristics that the people must have in order for the system to be accountable to them. The democratic system will not have the necessary conditions unless the people possess the appropriate characteristics, characteristics subsumed under the term "civic culture."

"Constitutionality" exists when basic norms of the system establish how authorized public servants are chosen and how the policy structure of the regime is made accountable. The constitution structurally sets up a democracy as an institutionally mixed regime. Although the term "mixed regime" is not used in the definition, the concept of constraints and checks and balances makes the mixed regime a necessary component of a democracy and therefore properly defines a democratic republic. In the mixed regime, the legislative, executive, and judicial functions must be independently accountable, either directly or indirectly, to the people. These components of the mixed regime must also be mutually restraining. In short, certain types of institutions and arrangements among institutions give effect to public accountability in the democratic regime.

Another empirical condition for a working system is the existence of free elections. For elections to function there must exist a free choice between two or more competitive parties where freedom of speech and press is present. Political parties are empirically and systematically necessary for democracy. Parties act as representatives of the people not only with regard to who and what are represented but also in regard to the actions they take. The function of parties is not to keep elites permanently in power but to act as the agents of the electing people. Parties make sure that the people's wishes, rather than the elites' wishes, are respected. The democratic concept of "good" laws and policies are those that are authorized by the people.

The definition of the democratic republic must also meet the problems arising from the globalization of the world economy and that economy's capacity to restrict democratic decision making. A modern theory of democracy must incorporate the idea of an accountable relationship between the institutions of the world economy and the state.

Avoiding Accountability in a Consolidated Democracy: The Swiss Case

Elitist dominance in democracies in the contemporary environment arises from the fact that external transnational elites and domestic elites are capable of blocking accountability. Transnational elites seek influence over parliaments, media, and academia in conjunction with domestic elements, hoping to free themselves from accountability. These transnational elites are ensconced in financial capitals that evade nation-state controls. Sometimes termed "the overworld," those elites outside the control of individual states see themselves as managing the global economy and influencing attitudes worldwide.[15] An example of the interaction between overworld and domestic elites and underworld interests in transforming the accountability of a political system occurred in Switzerland in 1997.

Switzerland is generally thought to be an idyllic country, with a modern, civilized, highly educated population living peacefully in a drug-free society with a model democratic system. However, another picture is emerging. There is crime in the villages, urban decay in the cities, and widespread drug consumption and decline in educational standards throughout the country.

Zurich, the finance capital of Switzerland, provides a case in point. Before 1989 there were only three hundred methadone addicts in the canton of Zurich. In the mid-1980s a socialist-environmentalist coalition took over Zurich's town council. One of the new councilors, Emilie Lieberherr, was linked to the Radical Party, an Italian party that founded the International League against Drug Prohibition, which seeks the liberalization and the legalization of narcotics.[16] The Radical Party has openly courted Italian criminals and has sponsored membership drives in Italian prisons. It is funded by convicted murderers and organized crime figures. Voting analysts have demonstrated that its support has come from areas of so-called high-density mafia vote.[17]

In any event, the subsequent liberalization of drugs in Zurich resulted in a needle-exchange program, followed by the opening of Needle Park (Platzpitz), where fifteen thousand syringes and sixty-eight hundred substitute needles were distributed daily. Three thousand addicts received methadone; of twenty thousand addicts, four thousand were HIV positive. Despite the drop in the price of drugs stemming from the government's subsidized program, organized crime continued to control a piece of the market.[18] During this period, crime increased, and the death rate among addicts who took legal drugs was 2.4 times higher than among those who did not.[19] Authorities were eventually forced to close Needle Park in February 1992.

Despite this experience—and despite a strong antidrug sentiment among Swiss citizens—advocates of drug legalization continued to advance harm reduction as the preferred way to manage the drug problem. The government opened a second drug park in the summer of 1992 at Letten Station, an area where close to fifty thousand students pass by on their way to school and the university. Approximately fifteen thousand syringes were distributed there daily. The number of drug addicts in the country had doubled by May 1995 and had doubled again by November 1996.[20]

Swiss lobby groups, such as the Verein Zur Forderung Der Psychologischen Menschenkenntris (VPM), called for a referendum against legalization and attempted to block the open needle-supply centers and shooting galleries. Opposition to the September 28, 1997, referendum came from an alignment of government officials, the press, and prominent business leaders.

Roland C. Rasi, general manager of the Swiss Bank Corporation (SBV), one of Switzerland's largest banks, took the lead in persuading many business leaders to sign an antireferendum document. A press conference supporting the legal distribution of heroin was held at the SBV's headquarters in Zurich on November 9, 1995.[21] The business leaders endorsed the employment of addicts in the workplace and their integration into society while maintaining their addiction through heroin distribution projects throughout the country.

The support of the business community gave respectability to the antireferendum forces and contributed to the success of the legalization movement. Their strategy succeeded when 71 percent of the voters rejected the prohibition against legalization. However, those voting represented only 30 percent of eligible Swiss voters. The health ministry then attempted to put state distribution of heroin to hardened addicts on a permanent legal footing. "We will propose a change in the narcotics legislation to the cabinet as soon as possible," director of the Health Ministry, Thomas Zeltner, announced.[22]

The legalization movement in Switzerland openly seeks to bypass the checks of the electorate. In the words of Councilor Lieberherr, "We are looking for a way past the people."[23] This search for "a way past the people" has the support not only of business leaders and the liberal press, but also of public health officials, including the Swiss minister of health and family affairs, some police chiefs and government advisors backing a narcotics policy of "harm reduction," mafia fronts, and other marginal groups.[24] The existence of such an alliance reveals how narcostatization evolves and the extent to which Switzerland is undergoing the process of narcostatization.

The fluidity of the situation in Switzerland is demonstrated by the failure of the prolegalization movement in the November 29, 1998, referendum. In that referendum 74 percent voted *against* a constitutional amendment that would have legalized "the consumption, cultivation or possession of drugs and their acquisition for personal use." The proposed amendment to the constitution stated in addition that narcotic drugs consumed for nonmedical reasons be made available without prescription [Articles 32.1 and 32.2]. It is interesting to note that a public letter to UN Secretary-General Kofi Annan, which was published in the *New York Times* on June 8, 1998, stating that "the global war on drugs is now causing more harm than drug abuse itself," was republished in Switzerland's largest German-language newspaper, *Neue Zürcher Zeitung*, three days before the referendum. Among the signers were members of the Drug Policy Foundation and the Lindesmith Center, John Sperling of the Apollo Group, and George Soros, chairman of George Soros Management.[25]

The case of Switzerland illustrates that if the public servants are not accountable, the regime is a pseudodemocracy or an elitist system, even if it has the formal attributes of elections. According to the Index of Narcostatization Indicators (see chapter 7), Switzerland is at level 2, the developing stage of narcostatization, while already harboring one element each from levels 3 (serious) and 4 (critical).

The Spreading Campaign for Legalization

Why the push for legalization in Switzerland? One theory is that Switzerland has been under international pressure to adopt legalization. This theory views Switzerland as a pilot project for experimenting on how to bring about drug legalization in a highly developed, moral, independent, and democratic country.[26] According to this theory, if a country widely known as both conservative and humane can be brought to legalize drugs, then others will undoubtedly follow. Prolegalization forces view Switzerland as a laboratory for experimentation and a first domino.

A second theory is that Switzerland is important for the money-laundering interests of the drug trade. Carla del Ponte, the Swiss public prosecutor, argues that "a liberalization or legalization of the sale and consumption of drugs will lead to an influx of drug money in Switzerland because the money, after legalization, will no longer be dirty, but clean."[27] This movement can be traced to 1990 when four cities—Zurich, Frankfurt, Hamburg, and Amsterdam—founded the European Cities on Drug Policy (ECDP) and adopted the Frankfurt Resolution, which calls for the distribution of heroin to addicts, the legalization of marijuana, the introduction of "shooting galleries," and the termination of the 1961 UN Single Convention. The ECDP cooperates with Italy's Radical Party, the International League against Drug Prohibition, and the U.S.-based Drug Policy Foundation. Since its founding, ECDP has established membership in thirty European cities in addition to Switzerland's six largest German-speaking cities.[28]

NARCOSTATIZATION AND THE DEMOCRATIC REPUBLIC

Narcostatization operates against the empirical and logical conditions that make a democracy real rather than formal. The following five components of the corruption of democracy show how narcostatization undermines the necessary conditions for a democracy to serve its intended purposes:

1. The narcostatization process undermines a people's civic culture. The key role for the civic culture in a democratic civilization is to maintain stability. Evidence suggests culture does not cause the creation of the democratic regime but constrains the behavior of political officials.[29] As more people use drugs, commit crimes, and embrace values demonstrating indifference to political participation, then the portion of the adult population that has the desire and the economic and political capability to hold elites accountable decreases. Note that less than 24 percent of all eligible Swiss voters supported heroin distribution in an election in which 70 percent of the Swiss did not vote.

2. The narcostatization process impacts on party competition as the contending parties for high office become dependent on subsidies from drug traffickers to fund their campaigns. These subsidies indicate that despite rhetorical and, in some cases, sporadic enforcement measures, the parties become more responsive to the interests of the cartels than to those of the people. This result indicates that the pact or pacts that set up the rules constraining public officials' behavior is unraveling. When citizens do not act in concert to protect their culture, a ruling group may

emerge and gain public acquiescence to activities the public did not initially support.

3. The narcostatization process undermines the institutional checks of the executive, legislative, and judicial powers on the ruling elites. As the major institutional centers find themselves compromised by narcotics, they are increasingly unlikely to restrain other institutions in this activity. This result is particularly alarming for an ethnically divided society such as found in Switzerland, which devised provisions explicitly to check the effects of ethnic and religious differences. If it becomes widely understood that limits are not enforceable against public officials, then ethnic and religious trust may be one of the casualties as well.

4. The narcostatization process undermines elite accountability and transforms public servants into a ruling class. The intention of the democratic regime to avoid tyranny and to produce good laws and policies is defeated as both the procedural and substantive components of the democratic republic are fused with the protection of and dependence on organized criminal behavior.

5. To the extent the democratic state does not have a responsible relationship with the transnational system of global governance, its governing class becomes more dependent on external forces than domestic ones. Where the transnational economic system is corrupted and the democratic state does not assist the institutional mechanisms for controlling corruption, its elites may be incorporated into a criminalized world system.

The processes undermining the five major components of the democratic republic permit an understanding of how narcostatization can reveal what is occurring. On the other hand, if the procedural definition of democracy is used, awareness of what is happening will be postponed until the process may well be irreversible.

In summary, the erosion of the civic culture, the decay of the party systems, the fragmentation of the permanent institutions of the regime, the change from serving to ruling in the principles of the governing elites, and the forging of ruling rather than serving transnational elite alliances are signs of the eclipse both of the democratic republic and of a more peaceful international environment. Understanding the corrupting role of narcotics trafficking provides a warning mechanism for detecting the transformation of apparently democratic regimes and for heading off the possibilities of increasing conflict within and between states.

The narcotics trafficking industry works synergistically with modernist and postmodernist intellectual and cultural trends to transform mass culture. It changes mass culture from one embedded in metaphysical norms to one fostering libertarian permissiveness and individual economic concerns. It pulls party competition away from its system-sustaining role since the shared norms limiting behavior no longer exist in the civic culture. If the loss of a common normative civic structure inhibits people from acting jointly for the public good, the rule of party factions supported by corrupt private interests may be expected.

With the drugging of the general population, governing elites come to see themselves as a ruling class and not as public servants accountable to a public that believes in limits on private and public behavior. And, finally, as these unaccountable elites forge alliances with their counterparts in other countries, a transnational alliance of finance capital is facilitated, an alliance freed of democratic republican accountability. Borderless and unchecked capital is thus available for speculative assaults on states resisting the agendas of unaccountable money interests.

The above description distinguishes between actual democratic and pseudodemocratic regimes. It identifies how corruption subverts the power-checking purpose of the democratic regime. It focuses on the logical and empirical conditions necessary for democracy to work. And it recognizes that forms alone are not sufficient.

PART II

Governments, Organized Crime, and International Finance

CHAPTER 4

GOVERNMENTS: FROM THE OPIUM WARS TO THE COLD WAR

THE AMBIGUOUS ROLE OF GOVERNMENTS IN CRIMINAL ACTIVITIES

An understanding of governmental involvement is essential to an understanding of the narcotics problem. The economic model alone does not include an awareness of governmental support of and protection for drug trafficking.[1] Furthermore, it impedes an enhanced understanding of the embedded nature of criminal activity within the political system.

As mentioned before, the standard economic model focuses solely on supply, demand, and profits and explores only those areas where the system is vulnerable in controlling drug trafficking. Proponents of this model center their debate around the relative merits of targeting crop eradication, interdiction, and interruption of profit repatriation. Thomas B. Fowler suggests the key to disrupting the drug trade lies in severing the flow of money from smugglers to drug barons. (See figure 3.) "Interception of laundered money or the flow of money back to the drug barons," Fowler has said, "has much greater promise of achieving the desired goal of making drugs unavailable and can be carried out at a cost which is significantly less than that of drug interdiction efforts."[2]

But the purely economic model ignores the mutual dependency among governments, organized crime, and transnational capitalism. Governments may operate in the international environment to insulate themselves from domestic accountability. Historically, governments have

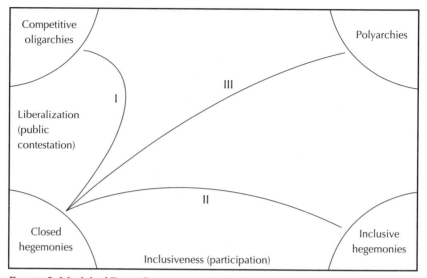

FIGURE 3. Model of Drug Operations (From Thomas Fowler, "Winning the War on Drugs," *Journal of Social, Political, and Economic Studies*, Winter 1990.)

had an interest in the drug trade for reasons of revenue. In 1797, during the war against Napoleon Bonaparte, Great Britain decided to formally supervise narcotics trafficking in the Far East to ensure the nation's revenues and tea supply. British Prime Minister William Pitt the Younger placed the management of the East India Company under a government-appointed board, the Calcutta Council. (The center of opium production in India was in the Bengal where Calcutta served as the capital.) Although the Calcutta Council officially prohibited the import of opium into China, it rescinded the company's direct control of the opium business because it was not being run with sufficient profitability. Thus the council appropriated that share of the profit that the contractor had previously enjoyed, and, more important, it was in a position both to supervise and restrict production.[3]

The British government's involvement illustrates how trade in opium began as a government-protected monopoly and later became a fully government-controlled business. The Calcutta Council officially recognized its duty to discourage the sale and consumption of opium, except for medicinal purposes, when "in fact, it would be using it as an additional source of revenue, . . . making the government of British India still more dependent upon its production." Consequently, the British government, "needing some commodity which would sell in sufficient quantity in China to maintain the balance of trade, was equally involved. As it held the controlling interest, parliament, in a sense, had become the chief shareholder in the opium business. And the government had again to consider how best to protect it."[4]

This pattern of government-granted monopoly or direct government management has become a model for organized crime. Governments sometimes protect the illegal activity or knowingly permit it through a lack of regulation or enforcement. The opium wars (1840–42 and 1858–60) between Great Britain and China demonstrate a government's historical involvement with the narcotics trade and willingness to engage in war to protect it.

THE OPIUM WARS

Early in the seventeenth century, Great Britain's East India Company secured trading rights to buy tea from the emperor of China. As British demand for tea increased, a balance of payment deficit resulted between the two countries. Opium smuggled into China provided the needed revenues to offset the British deficit. The Imperial Court became disturbed over the spread of opium smoking among the population and placed a ban on its importation in 1729. When the Chinese government pleaded with the British government to desist in the opium trade, it was completely rebuffed, and the East India Company continued to allow "country ships" of independent "country firms" to ply the opium trade under its license. Technically, the goods the country ships sold to China did not belong to the company. However, these ships could only obtain their commodities with the permission of the company. The allegedly independent country ships were the means by which the East India Company plausibly denied its involvement in the drug trade.

However, the company remained fearful that if it was found importing the drug illegally it would lose its trading rights in China. Therefore the Select Committee, the East India Company management board at Canton, wrote on September 3, 1827,

> The very extensive Contraband Trade now carried on at the anchorage of Linting [sic], not only in the Importation of Opium, but in the transit of goods of every description to and from Canton,

by means of such vessels as are entering the river, renders it necessary in our opinion to issue a strict prohibition against any communication between our ships and the above vessels, which might
eventually form a subject of discussion to the Officers of Government
and a pretense for levying exactions upon the Hong Merchants.[5]

Initially, neither the Chinese emperor nor the British viceroy seemed
to comprehend the full extent of the traffic, which had been gradually
growing, fostered by the East India Company, ever since the 1600s.
Although opium had been cultivated in Bengal for centuries, the cultivation of the drug increased with British involvement. The British chose
not to sell opium to their Indian subjects, but to the Chinese who had
been purchasing it from the Portuguese for generations. The Portuguese
had operated out of Malwa, on the Indian coast north of Bombay. When
the British drove the Portuguese out of the market, the East India
Company gained the trade monopoly.

Recognizing the emperor's edict forbidding the importation of opium,
the company found a way of selling it that would avoid censure against
them and their commodities. The British country firms that had traditionally managed trade inside Asia assumed the risk of marketing the
opium. They worked out a policy with Parliament by which they were
able to sell ever-larger quantities. By 1793 revenues were a quarter of a
million pounds, and by 1832 they were nearly 1 million pounds, which,
according to Maurice Collis, represented "about a sixth of the whole
Indian revenue."[6]

One of the principal country firms, Jardine and Matheson, had an
elaborate organization, which included a fleet of armed ships, clippers
that carried the opium from Calcutta to Lintin, a number of storage or
receiving ships to which the opium was transferred from the clippers, and
an office in Canton where Chinese smuggling contacts paid for opium.
When the Canton market was saturated, Jardine and Matheson acquired
a second fleet of ships that distributed opium farther up the coast and
eventually replaced the Chinese smuggling fleets. Out of reach of Chinese
governmental control, the coastal trade grew. As Collis reports, "That
Government, having no deep-sea fleet, could not prevent the opium ships
prowling along the coast; and even had local officials been honest, the
coast was so long, and cover and inlets so numerous, that the most
efficient preventive service could hardly have stopped smuggling."[7]

The opium trade represented a clear and present danger to the Chinese government. A substantial part of their population and even their bureaucracy had contributed to the opening of China to Western trade, not for political reasons, but because they were addicted to the drug and the profits that went with it. This sector now represented a considerable challenge to the government's official policy and authorities. This was especially threatening to the emperor, since his Manchu dynasty was not native to China. In addition to threatening rebellion, a sizable part of the bureaucracy was acting independently of the central dynasty. While the official policy was to prevent corruption, elements of the government were benefiting from the trade and resisting enforcement.[8] This is an early example of intrastate conflict: conflict within the government and between elements of the government and the population.

The century-and-a-half-long monopoly of the East India Company's trade with China came to an end with an act of English Parliament on August 28, 1833. Numerous factors brought the end of the trade monopoly, but they did not halt the company's monopoly on opium in India. The new British concerns then permitted to operate in China with a larger network of distributors actually increased the supply and subsequent demand for opium in China.[9] The central Chinese government resisted pressure from the new fleet of private companies seeking access to their market, and the British continued to flout their edicts.

Consequences of the opium trade for Chinese society were tremendous. According to reports of the time, "The class of people who consume opium in China are those of the male sex, chiefly between twenty and fifty-five years old. It affects soldiers very much, render[s] them weak and decrepit." It was estimated that opium smokers "constituted 10 to 20 percent of the officials in the central government, 20 to 30 percent of those in the local government, and 50 to 60 percent of the private secretaries . . . who handled law, punishments . . . , and taxes."[10]

In addition to corrupting the government and the army, the opium trade promoted prosperity in the financial system, though it impacted unfavorably on the country's balance of trade. A side effect was to make China's banks rich and its overall economy weak. By 1836 all the political leaders, whether in favor of legalization or prohibition, agreed that the drug trade caused a massive outflow of money. For the first time in its trade with the West, China ran unfavorable trade balances. It was this concern that caused China to demand a new policy restricting the importation of opium.

The new superintendent of British trade, William John Napier, further aggravated Great Britain's relationship with the Chinese central government. Instructed to seek the extension of British trade in China, he offended Chinese sensibilities with his brusque approach. The Chinese government responded by decreeing further controls on the opium trade and ordering Lord Napier to leave Canton. Napier refused and continued to press the Chinese government to open more ports for trade. The government retaliated by cutting off supplies to the British ships in port and prohibiting the entry of British ships. The British warned that this was a near act of war and that if any ships were fired upon, they would respond.

The clash intensified as British merchants influenced a more aggressive foreign policy, and insistence upon ending the drug traffic grew within the Peking government. Advocates within the Chinese central government called for capital punishment for opium smokers who did not stop consuming the drug within one year of the proposed law prohibiting it. The resulting law in 1838 called for the beheading of wholesalers and the strangling of smugglers, corrupt public servants, and those operating opium dens. An additional law ordered the beheading of foreign offenders. There was a considerable reduction in the smuggling trade as a direct result of these domestic laws. On January 30, 1839, a British representative in China reported to the British foreign minister, Viscount Henry John Temple Palmerston, that the opium traffic had come to nearly a complete halt.[11]

China's continued problems with opium had more to do with its failure to restrain the British than with its lack of success in repressing demand at home. The supervising government official, Commissioner Lin, hoped to continue legal trade with the British but did not realize that a decline in the opium trade would make it difficult for the British to buy Chinese commodities. Furthermore, he did not understand the British government would back the opium traders in China. His misunderstanding of Great Britain's intentions is illustrated in the letter he sent to Queen Victoria in the spring of 1839:

> We are of the opinion that this poisonous article is clandestinely manufactured by artful and depraved people of various tribes

under the dominion of your honorable nation. Doubtless you, the honorable sovereign of that nation, have not commanded the manufacture and sale of it. . . . And we have heard that in your honorable nation, too, the people are not permitted to smoke the drug, and that offenders in this particular expose themselves to sure punishment. It is clearly from a knowledge of its injurious effects on man, that you have directed severe prohibitions against it. But in order to remove the source of the evil thoroughly would it not be better to prohibit its sale and manufacture rather than merely prohibit its consumption?

Though not making use of it one's self, to venture nevertheless to manufacture and sell it, and with it to seduce the simple folk of this land, is to seek one's own livelihood by exposing others to death, to seek one's own advantage by other men's injury. Such acts are bitterly abhorrent to the nature of man and are utterly opposed to the ways of heaven. . . . We now wish to find, in cooperation with your honorable sovereignty, some means of bringing to a perpetual end this opium, so hurtful to mankind: we in this land forbidding the use of it, and you, in the nations of your dominion, forbidding its manufacture. . . . Not only then will the people of this land be relieved from its pernicious influence, but the people of your honorable nation too (for since they make it, how do we know they do not also smoke it?) will, when the manufacture is indeed forbidden, be likewise relieved from the danger of its use.[12]

Commissioner Lin kept Queen Victoria informed of his government's opposition to the drug trade and reported to her the new statute of capital punishment for foreign merchants found guilty of importing opium. He urged her to abolish the cultivation of the poppy in her dominions and to replace it with alternative crops. As Chinese naval forces were insufficient to block trade, Commissioner Lin chose to control trade by imprisoning British smugglers and holding them hostage until its termination. Massive amounts of opium were turned in and destroyed. From the British point of view this was an act of piracy and a threat to its power and prestige that justified a military response. The British government and merchants sought retaliation for the imprisonments, the opium losses, and the alleged insult. The first shots were fired when a British fleet was rejected in its demand for provisions at Kowloon. The British sent an expeditionary force, which blockaded Canton in the summer of 1840 and the first Opium War officially began.

The British military was overwhelmingly successful. China capitulated in May of 1842 and trade was resumed. The Treaty of Nanking forced the Chinese to grant the British everything they sought through the policies that foreign minister Palmerston formulated. Hong Kong was ceded to the British crown, five ports were opened up for opium trade, and the Chinese paid indemnities of $6 million for opium seizures and were forced to compensate the imprisoned British subjects. Hong Kong became a colony dependent on opium trade revenues.

Despite general support in Britain for enforced opium trade with China, there was some internal criticism of the British position. The *Times* of London stated in an editorial that moral compensation was owed to China "for pillaging her town and slaughtering her citizens in a quarrel which could never have arisen if we had not been guilty of an international crime."

Nonetheless, British policy continued to promote the opium trade with China. From 1839 until 1850 opium sales rose two and a half times. By the time the second Opium War began in 1858, Chinese addiction had risen to a correspondingly higher percentage of the total population. Despite British dominance after the first Opium War, the Chinese government still refused to legalize the opium trade. The second war finally compelled it to accept legalization.

STRATEGIC USE OF NARCOTICS BY RED CHINA, THE SOVIET UNION, AND CUBA

The origin of the ongoing cooperation between Chinese secret societies and the British dates from the time of the opium trade. With their control of river commerce and desire to overthrow the Manchus and restore the Ming dynasty, these societies were ideal partners to help the British. Most of them in southern China had been formed in opposition to the Manchu dynasty. The principal secret societies were the Heaven and Earth Society, a.k.a. the Three Dots Society; the Elder Brothers Society, which controlled the Yangtze-Shanghai area; and the Three United Society. The familiar designation of these societies as "triads" is derived from the latter group. In addition to trafficking in China's river system, the triads controlled gambling and prostitution. With British backing they became strong enough to stage revolts and gain control of some of the coastal cities. They were deeply implanted in the Fukien and Kwantung provinces, and from these provinces they emigrated overseas, creating a transnational network of secret societies protecting drug trafficking and other criminal activities.

Chinese leadership understood well its vulnerability when the triads allied themselves with foreigners. They also understood the foreigners' vulnerability when the triads were allied with the Chinese government. It should not come as a surprise then that once the opportunity arose Chinese leaders used narcotics as a weapon. As early as 1928 Mao Tse-tung, the Chinese Communist leader, supported using opium against the "imperialists," as he termed the Western powers. In fact, two of Mao's generals, Chu The and Ho Lung, were members of a triad, the Elder Brothers Society.[13] According to Joseph D. Douglass, Jr., Mao used narcotics to attack the United States, U.S. military forces in the Far East, Japan, and other Asian neighbors shortly after he secured mainland China in 1949. "The primary organizations involved in the early 1950s," Douglass noted, "were the Chinese Foreign Ministry, the Trade Ministry, and the Intelligence Service. North Korea was also trafficking narcotics in cooperation with China at this time and was directly connected with the flow of drugs into Japan and into the U.S. military bases in the Far East."[14]

The growth in drug trafficking and abuse within the United States and elsewhere correlates strongly with the support of governments that promote and protect it. Douglass revealed how drug-related deaths and addictions in New York and San Francisco jumped dramatically in 1949–50 when Mao's international narcotics strategy was organized. A second jump occurred in 1960 when Chinese operations were intensified and Soviet narcotics trafficking operations began.[15]

Hearings before a subcommittee of the U.S. Senate Judiciary Committee in 1955 described in great detail the role of the Chinese government in organizing the country's narcotics operations.[16] The Chinese Ministry of Agriculture was in charge of producing better varieties of poppies, the Ministry of Commerce organized storage and export, the Ministry of Foreign Trade managed external trade, the Ministry of Foreign Affairs assisted marketing, and the Ministry of Public Security provided security. According to Douglass, "The trafficking tradecraft included classical smuggling; transport by shipping companies (both knowingly and unknowingly); use of communists and ethnic Chinese abroad; collaboration with international organized-crime syndicates; use of foreign posts of mainland parent organizations; abuse of diplomatic privilege; use of normal branded merchandise as a cover; transport by mail; and forgery or packaging with misleading trademarks."[17]

In short, the Chinese government was involved in the production and distribution of drugs to undermine its enemies and to increase its national income. From the time of the opium wars, the Chinese had known very well that the consumption of drugs weakened their people, corrupted their government, and destroyed their morale. They made a conscious decision to use drugs as a weapon.

Extensive evidence indicates the Soviet Union also utilized narcotics strategically to penetrate and weaken other countries. To that end, it used the considerable power of the KGB and other Warsaw Pact intelligence agencies. According to Gen. Maj. Jan Sejna, who defected from the former Czechoslovakia's intelligence services to the United States on February 25, 1968, Soviet strategic use of narcotics emerged during the Korean War. Sejna identified five stages in Soviet strategy that incorporated narcotics trafficking. The first two stages were to select and train leaders for revolutionary movements. In the third stage, drugs were used to undermine morale within the targeted countries and to recruit agents for the revolution. The fourth step was to infiltrate organized crime and the fifth was to plan a worldwide network for sabotage. The Soviets crafted this strategy from 1954 to 1956. The decision to penetrate organized crime was made in 1955. As Douglass has said,

> The main reason for infiltrating organized crime was the Soviet belief that high-quality information—information of political corruption, money and business, international relations, drug trafficking, and counter-intelligence—was to be found in organized crime. The Soviets reasoned that if they could successfully infiltrate organized crime, they would have unusually good possibilities to control many politicians and would have access to the best information on drugs, money, weapons, and corruption of many kinds. A secondary reason was to use organized crime as a covert mechanism for distributing drugs.[18]

Czechoslovakia was assigned an important role in the operation. Its intelligence agents were told to infiltrate seventeen different organized crime groups in addition to the mafia in Germany, France, Italy, Austria, and Latin America. Terrorism was incorporated in conjunction with drugs in order to destabilize the targeted countries.

Cuba was brought into the operation in the summer of 1960, barely eighteen months after Fidel Castro had gained power. Castro's brother, Raul, had been recruited by Czech intelligence in the early 1950s when, during a visit to Czechoslovakia, he agreed to cooperate with the revolutionary strategy. During the 1962 Second Havana Conference, the joint intelligence group was appointed to collect data on individuals corrupted by drug trafficking who could be used as spies or agents of influence. An enormous amount of data was obtained on drug trafficking in Latin America. At the same time, the group identified a large number of companies in Mexico "whose main business was drug smuggling, including pictures of the trucks and names of the drivers used to transport the drugs into the United States."[19]

The Tri-Continental Conference held in Cuba in 1966 heralded the decision to have Cuban intelligence agents infiltrate all Latin American operations. Cuba set up narcotics operations in Mexico and Colombia and cooperated with Czech agents in Panama and Argentina. The Soviet-Czech-Cuban operation also targeted the Andean region, Central America, Chile, and Brazil. Mexico was of particular importance because of its two-thousand-mile border with the United States.

THE UNITED STATES GOVERNMENT AND NARCOTICS

In at least three instances the United States may have cooperated with narcotics trafficking for political and strategic purposes. The first came during the Vietnam War. The United States picked up the support of various groups resisting the communists in Vietnam by helping them market opium. Alfred W. McCoy has written,

> At a time when there was no ground or air transport to and from the mountains of Laos except CIA aircraft, opium continued to flow out of the villages of Laos to transit points such as Long Tieng.

There, government air forces, this time Vietnamese and Lao instead of French, transported narcotics to Saigon, where close allies of Vietnam's political leaders were involved in both domestic distribution and international trafficking. And just as the French high commissioner had found it politically expedient to overlook the Binh Xuyen's involvement in Saigon's opium trade, the U.S. embassy, as part of its unqualified support of the Thieu-Ky regime, looked the other way when presented with evidence that Saigon's leaders were involved in the GI heroin traffic.[20]

Charges of CIA covert operations in alliance with drug lords and tribal leaders led to congressional concern and a review of the agency's activities. In testimony before a U.S. committee in June 1972, the U.S. inspector general concluded that the agency did not support drug trafficking "as a matter of policy." The agency, however, cooperated with drug trafficking for other purposes besides policy. According to McCoy, the revelations of the inspector general support the view that the agency's relationship "involved indirect complicity rather than direct culpability."[21]

A second allegation of U.S. involvement in drug trafficking has to do with supplying arms to the Afghan resistance during the Soviet invasion in December 1979. The Pakistani government's intelligence agency cooperated with the CIA to provide guns and ammunition for the Mujahedin. The trucks taking the incoming weapons from Pakistan to Afghanistan returned with narcotics stashed among sacks of grain and other legitimate goods. The guns and drug trade in Afghanistan was protected by Pakistani army officers and assisted by the now-defunct Bank of Credit and Commerce International (BCCI). The war in Afghanistan led to a ten-year partnership between the intelligence agency of the Pakistan military (the ISI), the CIA, and Saudi intelligence. The Saudi intelligence chief, Prince Turki bin Faisal, was a BCCI shareholder and distributed more than $1 billion in cash to the Mujahedin in the 1980s. The war coincided with an upsurge in drug trafficking in Pakistan. By the mid-1980s an estimated 80 percent of all heroin consumed in Britain and 30 percent in the United States came from Pakistan. During the same period, Pakistan's drug revenues were estimated at between $8 billion and $10 billion. Much of this money was being laundered through BCCI.[22]

Two other students of the Pakistani connection, Jonathan Beaty and S. C. Gwynne, write,

> Poppy cultivation boomed in Afghanistan during the war years, as did Pakistan's own opium crop in the remote frontier area. Traditionally, opium had moved out of Afghanistan through Pakistan, Iran, Turkey, and India, but because of a drug crackdown in Turkey, the Islamic revolution in Iran, and the Soviet invasion of Afghanistan, virtually all west-flowing opium was being diverted through Pakistan. With the war as a cover, it also became profitable to process the opium into heroin before it began its journey, and hundreds of small laboratories sprang up on the frontier. Soon the Pakistani market was glutted with cheap narcotics, and drug barons penetrated the politically unstable and economically weak society. (In 1979 Pakistan's drug addiction rate was negligible; by 1992 addicts numbered at least 800,000.) By 1984 an estimated forty drug syndicates were flourishing, and Pakistan was the origin of 70 percent of the world's supply of high-grade heroin.[23]

A third circumstance of alleged U.S. support of drug trafficking concerns the financing of the Contras in Nicaragua. This occurred after the October 1984 Boland Amendment cut off U.S. military aid to the Contras. The motivation behind the autonomous CIA operation was the curtailment of congressional support for covert operations. Lieutenant Colonel Oliver North testified before the U.S. Iran-Contra committee that CIA chief William Casey wanted an "off-the-shelf, self-sustaining, stand-alone entity that could perform certain activities on behalf of the United States." In other words, the need for an independent source to finance covert operations required a mechanism permitting the operation to be independent of congressionally appropriated funds.

According to Peter Dale Scott and Jonathan Marshall, the CIA-Contra drug connection extended to Honduras, Panama, and Costa Rica. They write that "each major faction in the Contras had its own cocaine connection and that the rise of each connection corresponded to a change in the management of the U.S.-Contra relationship." These writers claim that at least two of the Contra drug connections received their cocaine from the Cali cartel, and they conclude, "There are documentary indications that, as far back as 1983, Washington used or at least condoned many or all of these different Contra drug connections to maintain Contra support operations. At a minimum, the U.S. Government and the CIA were well aware of the drug problems. . . . North's notebooks and Robert Owen's memos to North both refer to them, as do other internal documents of the Reagan administration."[24]

Documentary evidence indicates that the private resupply effort of the Contras involved many of the same people who had maintained the tribal resistance effort in Southeast Asia. Alfred W. McCoy writes,

> When Lieutenant Colonel Oliver North of the National Security Council formed a private network to fund the Contras after the aid cutoff, he recruited General Richard Secord, recently retired from the Pentagon, to establish a covert arms supply operation. Admitting his ignorance about infantry weapons, Secord, a career air force officer, recruited the ex-agency man Thomas Clines, whom he later described as "a very close associate of mine from CIA days." The phrase "CIA days" was, of course, a reference to their service together commanding the agency's secret war in Laos during the late 1960s.[25]

McCoy concludes that the CIA's Contra support operation coincided with a major expansion in the Caribbean cocaine trade and that the coincidence between cocaine trafficking and covert operations made the DEA's task of drug interdiction almost impossible.[26]

Assuming that the United States maintained the relationships in Southeast Asia, Pakistan, and Central America as described, the CIA inspector general's conclusion that the agency needed "an assessment of the possible adverse repercussions" of its relations with drug dealers seems mild. In any case, there is considerable evidence that individuals in the United States government have been consciously involved in the facilitation of narcotics trafficking for political purposes.[27]

CONTEMPORARY GOVERNMENT SUPPORT OF THE DRUG TRADE

Each of the three interrelated factors producing narcostatization are extremely important in understanding the full extent of the problem of the criminalization of the state. The mutual dependence of government policy, organized crime, and transnational capitalism may be considered a synergistic independent variable for three additional dependent variables: anocratization, international strife, and civil violence or insurgency.

The criminalization of government, society, and the international financial system supports inter- and intrastate conflict in a narcostate. The interpenetrating variables reinforce the factors that produce narcostatization and result in a vicious circle. In some cases, state corruption is used as a justification for insurgency. Or foreign states may become involved in the corrupt state's internal affairs in order to help defend themselves from that state's protected criminal activities.

An appropriate understanding of the drug problem requires avoiding a single image of "good" governments combating crime and criminal financial activity. Governments may simultaneously combat and support drug trafficking and money laundering. Of course, at the official and public level, governments, such as those of Colombia and Mexico, deny involvement in narcotics trafficking and the protection of money laundering. The public, not possessing sufficient knowledge of the circumstances or a reason to disbelieve its leaders, often accepts their denials. Yet it is inconceivable that some government officials are truly unaware of their government's involvement in criminal activities.

In conclusion, governments have four main reasons for supporting drug trafficking and consumption in other countries. First, the enormous profits earned by the drug trade not only maintain the financial systems of countries where liquidity has become a problem but also expand the economic influence of those nations. Second, the drug trade supports both a nation's agriculture and its commerce. The various narcotics plants are easily grown in remote areas, providing livelihoods for poor peasants, and the illicit trade assists commerce by providing extraordinary profits to a nation's commercial interests.

Third, states embrace drug trafficking as a means to secure intelligence and to financially support intelligence agencies. Drug income, precisely because it is illegal, remains anonymous and is a source of autonomy and independence for intelligence agencies. In addition, it provides access to criminal elements who can furnish the intelligence agencies with services such as assassinations, intimidations, and other activities the agencies wish to keep at arm's length.

Fourth, as demonstrated in the case of relations between the former Soviet bloc and Cuba and in U.S. activity in Afghanistan, governments support drug trafficking for strategic reasons. Some states embrace drug trafficking as a policy to destroy their enemies. The principal targets are the enemy's political institutions, its armed forces, and its society, particularly its most vulnerable classes and most important elites.

CHAPTER 5

THE DEVELOPMENT AND SPREAD OF ORGANIZED CRIME

Organized crime has spread with the internationalization of capitalism and the increase in global trade. Although it is not the only variable, organized crime plays a significant role in corrupting the state. Most observers are familiar with the problem of organized crime in large cities but do not consider it as having a statewide or international presence. Yet organized crime is embodied in modern and well-established international groups that infiltrate governments and financial institutions. The illegal activities of these groups extend beyond narcotics trafficking and money laundering. Organized crime, whether called a syndicate, mafia, or cartel, is at the root of "productive" criminality. It is an organization that manufactures or appropriates for markets both illicit and legitimate goods and services while seeking either the de facto or the de jure protection of portions of the government. This definition of organized crime draws on insights gained from numerous studies that demonstrate that its effective operation requires exploitation of the market and its cooperation with elements of the government.

In his study of the traditional Sicilian mafia, Henner Hess found that "The phenomenon of the traditional Sicilian mafia has combined in itself the characteristics of two types of crime: [those] of organized crime with those of repressive crime. In other words, those of an illegal enterprise for financial gain and profit with those of an illegal defense of economic and political privilege."[1]

Organized crime is intimately connected with people in the political structure who facilitate its activities. As authors Pierre Tremblay and Richard Kedzior note, "An admission that organized crime exists is an admission that political corruption exists and that power is exercised through patronage. On the other hand, the denial that organized crime exists may emanate from a conviction that patronage is no longer a part of the political process or that it will be harmful to admit that this is so."[2]

Organized crime's relationship with the government provides for political immunity from the law. The mafia or cartel boss operates at a midline between the upperworld and the underworld. Figure 4 illustrates a model of the relationship between upperworld and underworld mafia systems. In this model, the crime boss operates as a broker between local, regional, and national levels of the political system. Political connections in the upperworld protect the organization's production and distribution of goods and services while the organization's enforcement apparatus protects business in the underworld.

Sometimes enforcement mechanisms of the underworld ally themselves with the upperworld against political opponents. A three-level hierarchy of power is evident in both the upperworld and the underworld. The boss is clearly number 1 with respect to the underworld but, depending on the nature of the political system, the boss may or may not be subordinate to a more powerful political figure in the upperworld. These relationships are fluid and dynamic. Organized crime may be part of the productive economy and the social system in that it depends on mass markets and exploits the level of social tolerance for its products. The fight for legalization only promotes the social acceptability of the activity.

The evolution of organized crime in societies ranging from Japan and China to Italy and the United States indicates that struggles between the cartels are frequent and ongoing, as are the struggles between the political bosses. The conflicts between the underworld and the upperworld merge as the relationships between the mafias and politicians consolidate. This is occurring in Mexico and has been underway in Colombia since the early 1980s, as will be shown in later chapters.

The corruption stemming from organized crime provides a substitute source of wealth and power for the institutionalized privileges the elites once held as a bureaucratic oligarchy. While authoritarian elites are able to manage organized crime, newly privatized economies provide insula-

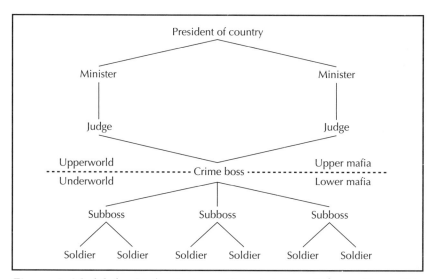

Figure 4. Model for Mafia Systems (Adapted from Henner Hess, "The Traditional Sicilian Mafia," in *Organized Crime: A Global Perspective*, edited by Robert J. Kelly. Totowa, N.J.: Roman & Littlefield, 1986.)

tion from electoral accountability. The former bureaucratic oligarchy becomes a ruling class that exploits and controls what is in effect a criminal capitalist class. The minimum definition of democracy, "procedural democracy," becomes the political formula by which the new ruling class justifies its rule to the rest of society and the international community.

The criminal-political relationship progresses from the local and regional to the national level of politics. After consolidating at the local and state level, the criminal relationship advances to the international arena. If organized crime develops in the social context of economic demand for illicit goods and political corruption, then the globalization of markets and politics allows organized crime to flourish where international society is anarchical. As governments become dependent on criminal organizations for profits and the acquisition of arms and other sinews of state power, the international arena becomes a new haven for organized crime.

In addition, corruption in the form of organized crime provides the authoritarian elite or bureaucratic oligarchy a means of gaining wealth and retaining power. An authoritarian elite in a democratic and privatizing economy may find organized crime useful for acquiring wealth and insulating itself from electoral accountability. An alleged transition from authoritarianism to democracy is frustrated when the former ruling elite continues to control the government as an elected class connected to the permanent government bureaucracy. In this way, the ruling elite remains largely independent of civil society, with a substantial part of that independence derived from exploiting and controlling organized crime.

The role of organized crime in corrupting democracy goes beyond the authoritarian elites' cooperation to preserve their power in democratic transitions. Existing consolidated democracies may find elements of the elected establishment forging ties with organized crime in order to cushion the country from external economic shocks. These alliances protect sectors of the economy dependent on the financial benefits of organized crime. Society's support for a corrupt government may increase in situations where the income derived from the narcotics trade allows the government to pay its debts and provide much-needed social services. In this vicious circle then, the resources organized crime provides to the government assist elites to gain and maintain power.

The subversive relationship between government and organized crime suggests that a state with democratic features may not in essence be an accountable and responsible political system. For a regime to be considered fully democratic, the electoral process must in practice maintain accountability. Where the governing elites rely on criminal oligarchs to finance and privatize state entities, the maintenance of accountability through the electoral process becomes questionable. This distrust of genuine democratic accountability is present for regimes in transition, such as Russia, as well as for long-term consolidated regimes, such as the United States.

THE RUSSIAN MAFIA

According to Stephen Handelman, an expert on Russian crime, organized crime in Russia long antedates the former Soviet Union. The criminal gangs of czarist times served as prototypes for the future Bolshevik organizations. Later, Stalin used gang leaders for his revolutionary activities and recruited some of them for his secret police. In the gulag system, gang members informed on political dissidents.[3] The Russian mafias were in some cases protected by the state to help keep the Soviet economy afloat through their skill in black market activities. They were also involved in arms trafficking, prostitution, and money laundering.

During the Perestroika period of the late 1980s, the gangs forged ties with regional political regimes and cooperated in the restructuring of the economy by legitimizing their profits in stock exchanges, joint ventures, and banks.[4] Claire Sterling, in her book *Thieves' World*, notes that the mafia moved from "merely feeding off the economy to owning it." Illicit activities of the Russian mafias became more noticeable after the fall of the Berlin Wall. East German delinquents drew their power from contraband alcohol and cigarettes, automobile theft, fraud, prostitution, sales of arms and drugs, extortion, and assassinations.[5]

During the final years of the Soviet Union, the mafia's volume of transactions increased from less than 1 billion rubles in 1989 to 130 billion rubles in 1991, a sum equivalent to the national deficit of the USSR. In 1992, organized crime controlled between 30 and 40 percent of the GNP of Russia. As of 1994 there were five thousand Russian mafia bands with 3 million accomplices spread throughout the fifteen ex-Soviet republics, over one-sixth of the world. And, like most powerful mafias, the Russian mafia spread into other parts of the world. It penetrated Los Angeles, San Francisco, Chicago, and Philadelphia, as well as a dozen other cities in the United States and Canada. The FBI described the Russian mafia as prone to violence and considers it one of the most brutal criminal organizations ever in the United States.[6]

Criminal activity increased sharply amid the economic and political chaos that developed after the fall of the Soviet Union. As the Soviet regime collapsed in Russia, the Russian ruling class, or *nomenklatura*, merged with elements of the criminal class. Stephen Handelman writes,

> The two criminal societies made a natural fit. Already strikingly similar in organization, they presided over the two major streams of capital available to post–Communist Russia: black-market profits and the wealth of the Communist Party. The old formal barriers between the *vorovskoi mir* and the Party hierarchy were erased by new alliances of convenience. The process was most visible in Russia's regions, where the crime lords and the bureaucrats shared the common aim of resisting the attempts of the central authorities to break the power of the large state enterprises.[7]

Whether or not there is a central command controlling Russia's various mafias is a topic of much discussion. There are approximately two hundred Russian crime groups operating in twenty-nine countries outside the former Soviet Union. According to the Russian Interior Ministry, these groups run prostitution rings in Macao and Guangxhou, China; narcotics trafficking in Uzbekistan and Tajikistan; money laundering in Cyprus; money laundering and welfare fraud in Israel; illegal alien smuggling in Sweden; money laundering, car theft, nuclear material smuggling, arms dealing, and prostitution in Germany; money laundering in Belgium and the United Kingdom; diesel fuel tax evasion, car and jewelry theft, insurance fraud, organized shoplifting, contract murders, gun running, crack vial manufacturing, money laundering, and prostitution in the United States; and car and jewelry theft in Canada. Robert H. Rasor, head of the U.S. Secret Service's financial-crime unit notes, "The Russians know the smart way to get money isn't by robbing banks but by quietly creating fraud schemes that involve millions of dollars. They take advantage of the weaknesses in systems."[8]

There is a clear hierarchy in the gangs. At the lowest level are the people who carry out the open illegal activity while at the top are the "godfathers" who plot the strategy. These chiefs may be allied with or themselves be government officials.[9] The major recent growth of the Russian mafias has come from sales of the former Soviet Union's control of various enterprises. These mafias control an estimated 60 to 70 percent of Russian industry.[10] Most of the eighteen hundred commercial banks in Russia are either partially or completely owned by the mafias.[11] The Russian mafia is not only involved in the distribution and marketing of illicit products, but also in the production of drugs. There are frequent reports of large poppy field cultivations in the southern republics of Russia. Kazakhstan grows opium, as do Ubezk and Kyrgyztan. There are also instances of Russians manufacturing synthetic drugs (Krokodil and Chert), which are a thousand times stronger than heroin.[12]

The Russian mafias have become particularly adept in arms sales. Thousands of cases of military weapons have been stolen and sold on the international black market. In addition to rockets, antitank missiles and hand grenades, the mafia has sold radioactive materials such as plutonium and enriched uranium. German and Swiss police have intercepted substantial shipments of nuclear weapons material.[13] According to reports in the Western press, Russian generals have been operating through state companies or legitimate front firms and have used the criminal networks to market radioactive material to Middle Eastern and North African countries.[14] The former Soviet mafia is now part of a network of organized criminal organizations encompassing the entire world, with connections to the Sicilian mafia.

THE SICILIAN MAFIA

The Sicilian mafia is a potent political force. Despite repeated efforts to defeat it, it remains resilient. It is present not only in the United States, Russia and other eastern European states, but also in France, Belgium, Germany, and Holland.[15] In the 1980s, the Sicilian mafia controlled 80 percent of New York's heroin market; had extensive investments in major financial companies, real estate, commerce, and agribusiness; and had an estimated gross domestic product (GDP) of $20 billion to $25 billion in Italy alone.[16] Its deleterious impact has been felt in the political arena, where it not only has made Italian politicians less accountable to the people who elect them but has created an alternative set of obligations to their interests. By controlling the illicit narcotics industry, the mafia has kept southern Italy economically backward.

The Sicilian mafia, one of the oldest criminal clans in the world, was born on the island of Sicily; its modern roots date back to the nineteenth century. It has expanded throughout Europe and is most notable for its involvement in criminal activities in Italy and Germany. Its leadership is in family units that have become the prototype for numerous criminal associations all over the world: the Corleone clan, the Madonia family in Palermo, the Giuseppe Madonia clan in Guela, and the Santapaola clan in Catania.[17]

European police sources believe the Sicilian mafia has about fifteen hundred members and close to fifteen thousand accomplices in Sicily, Calabria, Apulia, Campania, and Naples. Its main income is derived from cocaine and heroin trafficking. It created the new European cocaine market through an agreement with the Colombian drug cartels in which they gave the Colombians "exclusive rights" for trafficking South American cocaine in Europe. The Sicilian-Colombian pact was the first of similar agreements among other mafias in the world for illicit international transactions.[18] In 1992, the Sicilians introduced more than two hundred tons of drugs to Europe, with an income of about $10 billion. The economic power of the Sicilian mafia is so strong that the Cuntrera-Paolo and Pasquale brothers bought the Caribbean island of Aruba in 1980, acquiring hotels, land, banks, police, customs officials, government bureaucrats, and political leaders.

Matching this extraordinary economic influence is the control of literally thousands of politicians and businessmen. This corruption does not respect hierarchies, ideologies, or political parties. In the 1990s Italy implemented Operation Clean Hands on the initiative of several coura-geous prosecutors. The goal of Operation Clean Hands was to weed out mafia connections with government officials and end the corruption infesting every level of Italian government and business.

In the first two years Operation Clean Hands was put in place, more than fifteen hundred politicians and businessmen were arrested and many more placed under investigation.[19] They were accused of corrup-tion and collaboration with criminal groups. By 1993, one third of the nation's Parliament faced corruption charges and the head of Italy's state-run media company was under investigation. It was concluded that bribes in the 1980s and early 1990s had amounted to approximately $10 to $20 thousand million, and the scandal forced many important public figures to leave their posts.[20]

The Sicilian bosses (*capos*) are said to be responsible for the 1992 assassination of Italian judge Giovanni Falcone, considered one of the most valiant prosecutors of the mafia. His investigations demonstrated the involvement of prominent politicians in illicit transactions and led to extensive changes in the Italian political system. Even so, this extra-ordinary criminal enterprise has not been fundamentally defeated.

One of the most notorious capos in the history of the mafia was Salvatore "Toto" Riina, the brain behind one of the bloodiest fights against the Italian state. Responsible for the deaths of hundreds of people, his organization assassinated five judges, one attorney general, one states-man, two chiefs of police, and important politicians from the Christian Democratic and Communist parties. Riina took over and consolidated his rule within the mafia after Lucky Luciano's imprisonment in 1974. He established an intelligence network among the 150 mafia families and seemed to have an unassailable position until the murders of Judges

Giovanni Falcone and Paolo Borsellino. The public outcry over their deaths resulted in a major crackdown on Riina and the mafia, which exposed the Christian Democratic party's long-time cooperation with the mafia.[21]

The exposure of this network had a devastating impact on the Christian Democratic party and brought to the fore alternative political parties. Much of the network of party government and mafia was knitted under the cover of a secret Masonic lodge composed of top military police, secret service, judges, and cabinet ministers. The extensive corruption of Italian society and government reveals that the interconnection of politics and crime has enormous staying power. According to author Brian Sullivan,

> The world's most notorious and supposedly most powerful crime group actually has been dependent on official government support and after that protection was removed [it showed] how vulnerable it has been to government prosecution. . . . [International organized crime groups] really may not enjoy much success without access to the resources and sponsorship of sovereign states. When such successful organizations are supposed to exist, I would be quite suspicious. I would investigate the possibility of covert government aid to such groups as the ready source of their strength.[22]

In the post–cold war era the Sicilian mafia, which was thought to have no equal, was joined by other major mafia players. The most prominent ones, besides the Russians, were the Chinese triads and the Japanese yakuza. Claire Sterling believes that these three mafias, together with the American and Colombian mafias, have been forming a worldwide criminal consortium.[23]

THE ASIAN SYNDICATES

Of all the criminal mafia groups, the Chinese triads are probably the oldest. Historians of the triads have identified secret societies as early as the fifth century B.C. and have found them involved in the nineteenth-century Taiping Rebellion, the 1911 revolution of Sun Yat-sen, and the 1937–45 struggle against Japan.[24] During the opium wars the triads made almost as much money as the British trading companies. After China banned opium they were able to survive by marketing heroin. A faction of the triads made an alliance with Generalissimo Chiang Kai-shek, and others established themselves in the Shan states of northern Burma.

The trafficking and sale of heroin remains the main business of the Chinese triads, which own two-thirds of the world heroin market, with the United States as their principal client. They also deal in the lucrative trafficking of illegal immigrants in Southeast Asia, Europe, and the United States.[25]

The triads have grown at a remarkable rate. Hong Kong has been their window to the world for more than a century, and many of the more powerful gangs are in Hong Kong, where such brotherhoods as the Wo Shing Wo and the Sun Hee On have a notorious presence. The Hong Kong–based triads are prominent in managing immigration to the United States and operate in every criminal activity from drugs and prostitution to loan sharking. Law enforcement has had considerable difficulty dealing with the triads because their members easily transfer from one syndicate to another for a fee.[26]

Not as ancient, but certainly as widespread, are the Japanese organized criminal gangs, the yakuza—the word yakuza literally means "trash" in Japanese. Founded three hundred years ago, the yakuza was a criminal organization of gamblers and assassins that transformed into a fighting force during clashes of local and regional leaders in the seventeenth century. After World War II, they assisted right-wing political forces and allied with the CIA in persecuting militant leftists, independent syndicates, and the autonomous press, in exchange for control of the black market and freedom to continue with their criminal activities. In 1955, they participated in the creation of the Liberal Democratic Party (LDP) of Japan, and their top leaders began to dabble in the construction, entertainment, and prostitution industries.[27] In the past twenty-five years, the yakuza have extended into Asia, North and South America, Europe, and the former Soviet Union. They expanded in the early 1970s into Korea and the Philippines, then Hawaii and California, before hitting the rest of the Americas and Europe.

The yakuza's principal activities include gambling, prostitution, drugs, and real estate investments in the Philippines, Taiwan, and Thailand. One of their operations consists of laundering money and trapping clients in loans with exaggerated interest rates. The yakuza have been cooperating with the Cosa Nostra since 1960, when they first began working as waiters, dishwashers, and cooks in Hawaii, the nearest occidental entrance to the United States.[28] Their annual income from arms and cocaine and heroin contraband is estimated at more than $20 billion. The total income of the yakuza has been estimated at over $71 billion.

A coalition of several thousand organized gangs, the yakuza claim more than one hundred thousand members. Besides being one of the economic and financial pillars of Japan, the yakuza have laundered hundreds of millions of dollars in real estate and other investments in Hawaii, California, Nevada, Arizona, and New York.[29] For comparative purposes, Japan's largest bank, Dai-Ichi Kangyo Bank, employs nineteen thousand people and in 1993 had profits of nearly $384 million. Japanese businesses have been so beleaguered by the yakuza that they employ a private firm, the JSS company, for the protection of company executives. The severity of the situation prompted the United Nations to hold a crime conference in Naples the week of November 20, 1994, which focused on programs to combat the yakuza, the Sicilian mafia, and the other transnational crime organizations.[30]

According to the Japanese investigator Ranko Fujizawa, "the political elite of the main parties and the mafiosos constitute the two faces of power which, with an intricate collaboration and exchange of favors, [have lived] harmoniously together for many decades." In October 1992, one of the most powerful political parties in Japan was divided by a corruption scandal, as a result of which the prime minister, Kiichi Miyazawa, fell.[31]

U.S. commercial interests became aware of the power of the Japanese yakuza when the U.S. Federal Maritime Commission imposed a $100,000-a-visit fine on Japanese vessels because of the delays on U.S. shipping imposed by the Japan Harbor Transportation Association (JHTA). The JHTA allegedly has ties to the Yamaguchi-gumi syndicate, which has the power to delay the unloading and loading of U.S. ships even if it does not exercise it. This "prior consultation" system prevents a shipper from shopping around for cheaper unloading services and thereby operates as a sanctioned cartel. In effect, the arrangement between the JHTA and the yakuza allows them to keep labor unrest under control and intimidate shippers from bucking cartel control of Japan's harbors. Some of the companies, such as Isewan Terminal Service Company in Nagoya, have been termed a *kigyo shatei*, "a yakuza-linked business," according to national-police documents.[32]

THE COLOMBIAN DRUG BARONS

The Colombian mafia originated in the mid-1960s when the first drug traffickers initiated their operations on a small scale in U.S. territory. After the boom in illegal drug consumption worldwide, the Colombian leaders began to experience considerable increases in earnings and discovered the immense lucrative possibilities. The Medellin and Cali cartels soon became the largest producers and distributors of cocaine in the world. In order to obtain maximum political and economic power, the Medellin cartel, with Pablo Escobar Gaviria at the helm, entered into a bloody fight against the Colombian government, bribing and assassinating police, judges, magistrates, journalists, and even presidential candidates.[33]

The Medellin cartel was responsible for the assassinations of Justice Minister Rodrigo Lara Bonilla in 1984 and Attorney General Carlos Mauro Hoyos in 1988. In 1989 the cartel informally declared war on the government and killed more than 550 people in a bombing campaign. The government essentially capitulated through lax jail sentences on notorious traffickers Pablo Escobar and the Ochoa brothers. Escobar was killed in 1993 after escaping from his luxurious prison accommodations.[34]

The Colombian government cooperated with the Cali cartel in its battle against the Medellin cartel. The Cali group provided intelligence to the government forces seeking to eliminate Escobar. As a result, the Cali cartel replaced the Medellin as the principal supplier of cocaine out of South America. In 1989, the Medellin cartel controlled an estimated 75 percent of the world's supply of cocaine. In 1993, they controlled only 40 percent, and a year later, the Cali cartel was estimated to be moving as much as 85 percent of the twelve hundred tons of cocaine shipped out of South America.[35] Now the dominant cocaine mafia in Colombia, the Cali cartel is run by several groups of kingpins. The older group of godfathers is led by Miguel and Gilberto Rodríguez Orejuela and Iván and Julio Fabio Urdinola. The rising younger group is led by Juan Carlos Ortíz and Juan Carlos Ramírez.[36] The Cali cartel has kept a low profile, bribing police and government officials to support their interests.

The dominance of the mafias in Colombia has led to the coining of a new term, "colombianization," defining a social situation generated by narcotics traffickers. A colombianization is characterized by the disintegration of political, economic, and social structures and a permanent state of violent crimes such as political assassinations, executions, and human rights violations.[37]

The Colombian mafias ally themselves with local capos in other countries such as Mexico to facilitate production, trafficking, and distribution. International agreements with the mafias of Europe and Russia have extended their business globally, with the United States as their principal market, making them one of the most powerful mafias in the world.[38] The global scope of the Cali cartel includes representatives from Japan to eastern and western Europe and, of course, throughout North, South, and Central America and the Caribbean. The cartel is vertically integrated in that it controls the purchasing, refining, wholesale, and distribution aspects of the cocaine trade. The sophistication of its distribution is demonstrated by its capacity to insert coca paste into concrete posts, plastic chairs, slippers, and other unusual products. These products are in turn shipped through legitimate businesses on cargo ships.[39]

DEA administrator Thomas Constantine notes, "It is unequivocally clear that the cartels control every aspect of the cocaine trade, from the amount of cocaine to be shipped on consignment, right down to the markings on each package." In 1994, the DEA partially lifted the secrecy covering its two-year investigation into the methods the Cali cartel used to move large amounts of cocaine from Colombia through Mexico and Los Angeles to distribution points throughout the United States. Over the two years of the investigation, 166 members of the alleged distribution network were arrested and more than six tons of cocaine and $13 million were seized. The traffickers used commercial and private planes, trucks, cars, and boats to smuggle drugs into and across the United States. William Mockler, chief of the DEA's major investigation section, stated that those arrested did not know the names of those higher up the chain of command and thus could not expose the whole organization in any plea bargaining arrangements. The cartel network operates on the basis of a cell organization that compartmentalizes the knowledge each member has of the organization.[40]

There is growing evidence of Cali cartel ties with the Russian mob. A Cali cartel member was spotted in Russia as early as 1992 and a year later a ton of cocaine from Colombia was seized in St. Petersburg. Several members of the Russian mob have been arrested in Bogota. The extent of the cooperation between the Russian and Colombian mafias led the foreign ministries of both countries to sign an agreement to exchange information in November 1997. One result of this cooperation occurred in January 1998 when Russia's federal security service, the successor to the KGB, discovered 265 kilos of Colombian cocaine in an underground vault between the Siberian town of Braskt and the port of Vladivostok. Forty tons of Colombian cocaine entered the territories of the former Soviet Union in 1997. When the 1998 World Cup was held in France, the Colombian-Russian cartels cooperated in inundating Europe with drugs.[41]

Besides the Cali alliance, the Russian mob has developed ties with the largest Colombian left-wing insurgency, the Revolutionary Armed Forces of Colombia (FARC). The Russian mob has been supplying FARC with sophisticated weapons, including rocket launchers and SAMs, handheld ground-to-air missiles.[42] The FARC threat has become increasingly severe, despite Pres. Andrés Pastrana's (1998–) offer to deal with the traffickers, and the United States continues to increase its military assistance to the Colombian armed forces.

Despite the deterioration of U.S. relations with Colombia in 1995 because of Pres. Ernesto Samper's alleged campaign financing from drug traffickers, White House drug czar Gen. Barry McCaffrey visited Colombia to offer U.S. support for the police and army who are "subject to guerrilla attacks." "It is undeniable," McCaffrey said, "that the Revolutionary Armed Forces of Colombia and the National Liberation Army are funded with millions of dollars in drug money."[43]

THE MEXICAN CARTELS

More than 20 percent of the heroin, 60 percent of the marijuana, and 50 percent of the cocaine imported into the United States come from Mexico, according to State Department estimates. In 1994 alone Mexican narco-traffickers laundered $3 billion to $6 billion through complex financial circuits.

The Cali cartel of Colombia has a dominant relationship with two of the major Mexican mafias, the Ciudad Juárez and the Gulf cartels.[44] The largest Mexican cartel, the Ciudad Juárez, was headed by Amado Carrillo

Fuentes[45] until he died July 4, 1997, after having "plastic surgery on his face and three and a half gallons of fat sucked from his body."[46] He had been described as the most powerful of the drug traffickers, and some analysts claim he was worth more than $25 billion. In Mexico there is speculation as to whether or not Carrillo was murdered with an intentional overdose of drugs or if he is even dead. Further elements add to the mystery. Carrillo's bodyguard and look-alike, Jorge Palacio Hernandez, was kidnapped two weeks before Carrillo's reported death, and the surgeons who operated on Carrillo were found four months later "embedded in concrete-filled barrels beside a highway." No matter what truly happened to Carrillo, his cartel continues to operate.[47]

The Gulf cartel was headed by Juan García Abrego until his conviction and imprisonment in the United States in 1996. The Mexican attorney general's office reports the Gulf cartel is worth over $10 billion. It has compromised federal and judicial officers, including the narcotics chief of the Federal Police of Mexico, Guillermo González Calderoni, and Deputy Attorney General Javier Coello Trejo.[48]

When the South Florida Tax Force, under then–vice president George Bush, cracked down on smuggling through the Caribbean into Florida, the Cali cartel forged ties with three major organizations. According to former Mexican assistant attorney general Eduardo Valle, the Gulf cartel was given a share in the profits based on the volume of its shipments through Mexico. Since it took its profits from both the Medellin and Cali cartels, it made more money than both those Colombian cartels.

The Tijuana cartel, headed by the Arellano Félix family, has also received international attention for its activities. In testimony before the Senate Foreign Relations Committee in October 1997, James Milford, deputy administrator of the DEA, stated that the Arellano Felix organization hired foreign mercenaries to train its private militia. Milford characterized the Tijuana cartel as "one of the most powerful, violent and aggressive trafficking organizations in the world."[49]

The Mexican mafias are responsible for about half the cocaine imported into the United States and receive 40 to 50 percent of the profit. According to the DEA, the principal centers of consumption are Los Angeles, Houston, Miami, and New York. The DEA estimates that the Cali cartel ships into the United States an estimated 560 to 800 tons of cocaine a year via Mexico. American agents maintain that the U.S.-Mexican border between Los Angeles and Houston is out of governmental control and almost exclusively in the hands of drug traffickers. DEA investigator Philip Jordani asserts the narcobusinessmen and the narcopoliticians "colombianized" Mexico under the presidency of Carlos Salinas.[50]

Jordani believes the assassinations of Roman Catholic Cardinal Juan Jesús Posadas Ocampo (1993), presidential candidate Luis Donaldo Colosio (1994), and party secretary Francisco Ruíz Massieu (1994) were meant to demonstrate the power of the narcotraffickers and terrorize the Mexican society and government. Their aim is to continue benefiting from the impunity granted them by the narcopoliticians in key positions of the administration. Since the presidency of Gustavo Díaz Ordáz (1964–70), the businesses connected with narcotics trafficking have consolidated their power with the help of politicians who hold key positions in the cabinet. Several members of Miguel de la Madrid's (1982–88) and Carlos Salinas de Gortari's (1988–94) cabinets—including the ex-secretary of defense Juan Arévalo Gardoqui, Enrique Alvarez del Castillo, Javier Coello Trejo, Guillermo González Calderoni, Manuel Ibarra Herrera, Miguel Aldana Ibarra, Rafael Aguilar Guajardo, and Elias Ramírez, among others—have allegedly protected traffickers. According to Jordani, the power of the narcotics traffickers has reached the most important and strategic levels of government.[51]

The Catholic Church in Mexico may also be touched by drug money. Nuncio Jerónimo Prigione, under public scrutiny on many occasions, drew attention to a possible Catholic Church connection because of his interview with two of the Arellano Félix brothers, leaders of the Tijuana cartel and two of Mexico's most wanted capos. Emmanuel Ruíz Subiaur, a specialist in religious matters, said, "there are indications the Catholic Church had money in the group represented by the banker Carlos Cabal Peniche," whose bank is among those investigated for money laundering through Operation Cobra, a joint U.S.-Mexico operation.[52]

As in the cases of Italy, Russia, Colombia, and Peru, the Mexican cartels and drug traffickers enjoy protection from the highest levels of the Mexican government. When DEA agent Enrique "Kiki" Camarena was kidnapped, tortured, and murdered in 1985, the investigation of the perpetrators revealed that high-level government officials had close ties to the cartels. Miguel Angel Félix Gallardo, one of the top figures in the cartel associated with Camarena's abduction and murder, was closely associated with top Mexican officials.[53] Enrique Alvarez del Castillo was governor of Jalisco at the time of Camarena's abduction. He later became

Pres. Carlos Salinas de Gortari's first attorney general. While governor of Jalisco, Alvarez was accused of allowing drug trafficking in his state and was considered an extraordinary choice to be in charge of the police forces that ran Mexico's drug interdiction efforts.

Another name that surfaced from the investigations into Camarena's murder was that of Rubén Zuno Arce, the brother-in-law of former Mexican president Luis Echeverría. Zuno Arce previously owned the house in which Camarena was tortured. According to DEA sources, Zuno Arce was a major trafficker in Guadalajara and was accused of shooting two Mexican federal police in 1978. When he was ultimately arrested in San Antonio in 1989 for drug trafficking, prosecutors allegedly dropped the case against him because of his political connections.[54] A year later he was convicted in Los Angeles.

Zuno Arce was a former associate of Rafael Caro Quintero and Ernesto Fonesco Carrillo. It is known that both these men were involved in the kidnap-killing of Camarena. When Caro Quintero, the head of the Guadalajara cocaine cartel, was finally captured, he had in his possession the phone numbers of several cabinet ministers, including the minister of defense.[55]

As the drug war in Mexico becomes militarized, there is growing concern that more of the nation's officers will be corrupted by it.[56] U.S. authorities have implicated high-ranking Mexican officers, Maj. Gen. Juan Poblano Silva and his executive officer, Lt. Col. Salvador de la Vega, in drug trafficking. They were linked to a high-ranking member of the Mexican ruling party and convicted drug trafficker Hector Manuel Brumei Alvarez and Jorge Carranza Peniche, grandson of former president Venustiano Carranza.

Another case of high-level military involvement concerned the firing in early 1997 of Gen. Jesús Gutiérrez Rebollo as head of Mexico's anti-drug agency. Highly praised by U.S. authorities and Pres. Ernesto Zedillo for his integrity, General Gutiérrez had been provided intelligence on U.S. strategies and informants in Mexico before it was belatedly discovered that he was on the payroll of the Amado Carrillo Fuentes–led Ciudad Juárez cartel, the nation's largest cartel. The Carrillo-Gutiérrez relationship led to the penetration of U.S. antinarcotic intelligence. Carrillo Fuentes, one of Mexico's wealthiest men, also financed the military's antinarcotics operations against his principal rivals.[57] After General Gutierrez's arrest, Carrillo Fuentes visited Chile, Russia, and

Cuba. At the time of his sudden death on July 4, 1997, he was forging ties with the Russian mob and allegedly setting up operations in Chile to sell drugs to New Zealand and Australia.[58]

THE U.S. NATIONAL CRIME SYNDICATE

Organized crime in the United States "(1) is not some random or episodic thing, but a patterned and structured activity; (2) finds and exploits opportunities for illicit gain; and (3) operates across time regardless of individual changes in personnel or leadership," one observer has claimed. According to Peter A. Lupsha, "Organized crime in the United States tended to be dominated by an Italian-American-Jewish coalition. . . . Charles 'Lucky' Luciano's group appeared paramount over all other so-called 'La Cosa Nostra' groups, and with its multi-ethnic leadership mix, it acted as the link connecting Jewish and Italian organized crime across the United States."[59]

The characterization of organized crime in America as uniquely Italian has led to a misdiagnosis of the range, extent, and multiethnic nature of the country's National Crime Syndicate (NCS), which was designed to protect its leaders from competition, to provide funds for political protection, and to tax regional bosses according to their ability to pay. When the U.S. Senate's McClellan Committee investigated organized crime in 1959, Meyer Lansky was identified as the head of the National Crime Syndicate.[60]

According to Hank Messick, the author of an in-depth study of Lansky, when a high-ranking Justice official was asked why the department placed emphasis on the mafia instead of the National Crime Syndicate, the man explained, "The Mafia was small and handy. The feeling was the American people would buy it with its family relations and blood oaths a lot quicker than they could understand the complex syndicate. You must remember, we wanted to get public support behind the drive on crime."[61]

Born Maier Suchowljansky in Grodno, Russia, Meyer Lansky came to the United States in 1911 when he was nine years old. In time he filled the vacuum left by the previous brain of organized crime, Arnold Rothstein, the fixer of the 1919 World Series, who was murdered on November 4, 1928, in the Park Central Hotel of New York. Lansky, who had traveled about the country meeting with the bosses from Philadelphia to Kansas City, subsequently inspired the 1929 gangland convention held at the Hotel President in Atlantic City to search for additional sources of income. Lansky was the informal leader of the New York delegation which included Lucky Luciano and Joe Adonis. Other city or state organizations represented at the meeting were those of Cleveland, Detroit, Philadelphia, Kansas City, and New Jersey. This Atlantic City meeting demonstrated the multiethnic character of the NCS.[62]

Although no formal organization was created at the Atlantic City meeting, Lansky initiated the New York group's cooperation with the Cleveland syndicate. From that time on, arrangements were developed with other gangs throughout the United States, with Lansky the de facto chairman of the board.

Organized crime expanded during Prohibition, and when it ended, the major distributors of alcohol made large fortunes in the legal market. Most of the hard-core criminals who stayed in illegal activities after Prohibition went into gambling. Gambling houses were often located far from major cities, in towns such as Covington, Kentucky, and Hot Springs, Arkansas. Gambling was facilitated by the nationwide wire service, which ultimately led the FBI to recognize organized crime as a national problem.

In addition to gambling, the NCS moved into Hollywood. Key to controlling Hollywood was dominance of the performing artists and their unions. In 1924, Julius Caesar Stein started the Music Corporation of America (MCA). He achieved his first great success when he signed Guy Lombardo and his orchestra to an exclusive contract. MCA gradually came to represent many of the major Hollywood stars, including Betty Davis, Joan Crawford, John Garfield, Betty Grable, and Jane Wyman. Stein's "enforcer" was Willie Bioff, who "specialized in disrupting the operations of theatres and nightclubs that refused to contract businesses with MCA."[63]

Julius Stein allied himself with James Caesar Petrillo, president of the Chicago chapter of the American Federation of Musicians (AFM). Stein and Petrillo were in turn connected to Al Capone, who ran the Chicago mob from 1925 until 1931 and who through his cousin Lucky Luciano was also connected to Lansky and his chief hitman, Benjamin "Bugsy" Siegel.

When Capone was tried, convicted, and imprisoned for income tax evasion in 1931, Frank Nitti became the figurehead of the Chicago mob, but Tony Accardo, Paul Ricca, Charlie Fischetti (Capone's cousin), and Jake "Greasy Thumb" Guzik were the real bosses. Guzik brought Sidney Korshak into the mob,[64] and Korshak was soon managing all labor problems with the movie industry. This was the beginning of the mafia's involvement with the unions and the studios.

When gambling was legalized in Las Vegas, Nevada, in 1931 to stimulate the economy, Korshak became the channel for the Teamster pension fund in the Las Vegas casinos,[65] in addition to being the main "fixer" in Hollywood. The casino operations for the mob in Las Vegas were pioneered by Bugsy Siegel, who had moved west with Lansky's approval. By the mid-1940s, Las Vegas was swarming with representatives of the NCS from New York, New Jersey, Cleveland, Boston, and Chicago.[66]

The NCS also took advantage of the opportunities opening in Cuba under Fulgencio Batista, who led a successful coup d'etat on September 4, 1933. With the legalization of gambling in Havana, Lansky forged a personal relationship with Batista and by 1935 was building the NCS empire there.[67] Lansky and Luciano hoped to make the Caribbean the center of their operations.

> During the 1930s Meyer Lansky "discovered" the Caribbean for northeastern syndicate bosses and invested their illegal profits in an assortment of lucrative gambing ventures. In 1933 Lansky moved into the Miami Beach area and took over most of the illegal off-track betting and a variety of hotels and casinos. He was also reportedly responsible for organized crime's decision to declare Miami a "free city" (i.e., not subject to the usual rules of territorial monopoly). Following his success in Miami, Lansky moved to Havana for three years, and by the beginning of World War II he owned the Hotel Nacional's casino and was leasing the municipal racetrack from a reputable New York bank. . . . Luciano's 1947 visit to Cuba laid the groundwork for Havana's subsequent role in international narcotics-smuggling traffic. Arriving in January, Luciano summoned the leaders of American organized crime, including Meyer Lansky, to Havana for a meeting, and began paying extravagant bribes to prominent Cuban officials as well. The director of the Federal Bureau of Narcotics at the time felt that Luciano's presence in Cuba was an ominous sign.[68]

Harry J. Anslinger, commissioner of narcotics and an expert on Lansky and Luciano reported that "The Isle of Pines, south of Cuba, was to become the Monte Carlo of the Western Hemisphere. Cuba was to be made the center of all international narcotic operations. We had a number of transcribed calls Lucky had made to Miami, New York, Chicago and other large American cities, and the names of the hoodlums who called him."[69] Later, when Luciano was released from prison and returned to Italy, Meyer Lansky became the supervisor of Luciano's operations in the United States.

Mob control of the casinos in Las Vegas was threatened by the 1947 gangland murder of Bugsy Siegel. Siegel's 1947 losses at the Flamingo in Las Vegas led to the NCS's decision to eliminate him. Nonetheless, Lansky retained control of Siegel's interests in the Flamingo Hotel and Casino. This occurrence was part of what the famous Kefauver Committee sought to investigate. Chaired by Sen. Estes Kefauver, the Senate Special Committee began its investigation of organized crime in May 1950. Sidney Korshak was subpoenaed by the committee on September 1, 1950, but never appeared as a witness. He may have blackmailed Kefauver and thereby kept any mention of himself from appearing in the committee's documents or transcripts. Several investigators claim the Chicago mafia engineered compromising pictures of the senator in his hotel room.[70]

The Kefauver hearings led to a crackdown on crime in various cities in the United States. Lansky now realized that to sustain his gambling operations they would either have to have legal status in the United States or be conducted offshore in the Caribbean. The benefit of legal status is underlined by the support Moe Dalitz received from the former head of the Nevada tax commission's gaming division, who claimed that men like Dalitz were not "gangsters in the true sense, but merely men who wanted to come to Nevada and do legally what they had been doing illegally in other states."[71]

After the collapse of his operations in Cuba with the ascent of Castro in 1959, Lansky chose the Bahamas as the site for his offshore gambling, narcotics, and money-laundering operations. He used the Mary Carter Paint Company based in Miami to buy Hog Island, later named Paradise Island. Subsequently, Mary Carter sold its paint division and emerged as Resorts International, Inc. Lansky's operations became further entrenched in the Bahamas when he backed Lynden O. Pindling of the

Progressive Liberal Party against the Bay Street Boys, the old guard of the islands, who were accused of corruption. With the removal of the corrupt backers of the Bay Street Boys, it was clear sailing for Lansky's NCS-backed Resorts International.[72]

The extent of the NCS's political connections to the various state and national figures is highly suggestive of the sub-rosa influence the mob had. Sidney Korshak had ties to powerful Democratic Party figures— including James Arvey, whose protégé was Adlai Stevenson,[73] and Paul Ziffren, once considered the most important force in the California Democratic Party. Ziffren later became a law partner of William French Smith, who himself became Reagan's attorney general.[74] There were also connections to Republican Party leaders. Former New York governor Thomas E. Dewey and his son invested in Mary Carter Paint through a complicated financing arrangement whereby they invested in the Crosby Miller Company, which merged with Mary Carter Paint and yielded fifty shares for each one held in Crosby Miller.[75] Dewey, of course, sponsored Richard Nixon in his bid for the vice-presidency in 1952.

An interesting aspect of NCS operations is the degree to which the mob has gained access to and protection from politicians. J. Edgar Hoover, the FBI's longtime chief, was reportedly "naive" with respect to the NCS. He attended gangster-owned racetracks in Miami, posed with gang bosses, and accepted money from Lewis Solon Rosenstiel, a notorious bootlegger allied with the Canadian Bronfman interests. Rosenstiel was head of Schenley's Distilleries and he endowed the J. Edgar Hoover Foundation with Schenley stock. As information on the NCS developed, however, Hoover created a special squad based in Miami to identify gangsters and supported antiraqueteering efforts of the FBI.[76]

Despite the multiethnic character of the NCS, the Kefauver investigations into organized crime in the United States gave the impression that it was predominantly an Italian-American operation. "The very use of the word mafia to describe the organization of these activities reflected the belief that the problem was a predominantly Italian one, a belief that would soon diffuse from these Senate investigations to the public at large. The committee further concluded that there were two major syndicates in the nation and that both were operating in Nevada."[77]

Nevada's casinos are an example of legal protection of gambling in the United States. Mormons, who came to control the state politically, settled the northern part of Nevada, particularly the areas surrounding

Reno and the capital, Carson City, in the late 1840s. The first Nevada institution to provide loans to casinos was the predominantly Mormon- and Jewish-owned Bank of Las Vegas, which later became the Valley Bank of Nevada.[78]

The principal tool the Gaming Control Board of Nevada used to prevent criminal control of the casinos was the *Black Book*, "a list of persons who are to be excluded from casinos in the state because of their perceived threat to the public image of gaming."[79] Because the majority of names in the *Black Book* were Italian, the impression given by the Nevada gaming board was that they had effectively barred organized crime from the gambling casinos. This impression was furthered by the McClellan crime investigations of 1957. Sidney Korshak, the first witness called before the McClellan Committee, was questioned by Robert Kennedy before the full committee on October 30, 1957. Kennedy was interested in a labor dispute that involved Korshak, who was tied to Willie Bioff, the "Hollywood extortionist." Previously, in an FBI inter- view, Bioff had cited Korshak's role and importance to the Chicago mafia.[80] Nonetheless, the committee concluded that, "there was a 'mafia' operating in the United States of largely Italian and Italian-American origins. It was believed that this mafia was organized into regional 'families' that were structured bureaucratically, and that these families conspired to monopolize gambling, prostitution, and various rackets. These conclusions formed the basis for an 'alien conspiracy theory' of organized crime."[81] The failure to recognize the multiethnic character of the National Crime Syndicate allowed large numbers of non-Italians associated with the NCS to control gambling in Nevada, while the public was led to believe that the "mafia" was excluded.[82]

The legitimacy granted by Nevada's gaming board assisted Steve Wynn, who operated the Las Vegas Golden Nugget, to move into Atlantic City. In 1975, when New Jersey voters approved casino gambling, Lansky's Resorts International bought the Chalfonte-Haddon Hall, at that time Atlantic City's largest hotel. When Atlantic City opened for business on June 2, 1977, it was the first casino in operation. Soon after, Steve Wynn bought the Strand Motel and built the Golden Nugget Atlantic City on that site. The New Jersey Casino Control Commission gave Wynn a license to operate in Atlantic City on November 13, 1981. A year later, it became obvious that the Golden Nugget Atlantic City was being used for money laundering. Anthony C. Castelbuono arrived at the

Golden Nugget on Thanksgiving Day 1982 with "suitcases filled with $1.187 million in small bills." After gambling and allegedly losing $300,000, "he left the casino with $800,000 in hundreds neatly bundled in $10,000 packets in Golden Nugget wrappers."[83] In 1987, Castelbuono was sentenced to fifteen years in prison for his role in laundering millions of dollars in another case involving a Sicilian-based heroin smuggling operation.

The Golden Nugget had other ties to organized crime. To finance his casino, Wynn had turned to Michael Milken, the junk-bond wizard of the Drexel Burnham Lambert corporate finance department. Introduced to Wynn by Stanley Zaks, chairman of Zenith Insurance, Milken provided him with $160 million in high-interest junk-bond financing.[84] Milken's junk-bond dealings came to an end when he pleaded guilty to six felonies in April 1990. One of those deals involved the Golden Nugget and the insider sale of MCA stock.[85] Milken's Drexel had funneled more than $5 billion in junk bonds into the hotel-casino industry in both Las Vegas and Atlantic City. When Drexel declared bankruptcy, more than fifty-five savings and loans failed, U.S. taxpayers were saddled with $1 billion in direct costs, and insurance companies faced more than $100 billion in losses.[86]

Wall Street's relationship to organized crime is generally depicted as one of victimization. *Business Week* described organized crime families as owning or controlling "perhaps two dozen brokerage firms that make markets in hundreds of stocks," driving prices up and then dumping them on the public. According to *Business Week*, "The Mob's activities seem confined almost exclusively to stocks traded in the over-the-counter 'bulletin board' and NASDAQ small-cap markets. By contrast, New York Stock Exchange and American Stock Exchange issues and firms apparently have been free of Mob exploitation."[87]

The financing of Steve Wynn and other casino owners of Las Vegas and Atlantic City illustrates how some of Wall Street's largest investment houses sustain businesses that, despite their legal gambling status, are frequently accused of money laundering. At the local level, organized crime controls some small brokerage firms and practices various financial scams. However, more important is the degree to which the large financial houses have backed the development of hotel-casinos with junk bonds.

In short, organized crime in the United States is a multiethnic national organization legally protected in numerous states. NCS gambling casinos assist the laundering of money obtained from narcotics trafficking and other illicit sources. In addition, the penetration of organized crime into Hollywood and its unions has allowed it to influence the U.S. culture industry. There is evidence that organized crime has connections to political bosses and to the funding of presidential campaigns, suggesting that its influence may reach into the highest levels of America's political system. For instance, there is the troubling example of John Rosselli's murder when he was called to testify before a congressional committee regarding President Kennedy's assassination.[88]

Why is it so difficult to thwart organized crime? Basically, the answer is endemic corruption—the combination of legalized gambling, the drug trade, the greed of financial institutions, the corruption of Hollywood, the growing dependence of politicians on large sums of money, the nationwide organization of crime, and the misleading perception that organized crime is run by a single ethnic group. The United States is witnessing the fusion of major money market centers, national and state political elites, Hollywood, legalized gambling, and the NCS. The United States is the leading country for laundering dirty money from illicit activities such as fraud and narcotics trafficking.[89] All of these are signs that in the United States the process of narcostatization may be well under way.

U.S. Intelligence, Organized Crime, and Narcotics

The intelligence agencies of various governments have explicitly promoted organized crime in the politics of international conflict. Before the cold war began, the United States intelligence agencies had forged a relationship with professional criminals. "Within three months of the Pearl Harbor attack," one observer has said, "the proposal to employ professional criminals in intelligence operations was made, adopted, and implemented. Collaboration between intelligence and organized crime clearly then was not forced upon America by the exigencies of the post-War world."[90]

At the beginning of World War II, the United States used organized crime elements in New York to help restrain labor unrest and to curb the sabotage and sinking of U.S. ships leaving port. The mafia's assistance to the U.S. government gave it new life after it had been crushed in Sicily by Mussolini's fascist regime. The resuscitation began on the New York waterfront with the burning of the French liner *Normandie*. This, along with attacks on U.S. ships by enemy submarines, led the Office of Naval Intelligence (ONI) to recruit local racket bosses to control sabotage in the Third Naval District, which included New York and New Jersey. Clearly, the ONI itself lacked the capacity to infiltrate and control the waterfront area, but it also quickly realized that it could not get the job done with middle-ranking racketeers and thus sought higher-ups. The key figure here was Lucky Luciano, who was serving time in Clinton State Prison in upstate New York. Luciano agreed to cooperate with the ONI. He suggested that Meyer Lansky, his partner in narcotics and bootlegging in Manhattan, serve as liaison between the U.S. Navy and the underworld.

Later, the ONI used the mafia for strategic intelligence in the U.S. invasion of Sicily, utilizing the organization to gain knowledge of the coastline and villages. After the invasion, the United States helped install mafia members in political positions in Italy as Allied forces drove out the fascists.[91] The United States continued supporting the mafia after World War II because of concern over the growth of membership in the Italian Communist Party. According to Alfred McCoy, the mafia was a natural anti-Communist ally, and it soon became a primary supporter of the Christian Democrats in southern Italy.[92]

The American intelligence community's cooperation with the mafia continued throughout most of the cold war. A legacy of the revitalized mafia was the massive corruption of the Italian state in the 1990s. Brian R. Sullivan considers this a warning that America should heed:

> There is reason to believe that the Italian Mafia benefited greatly from American governmental support in 1943–45 and possibly again in 1947–48. At that time, such cooperation with the Mafia could have been defended in the name of anti-Fascism, anti-Communism or simply as ragione di stato. But, weighing the gains and losses in the balance, it seems that American interests were far

more damaged by the mafia over the years than they were served. And the damage to the United States continues, particularly given heavy Mafia involvement in drug trafficking.[93]

Although many Americans believe that criminalization at the highest levels of the United States government could not occur, local experience with organized crime and growing evidence from the cold war indicate that the U.S. government may already have been compromised.

CIA involvement with organized crime includes entanglement in the global heroin traffic. According to Alfred W. McCoy, over the forty years of the cold war, CIA covert operations involved the agency in cooperation with narcotics smuggling and "often overwhelmed the interdiction efforts of the weaker U.S. drug enforcement agencies." The efforts of the Federal Bureau of Narcotics (FBN) and the Drug Enforcement Administration (DEA) to interdict the flow of heroin were inhibited by the CIA's logistic and political support for the drug lords. "At two critical junctures after World War II," McCoy writes, "the late 1940s and the late 1970s, when America's heroin supply and addict populations seemed to ebb, the CIA's covert action alliances generated a sudden surge of heroin that soon revived the U.S. drug trade." McCoy implicates the CIA in aiding the Corsican underworld in its struggle against the French Communist Party for control of the port of Marseilles; helping Hmong tribesmen battle the Laotian Communists by flying their opium to market; and supporting the Afghan resistance to the Soviets by expanding their opium market. "Unlike some national intelligence agencies," McCoy claims, "the CIA did not involve itself directly in the drug traffic to finance its covert operations. Nor was its culpability the work of a few corrupt agents eager to share in the enormous profits. The CIA's role in the heroin traffic was an inadvertent but almost inevitable consequence of its cold war tactics."[94]

In a sophisticated narcotics-state financial relationship, political elites, financial moguls, and narcotics traffickers work among themselves and with government agencies, well hidden from public scrutiny. The U.S. financing of the Nicaraguan Contras in their battle against the Sandinista government in the mid-1980s raised suspicion that corruption had penetrated to the highest levels of the U.S. government. In the 1990s, questions arose regarding the assistance given by former CIA operatives in the creation of a clandestine arms supply operation financed with narcotics money laundered in the state of Arkansas.

◆ ◆ ◆

With the help of economic globalization, organized crime is in a position to operate throughout the world with little political check. The various criminal organizations worldwide are well aware of each other and have developed methods to coordinate their activities. The Sicilian mafia, the Colombian drug cartels, the Turkish mafia, the Chinese triads, the Japanese yakuza, the new Russian mafia, and the NCS met in Aruba in 1987 and in Rome in 1992, where they agreed to avoid conflicts, plan common strategies, and peacefully divide the planet among themselves.[95] Orlando Cediel Ospina-Vargas, alias Tony Duran, leader of the Colombian cocaine mafias, planned to use these international connections to launder money in a professional, sophisticated and efficient manner.[96]

In short, it is clear that corruption infiltrates governments at the highest levels and that mafia cartels cooperate with each other much like states across international frontiers. Organized crime operates in terms of its own imperatives for economic expansion, for coalition building among its various national cartels, and for enforcement of its interests. To flourish, it depends on government protection and the opportunities provided by the globalization of international capitalism.

CHAPTER 6

THE CRIMINALIZATION OF THE INTERNATIONAL FINANCE SYSTEM

Organized crime and governments are interconnected with a third constituent part of narcostatization, the transnational financial system. This challenges two main assumptions regarding the international financial system and organized crime. The first assumption is that banks and the various national financial systems are essentially opposed to any activity that allows criminals to launder their profits and invest them in legitimate businesses. The second assumption is that the complexities of the globalized financial and trade systems make it difficult to control money laundering. However, the rise of criminal banks and the activities of legitimate banks undermine the first assumption and indicate that some components of the financial system are frequently willing participants, rather than victims, of money laundering. Furthermore, examples of cooperation across national borders provide proof of successful enforcement against money laundering and undermine the second assumption.

The breakdown of communism and state socialism and the incorporation of the former states of the Soviet Union into a worldwide capitalist economy have contributed to the expansion of global capitalism. Within this enlarged capitalist environment, the organized criminal elements of the West have been able to forge alliances and mutual financial relationships. The movement of illicit commodities and illegally obtained legitimate goods and the financing and laundering of profits have become global activities. In short, international criminal organizations and illicit drug markets could not operate successfully without the help of the international banking community. This financial community—both wittingly and unwittingly—has been used effectively to launder the profits generated by drug trafficking and other criminal activities.

THE GLOBALIZATION OF FINANCIAL MARKETS

International political economists debate whether the globalization of financial markets is the result of technological and economic developments or of state policies. Interesting as that debate is, it does not alter the reality that financial globalization has occurred. Policies of the most powerful states, together with the agreements of the major central banks, support globalization. However, the exploitation of the neoliberal international financial order undermines its legitimacy. This deligitimization arises from the enormous opportunities the new financial order provides the criminal organizations to launder their illegal money.

The Bretton Woods system since the mid-1940s intended the global financial system to be subordinate to the states' individual interests.[1] The agreement was supposed to prevent international capital flows from undermining welfare policies and trade liberalization. The Bretton Woods system requested that the Bank for International Settlements (BIS) be put out of business. Set up in 1930 under the sponsorship of private and central bankers to manage the international debt problem created by Germany's difficulty in meeting its reparation payments from World War I, BIS hosted meetings of private and central bankers on a monthly basis. At these meetings rules and procedures were developed for the BIS to act as the international lender of last resort in financial crises. With headquarters in Basel, Switzerland, the Bank of International Settlements served as a "central banker's bank" and permitted international payments to be made by moving credits from one country's account to another on the books of the bank. The Young Plan, the effort to solve Germany's reparation problem, embodied this arrangement. Owen D. Young, for whom the plan was named, was an agent of J. P. Morgan, the most powerful U.S. bank at the time.

Several governments that came to power in the 1930s blamed the international financial community for much of the economic problems of the period. Franklin Delano Roosevelt believed the Morgan financial empire was the major culprit in the financial decline, and the Glass-Steagall Act signed on June 16, 1933, divided commercial and merchant banking, which affected the House of Morgan. According to Ron Chernow,

> The Glass-Steagall Act took dead aim at the House of Morgan. After all, it was the bank that had most spectacularly fused the two forms of banking. It had, ironically, proved that the two types of services could be successfully combined; Kuhn, Loeb and Lehman Brothers did less deposit business, while National City and Chase had scandal-ridden securities affiliates. The House of Morgan was the active double threat, with its million-dollar corporate balances and blue-ribbon underwriting business.[2]

However, the private and central bankers did not share the hostility of the Bretton Woods system to the movement of financial capital across state lines. They supported the BIS as a positive influence in disciplining governments against inflationary policies. The resurgence of these central and international private banks was evident after the 1960 dollar crisis. At that point, the Europeans invited a representative of the Federal Reserve Board to attend the BIS monthly meetings. They also brought in representatives of the Banks of Canada and Japan.

The Bretton Woods system with its exchange control preferences became defunct in 1973. The U.S. government stopped backing the Bretton Woods system and began supporting the open system when its trade deficits grew and reversal did not appear likely. The open system preserved U.S. economic policy autonomy by forcing foreign governments either to buy U.S. dollars or to raise the value of their currencies. President Jimmy Carter's appointment of Paul Volcker in August 1979 to head the Federal Reserve Board made clear the U.S. commitment to financial openness. Beginning at this time, the United States asserted and maintained its financial preeminence vis-à-vis other countries while becoming increasingly disciplined by the growing global financial markets.

At the end of the Carter administration and throughout the Reagan administration the U.S. policy community accepted a system of floating exchange rates. This subjected domestic economies to international restraints that were coordinated through central banks and the BIS. The

BIS thus became critical to the management of a liberal international financial capital system. As a result of the liberalization of international capital markets, the financial power of the United States did not decline relative to other states, but it did decline in contrast with the growing power of global financial markets and their managers.

Much of the discipline of America's monetary policy developed because of the unregulated Eurodollar market based in London. To use this market, banks operated offshore, out of the control of the Federal Reserve. Then, in 1981, the Federal Reserve established tax- and regulation-free international banking facilities (IBFs) on U.S. territory, and U.S. banks were no longer obliged to go offshore to increase their participation in unregulated international capital markets. Some central bankers remained concerned about this globalization process because of its impact on domestic autonomy and stability. However, the central banks were encouraged that they could effectively maintain global financial stability because of the successful cooperation they had experienced through the BIS. Even so, international financial authorities realized that the criminalization of the global financial system represented a threat to the stability of the capital markets. As one observer said, "The development of efficient and stable capital markets requires that participants have full confidence in them. If markets were to be contaminated by money controlled by criminal elements, they would react more dramatically to rumors and false statistics, thus generating more instability."[3]

International Money Laundering in the Financial System

An estimated $500 billion, or 2 percent of global GDP, is illegally laundered each year.[4] Drug traffickers are not alone in using the international financial system to launder illicit proceeds. They are joined by arms merchants, corrupt political officials, and tax evaders. The international money-laundering market has exploded in terms of volume, sophistication, and access to legitimate financial resources. The ability of authorities to respond effectively has diminished. According to the U.S. Customs Office, at the end of 1992 there were more than 6,290 active money-laundering cases under investigation.[5]

At one time money laundering in the United States was a fairly simple process. "Launderers" would make large cash deposits openly in commercial banks. But, as laws regulating cash deposits evolved, the drug launderers moved to offshore banks located in nations with less stringent financial regulations. Among the most popular offshore bases known for their lax secrecy laws are Aruba, Bahamas, Barbados, Bermuda, British Virgin Islands, Cayman Islands, Costa Rica, Cyprus, Gibraltar, Guernsey, Hong Kong, Isle of Man, Jersey, Liberia, Lichtenstein, Nauru, Netherlands, Netherlands Antilles, Nevis, Panama, Switzerland, Turks and Caicos, and Vanuatu. Banks in these areas offer the benefits of easy access, no questions asked, and simple withdrawal. Less widely recognized, Canadian banks have also been used by drug-running organizations to launder substantial amounts of money.

An example of the magnitude of the problem was provided by the DEA's crackdown, code-named Casablanca, on Mexican banks. On May 18, 1998, a federal grand jury in Los Angeles brought charges against three Mexican banks and more than twenty Mexican bankers. This indictment was the first to charge Mexican banks as institutions that were knowingly helping the drug traffickers to launder their money. The three banks indicted were Bancomer, Mexico's second largest bank, Banca Serfin, Mexico's third largest bank, and Banca Confia, a top-twenty Mexican bank. Mexican authorities indicted Confia's chairman, Jorge Lankenau, for large-scale bank fraud only a few days after Citibank purchased Confia on May 11, 1998.

The Federal Reserve Board announced civil actions against five other Mexican banks with branches in the United States. These included Banco Nacional de Mexico (Banamex), the nation's largest bank; Bital, Mexico's fourth largest bank; and Banco Santander, the nation's fifth-ranking bank. The Federal Reserve charged that these banks had "serious deficiencies in their anti-money laundering programs."[6]

Sophisticated computer and telecommunications equipment simplifies the illegal movement of capital around the world, making these transfers difficult to detect. The money-laundering system has been further internationalized by the borderless European Union, which is connected to the numerous states of the former Soviet Union. In the Pacific Basin, Hong Kong, Macao, Thailand, and Japan move illegal money among themselves as well as with China. The development of unregulated global financial markets facilitates a system where crime syndicates based in the Americas, Europe, the Middle East, Africa, the Pacific Basin, and Russia launder money throughout the world and reinvest in legitimate businesses.

CRIMINAL BANKS

Legitimate banks can be used by criminal elements to launder illegal profits as part of their normal business practices. But outlaw banks knowingly use normal business practices to launder criminal profits. One of the most famous outlaw banks was the Bank of Credit and Commerce International (BCCI); another is the Banca Nazionale del Lavoro (BNL).

Meyer Lansky, the New York mafia leader, pioneered the modern techniques of money laundering. His methods included using offshore bank accounts in the Bahamas and Switzerland and layering account records. Before Castro's rise to power in 1959, Cuba was the major off-shore laundering site of the American mafia. After Fidel Castro took over Cuba and shut down U.S. mafia operations there, Meyer Lansky initiated a multistate laundering system, moving his operations to the Bahamas and continuing his practice of corrupting politicians. In the Bahamas, Lansky supported Lynden Oscar Pindling, the head of the Progressive Liberal Party (PLP), who came to power in 1967 as the leader of a Caribbean black power movement. When the Bahamas achieved full independence in 1973, Pindling became the central facilitator of Lansky's offshore operations.[7] It is indicative of the scant attention the British government gave to this problem that Pindling was knighted by Queen Elizabeth in 1983.

It was not long before the Colombian mafia also began using the Bahamas. By the early 1980s, nearly 80 percent of the cocaine and marijauna that came to the United States traveled through the Bahamas.[8] In addition, the Bahamas were identified as an important way station for heroin arriving from the Near and Far East.

The Bahamas have regulations that prevent authorities from examining bank records on the islands unless granted special permission by a Bahamian court. When money is deposited in a Bahamian bank, it can easily be transferred to other banks and escape detection from the legal financial system. This method owes its success to cooperation between the Bahamas and four major Canadian-owned banks—the Bank of Nova

Scotia, the Bank of Montreal, the Royal Bank of Canada, and the Canadian Imperial Bank of Commerce—which operate freely in the United States. These four banks control approximately 80 percent of the Bahamian banking business. Unlike U.S. banks, Canadian banks do not have a system for reporting large cash transfers and deposits of dubious origin.[9]

As charges of money laundering and government corruption in the Bahamas increased, Prime Minister Pindling was forced to call for a Royal Commission of Inquiry in hopes that it would exonerate him. The Royal Commission's report found no conclusive evidence tying Pindling to money-laundering schemes. However, there were enough irregularities and damaging information to force substantial Bahamian cooperation in cracking down on drug trafficking. This situation changed drug trafficking patterns and made Mexico the principal transit route for drugs into the United States. Rachel Ehrenfeld reported in the early '90s that

> One unintended consequence of Bahamian cooperation has been the development of alternative drug-running routes. In recent years Colombian drug traffickers have shifted their air routes from the Bahamas to other countries in the region, including isolated airports in Mexico's Yucatan or Baja peninsulas as well as the northern states of Chihuahua, Nuevo Leon, Sonora, and the northwestern state of Sinaloa. The cargo is transferred to cars and trucks and smuggled into the United States across the border. Puerto Rico, Panama, Brazil, and Guatemala, to name a few, are heavily used as drug transshipment points to the United States and to growing European markets.[10]

An additional problem in checking money laundering is the increasing use of nonfinancial institutions for the transfer of funds. Among the favorite money-laundering venues are money exchange centers and wire transfers through such legitimate agents as Western Union and American Express. It is estimated, for example, that as much as $5 million per month is transferred between the United States and Mexico through legal money exchange houses. Offshore casinos operating on American Indian reservations that are not subject to close federal oversight are also increasingly attractive money-laundering sites. And import-export transactions can be used to veil the transfers of illegal money.

Most prominently, however, drug traffickers take advantage of the developed transnational mafias, gain control over legitimate banks, and cooperate with banks that are completely outside the control of any state. An example of a criminal takeover of a legitimate bank is the Italian Banco Ambrosiano affair in the 1970s and early 1980s.

The Banco Ambrosiano

In the late 1960s, the infamous Sicilian banker Michele Sindona owned banks in Italy and Switzerland. Sindona got his financial start during the Allied invasion of Sicily in 1943 when the American-Sicilian mafia, headed by Lucky Luciano and Meyer Lansky, played a key intelligence role for U.S. forces. With the protection of the mafia, Sindona purchased a truck from U.S. forces to begin his illegal smuggling operations. Sindona was backed by Bito Genovese, a member of Lucky Luciano's Italian-American crime family, who provided Sindona his produce, papers, and safe routes. After the war, Sindona moved to Milan where he had an introduction from a Sicilian bishop addressed to the priest who became the archbishop of Milan, Giovanni Battista Montini, later Pope Paul VI.

The Vatican, an independent state in Italy, is a potential offshore banking resource for Italians. In 1942, Pope Pius XII created a bank called the Instituto per le Oppere di Religione (IOR), more commonly known as the Vatican Bank. During World War II many Italians protected their money from confiscation by the Germans by depositing it in the IOR. After Italy formally declared the Vatican a tax haven, the IOR moved funds out of Italy in support of church activities worldwide.

Sindona cultivated very carefully his Vatican contacts and in 1960 he purchased a small bank called Banca Privata that received deposits from the IOR. Three years later, in 1963, when Montini was elected pope, Sindona strengthened his relationship with the IOR. He induced the IOR to purchase shares in his other Italian bank, Banco Unione, and in his Geneva-based bank, Banque Financement.

In addition to his Vatican connections, Sindona forged an important tie with a major French Bank, Banque de Paris et des Pays-Bas. He also had powerful relationships with the Hambros Bank in London and the Continental Bank in Chicago. His connection with the Continental Bank gave Sindona access to Pres. Richard Nixon through the bank's chairman, David Kennedy, Nixon's secretary of the treasury after his election in 1968. Sindona was also a member of a secret Masonic lodge called Propaganda 2 (P2). P2's leader was Licio Gelli, who in 1965 was inducted into the Grande Oriente, a wing of Italian Freemasonry that supported ending the hostility between the church and the Masons. Pope Paul VI responded to this overture by permitting Catholics to join the Grande Oriente. Gelli maintained covert high-level ties with businesses, governments, and intelligence agencies in Italy and South America; he was, for instance, an economic consultant to Juan Perón. All these relations produced a positive synergy for Sindona, and in 1968 he was named one of the top advisors to the Vatican Bank, where he worked closely with Paul Cassimir Marcinkus, an American-born bishop who became the bank's president. All in all, Sindona's banking network proved to be "a convenient vehicle for the laundering of 'dirty money' earned from the heroin traffic and other mob-connected businesses."[11]

The Banco Ambrosiano had been founded at the turn of the century with the help of the Roman Catholic Church to compete with Italy's secular banks. Named after Saint Ambrose, it served Milan's Catholic bourgeois, small artisans, and traders who operated in northern Italy. Roberto Calvi, who would play an important role in corrupting the bank, joined Banco Ambrosiano in 1946. Calvi had considerable talents, and he rose in the bank initially on the basis of his professional skills, but he also got a boost from forces outside the bank through his contact with Michele Sindona, who had vast sources of power, some of them highly secret. He had, for instance, front companies in Luxembourg and Liechtenstein where bank secrecy was nearly absolute.

In November 1970, Ambrosiano bought an offshore company from Sindona and named it Banco Ambrosiano Holding (BAH). Calvi was now in a position to use BAH to operate in the Italian market as well as to control other banks and companies outside Italy. Not surprisingly, one of the offshore banks set up by BAH was in the Bahamas. This bank, Cisalpine Overseas Bank, was founded in March 1971 in Nassau. Later it was renamed Banco Ambrosiano Overseas and was owned by BAH with a minority holding by IOR. Bishop Marcinkus was named to the board of directors. This appointment further strengthened Calvi's ties to the Vatican, and he moved to extend his holdings in Italian banks. Soon his bank was seen as part of a major up-and-coming financial empire.

The beginning of the troubles for Banco Ambrosiano came with the collapse of Sindona's empire. In July 1972, Sindona acquired the Franklin National Bank—which at the time was ranked the twentieth largest bank in the United States—for $40 million. Unfortunately for Sindona, Franklin was not a healthy bank. Large amounts of its loans were considered dubious and hints of Sindona's mafia connections further undermined investor confidence. The October 1973 Arab oil embargo hit Franklin hard. Sindona was able to get some support from David Kennedy and President Nixon's former New York law firm, but despite this help and additional support from his Italian allies, including former prime ministers and the P2 lodge, Sindona could not prevent the collapse of his empire. Franklin Bank suffered insolvency on October 8, 1974.

Franklin Bank's bankruptcy is an example of how the criminal take-over of a legitimate bank can bring about a financial crisis. Warnings of the near collapse of Franklin National Bank in May 1974 threatened bankruptcies of associated banks. Further collapse of the financial sector was prevented by the intervention of the U.S. Federal Reserve Bank and the cooperation of foreign central banks facilitated by the BIS. The Fed provided a large loan to the Franklin National Bank and permitted it to use these funds in its foreign branches, including Nassau. In addition, the Federal Reserve guaranteed Franklin's foreign exchange contracts and found a buyer for the bank.

At the May 1974 BIS meeting, the foreign central banks in the G-10 countries agreed to defend the dollar against speculation caused by rumors of the Franklin Bank's problems. This meeting showed the international financial community's ability to react successfully to a criminalized bank's troubles. It also illustrated how the U.S. government, the Vatican, and the international capitalist system can in turn be threatened by the criminalization of the financial system. The Franklin Bank's failure could also have exerted an independent impact on the macroeconomy.

With Sindona's disgrace, the Vatican turned to Roberto Calvi as its principal financial advisor. Sindona blamed Calvi for not helping him save his Italian financial empire and started a vendetta against him. In order to protect himself, Calvi, among other things, provided money to the political leaders of all the major parties and gave generous loans to P2 members. In spite of these precautions, his power began to crumble when a police raid accidentally turned up the membership list of P2, which revealed the extensive corruption of the Italian political elite. The list in Italy included Victorio de Saboya, the son of the former king, Umberto; 3 members of the cabinet; 43 members of parliament; 30 generals; 8 admirals; the editor of Italy's leading newspaper, *Il Corriere della Sera*; 58 university professors; the directors of the top three intelligence agencies; 183 officers of the armed forces; and other members of the establishment—a total of 953 people.[12] In Argentina the list included Gen. Carlos Suarez Mason and Adm. Emilio E. Massera.[13] The list helped a magistrate investigating Calvi's Ambrosiano Bank determine the means by which Calvi avoided Italy's foreign exchange laws and led to Calvi's arrest, trial, and conviction for violation of these laws. While Calvi was free on bail during an appeal, his body was found hanging from Black Friar's Bridge in London.[14]

The BCCI Case

The Ambrosiano Bank case illustrates how an established bank under state regulation can be corrupted and become part of an illegal international financial system. The case of the Bank of Credit and Commerce International (BCCI) is an example of drug traffickers working with a bank that was completely outside the control of any state's regulatory system and shows how a transnational financing system can be set up with an illegal purpose and activity at its heart.

Agha Hassan Abedi, a Pakistani financier, founded BCCI in 1972. Abedi and his family had moved to Pakistan from India where, as Muslims, they felt threatened by the Hindu-dominated state. Deeply influenced by Islam's hostility to secular, Zionist, and Christian dominance in world finance, Abedi wanted to forge an Islamic third world institution that could compete with the developed world's financial power. And indeed, he founded "a globe-straddling, multinational Third World bank that would break the hammerlock the giant European colonial banks held on the developing world."[15]

BCCI provides one of the most dramatic examples of how the globalization of international economy has permitted underworld networks to operate globally. It was "the largest criminal corporate enterprise ever, the biggest Ponzi scheme, the most pervasive money-laundering operation in history, the only bank—so far as anyone knows—that ran a risky sideline business in both conventional nuclear weapons, gold, drugs, turnkey mercenary armies, intelligence and counter-intelligence, shipping, and commodities from cement in the Middle East to Honduran coffee and Vietnamese beans."[16]

Principal backing for the bank, which was incorporated in Luxembourg with branches in London, came from Zayed bin Sultan al-Nahayan, the head of Abu Dhabi's ruling family and president of the United Arab Emirates, who invested $1.875 billion. From its beginning, the BCCI was also backed by A. W. "Tom" Clausen, the chairman of the Bank of America, at that time the largest bank in the world.[17] The Bank of America took a 30 percent share in BCCI on the basis of a $625,000 investment. The bank flourished after the October War in 1973, when the Arab oil embargo against the West produced a massive transfer of wealth to the Arab oil-producing countries.

Abedi knew that stateless Eurodollars[18] permitted BCCI to operate beyond the control of any government. In 1976, he set up another independent entity, the International Credit and Investment Corporation (ICIC) in the Cayman Islands. This new multinational stateless corporation permitted Abedi's enterprise to compete with the established international banking system and to operate a shadowy political, economic, and criminal enterprise. He was also able to penetrate and violate American banking laws, purchasing the American Banking Holding Company in Washington, D.C., through middlemen like the influential Clark Clifford, who acted as his attorney and representative.[19]

When the massive profits from petroleum declined in the 1980s, BCCI generated financial revenues by forging relationships with intelligence agencies and supporting the arms and drug trades. It provided very important services to U.S. intelligence agencies. One of the most important was its aid in transferring money to the Afghan resistance after the Soviet invasion in 1979. BCCI also facilitated various mob activities. Its basic role in these activities was to provide commercial letters of credit that provided cover for smuggling and money laundering. BCCI became the world's leading under- and overworld bank. Since the underground economy is estimated to be between $350 billion and $500 billion a year, such a stateless offshore facility was an enormous support to international crime and all those who sought to escape taxation, law enforcement, and legitimate regulation.[20]

One of the more sensational activities of the BCCI was its help in acquiring three Columbine warheads that were sold to Iraq. These devices, one of the most closely held technologies of the United States, are triggers for the fuel air bomb sometimes identified as the "poor man's hydrogen bomb." The "Black Network," another aspect of Abedi's empire, was facilitated by ICIC. The Black Network operated as a global intelligence and enforcement agency centered in Karachi, Pakistan, with about fifteen hundred employees. It has been accused of such crimes as extortion, kidnapping, bribery, and murder. It was logistically supported by Abu Nidal and other terrorist organizations, and it assisted Pakistan's nuclear program by obtaining blueprints for a uranium enrichment factory and the high-speed switches designed to trigger nuclear weapons. In addition to these enterprises, BCCI assisted the Palestine Liberation Organization (PLO) in providing $12 million during the 1980s to the Sandinista government of Nicaragua in its struggles against El Salvador. BCCI also supported narcoterrorist groups in Peru by facilitating drug trafficking and arms trade in that country's chronic internal wars.

Despite these many connections, the BCCI enterprise collapsed when British and American regulators closed down its U.S. operations in 1991. The key figure in exposing BCCI was Manhattan district attorney Robert Morgenthau. By the DEA's own account, "sixteen deaths around the world were related to the BCCI investigation."[21]

More than one analyst rejects the argument that "BCCI was masterminding spy operations, terrorist activities, drug conspiracies, illegal arms sales, or tax evasion conspiracies." These analysts claim that BCCI merely provided a convenient and friendly place for individuals involved in illegal activities.[22] And, of course, in Abedi's view, BCCI was to be a mighty force for good in the third world.

The culture of the BCCI operation made regulation difficult. It operated very much on personal relationships and on providing money to non-specified charities. In 1987 alone it donated over $21 million to charity. This, together with prize giveaways, was seen as a way of making friends. In 1979, BCCI endowed a $10 million third world prize, placing members of Indira Gandhi's family on the prize committee. Gandhi herself gave the prize away, and, despite customary opposition in India to a Pakistani-headed bank, BCCI received permission to open a branch in Bombay's financial district in 1983. In 1987, the Bombay branch of BCCI contributed nearly 10 percent of the entire network's aftertax profits to charities.

BCCI was successful in other regions around the world. It boasted thirty-three branches in Nigeria and thirty branches in Hong Kong. It owned 99 percent of the Banco de Credito y Comercio of Colombia, which operated thirty-one branches, two of them in Medellin. According to the parent company's annual report, the Colombian operation alone turned in a pretax income of $5 billion.[23]

LEGITIMATE BANKS AND MONEY LAUNDERING

Substantial evidence from the Banco Ambrosiano and BCCI cases show that these banks were consciously involved in criminal activity and that top officials knowingly supported this activity. There is also abundant documentation of the involvement of major legitimate American banks in money laundering.

In February 1985, the U.S. Justice Department filed criminal felony charges against the First National Bank of Boston, the largest bank in New England. The Bank of Boston was indicted for "knowingly and willfully" failing to report to the federal government the movement of over $1 billion between the bank's home office and several Swiss banks. The third point in the indictment read:

> From on or about July 1, 1980, and continuing through on or about September 30, 1984, in the District of Massachusetts, the defendant, Bank of Boston, a banking institution engaged in the business of dealing in currency, knowingly and willfully failed to file, and caused the failure to file, Currency Transaction Reports (IRS Forms 4789) with the Commissioner of the Internal Revenue Service, for currency transactions it engaged in, as required by law.[24]

The indictment was signed by William F. Weld, the U.S. attorney and later Republican governor of Massachusetts, and Jeremiah T. O'Sullivan, then chief attorney of the New England Organized Crime Strike Force. The investigation revealed that the New England Angiulo crime family had exchanged $50,000 in old $100 bills for five $10,000 cashier's checks beginning in February 1980. But that was nothing: By the time the charges were brought, approximately $1.218 billion in cash had been laundered at the bank.[25]

The case did not go to trial. The bank pleaded guilty to the felony charge before U.S. District Judge A. David Mazzone, who imposed a fine of $500,000. No individuals were indicted after the plea bargain agreement and responsibility for the money laundering was never assigned. Judge Mazzone later questioned why no individuals were charged.[26]

Further supporting the trend toward the criminalization of the international financial system was the 1996 Citibank case. The bank helped Raúl Salinas de Gortari, the brother of the former president of Mexico, Carlos Salinas de Gortari, launder more than $80 million. Raúl Salinas approached Citibank for assistance with his finances in early 1993.

> The basic principles for handling Mr. Salinas's money were straightforward, and designed to get his money to a safe haven without being traceable. Cashier's checks from Raúl Salinas would be sent to the Mexico City office of Citibank, mostly drawn from the accounts of Banco Cremi, a local Mexican bank. . . . [T]he money went electronically to the bank's own accounts in New York, and then was routed to a Citibank subsidiary in Switzerland. . . . The money was deposited in accounts bearing the name of companies set up in the Caymans, Caribbean islands whose secrecy laws make it possible to create corporations without disclosing their owners. . . . The bank] transferred tens of millions back and forth from Switzerland to England when money market rates in London were at their peak.[27]

Raúl Salinas has been tied to an additional $240 million trust fund in Switzerland. Under interrogation by Mexican authorities, Salinas acknowledged having accounts in either his name or a pseudonym in four Swiss banks, including Pictet & Cie., Bank Julius Baer in Zurich, and Banque Edmond de Rothschild.[28]

Between 1989 and 1993 Citibank was under the effective receivership of the Federal Reserve Board of Governors. The bank's procedures indicate that the movement of Salinas's millions required the approval of higher-ups. These higher-ups would be the Citibank executive vice president in charge of the international private banking group and the chief of the Europe and North America division who directly reports to Citicorp chairman John Reed. Reed has been described as a personal friend of President Salinas who was warmly received at the presidential residence whenever he visited Mexico. Also, William R. Rhodes, one of Citibank's vice presidents, had negotiated Mexico's historic debt-reduction agreement on behalf of hundreds of foreign banks in the 1980s and was a trusted advisor to the Salinas administration.[29] *Money Laundering Alert*, an industry journal, reported that "senior international bankers . . . say it is 'virtually impossible' that the chairman of a bank, even one of Citibank's size, not know about a new customer who met the Salinas pattern."[30]

When an internal probe was begun into the transfer of Salinas's money out of the country, Citibank's top money-laundering compliance officer, Jane Wexton, was excluded from participating. It was then that Michael Zeldin, head of the Justice Department's money-laundering section until 1992, stated, "Within banking, Jane is among the best in-house compliance people at any bank in the U.S. . . . If there was a problem, she should have been one of the people consulted, and the fact that there apparently was a problem leads me to believe she wasn't consulted."[31]

In July 1996 Citibank hired Robert Fiske to defend the bank in the Raul Salinas money-laundering case. A congressional report released on December 3, 1998, criticized Citibank for secretly transferring nearly $100 million for Raul Salinas without examining the source of the funds or Salinas's financial background. A Citibank official told the U.S. government that the failure to conduct the background check violated Citibank's internal "know your customer" policy. To prove criminal wrongdoing prosecutors have to demonstrate that an institution was "willfully blind" to the fact that funds came from an illegal source. If a bank willfully ignores its own policy, it makes "willfull blindness" easier to prove. It was also alleged that Citibank failed to tell the government about the network of foreign shell companies and offshore accounts that it had set up to shield the Salinas fortune.[32]

Besides the interest legitimate private banks have shown in servicing clients with large amounts of money from questionable sources, there may be lack of due diligence within the U.S. government itself. The effectiveness of the federal oversight of legitimate banks is called into question, particularly after the unfortunate experiences of Franklin National Bank and Citibank. The report of the General Accounting Office, the investigative arm of Congress, on Salinas demonstrates a U.S. government attempt to rectify its oversight failures with respect to legitimate banks.

The U.S. Treasury is also under observation. It is vulnerable because it fears the loss of substantial benefits if it seriously reduces underground financial flows. According to Christopher Whalen,

> Within the domestic finance division of the Treasury, the dollarization of local economies from Tijuana to Shanghai is viewed as a considerable source of revenue for the U.S. government. . . . [A] related concern for the successive Republican and Democrat-controlled Treasury chiefs has been the worry that any disruption of the international market (for example, by clamping down on transactions between the New York money markets and banks located in the Cayman Islands or Moscow) will raise U.S. interest rates and scare skittish investors already worried by Washington's spendthrift nature.[33]

KEEPING THE SYSTEM CLEAN

The dilemma facing the United States and the managers of the globalized financial markets is how to keep a liberal financial system open and yet prevent the corruption of that system and the states. There would be serious consequences if the international financial system became corrupted. First, there would be an increased likelihood that criminal elites would gain control of both the market-regulating system and governments. Second, there would be increased opposition to policies espousing traditional morality and accountability. Finally, there would be an inevitable nationalistic and protectionistic reaction to the global capitalist system, despite its antistatist and liberty-producing benefits.

The implication of both the criminalization of legitimate banks and the creation of criminal banks is that the international capitalist environment provides a structural incentive for banks to launder dirty money. The combination of the structural nature of the international economy with the anarchical structure of the international political arena makes it rational and possible for states to cooperate with criminal enterprises.

These structural implications could be transformed if a powerful state, such as the United States, assumed leadership and sought the cooperation of other major states and the central banks. An international system could emerge that would check money laundering and relieve the anarchical pressures on states to behave criminally. Such an international system under the leadership of the United States would strengthen an anti-money-laundering regime and provide incentives for cooperation. This country has sufficient leadership capability to forge cooperative relations with other states and to develop an effective international monetary regulatory system. Unless the United States vigorously pursues this agenda, the prospect of other states assuming the responsibility of combating the criminalization of states and the world economy is unlikely.[34]

The United States has in place a system of certification of foreign nations. Under the U.S. Foreign Assistance Act (Section 490), the president of the United States must certify foreign countries as either cooperating or not cooperating with the United States in the war on drugs. To be certified as fully cooperating, a country must fulfill the following requirements: It must seize illegal narcotics, restrain money laundering, eliminate corruption, prosecute drug lords, eradicate illegal crops, and break up drug cartels. Countries where the narcotics business operates with de facto government protection do not receive U.S. certification. Countries that cooperate receive bilateral aid, and the United States supports their loans from multilateral lending institutions such as the IMF and World Bank. The countries that are "decertified" lose U.S. bilateral aid and U.S. support for funds from the multilateral lending institutions. Some countries may be certified as not cooperating but receive a "national security" waiver, a decision made at the discretion of the president.

The process of corruption in democratic and democratizing states suggests the United States will be faced with more and more difficult decisions in certifying states as cooperating in the fight against drug trafficking.

PART III

Corrupting Democratic Transitions and Consolidations

CHAPTER 7

DEMOCRATIC TRANSITIONS AND ORGANIZED CRIME: RUSSIA AND THE ANDEAN REGION

Governments, organized crime and the criminalization of the global financial system have synergistically supported the rise of narcostatization. As asserted earlier, narcostatization may occur during a government's transition from an autocracy to a democracy or after a presumed democratic consolidation. Allegedly democratic transitions come into question when the corrupt elites from former authoritarian regimes continue in power after elections. An anocratic or pseudodemocratic state is one where the formal democratic procedures, such as contested elections, and the formal institutional structures, such as legislatures and independent judiciaries, are in place. Elections in an anocracy do not produce accountability, and institutional structures do not reliably check central power. A further feature of an anocratic state is that the shared norms needed to hold representatives accountable are not sufficiently widespread.

Corruption produced by narcostatization can lead either to an authoritarian state becoming anocratic when allegedly democratizing or to a consolidated democracy becoming anocratic because of the corruption of its institutions, electoral system, and civil society. Both authoritarian and democratic governments may converge toward anocracy. A subsequent chapter will explore how the anocratization process undermines the democratic peace thesis.

If the move from authoritarianism to procedural democracy, as defined in Robert Dahl's polyarchy (see chapter 2), is really an anocratization process, former authoritarian elites are able to cooperate with organized crime to stay in power despite the establishment of contested elections. Democratic changes conceal the corrupt reality of an anocratic state.

The anocratization process impacts differently on democracies and autocracies. It makes a democracy less democratic and an autocracy more democratic. In both cases, anocratization means that the democratic procedures disguise the existence of unaccountable ruling elites. (See table 1 in chapter 3.) Narcostatization is another form of anocratization, and not all anocratizations are caused by narcostatizations.

INDEX OF NARCOSTATIZATION INDICATORS

There are varying degrees of narcostatization. As the problem of corruption becomes globalized, it becomes increasingly necessary to evaluate and measure narcostatization uniformly in all countries. Without a guideline, the United States and the international community are unable to hold individual countries to a single objective standard. As has been seen, the United States decertifies those countries that do not cooperate in the fight against drugs. A standardized scale would help other countries understand how and why the United States makes its decisions.

The Index of Narcostatization Indicators (table 2) provides a scale that allows states to be classified according to their degree of corruption and decreased accountability. It establishes the development of narcostatization in a given state. The index does not represent an irreversible process. It is possible, even likely, that states will move up and down the scale according to changing conditions. The table introduces five levels of narcostatization: incipient, developing, serious, critical, and advanced, specifying increasing levels of narcostatization.

CRIMINALITY IN RUSSIA

Post–Communist Russia exemplifies how an alleged transition from autocracy to democracy can create an anocracy. Serious students of Russian criminality, such as Stephen Handelman and Claire Sterling, depict a country in the grip of corruption. Despite democratic elections

TABLE 2.

INDEX OF NARCOSTATIZATION INDICATORS

Level 1   Incipient

- Bribery of low-level officials
- Widespread drug consumption and inability either through lack of capability or will to reduce demand
- Increasing cultural support for drug consumption

Level 2   Developing

- Increasing governmental support for drug consumption
- Antidrug activists removed from educational and cultural institutions
- Government institutions (e.g., security, judicial, health, education) infiltrated or run by prodrug officials

Level 3   Serious

- Massive bribery and corruption of public officials
- Substantial intimidation, including murder, of resisting officials
- Corruption of local and regional police and judicial officials

Level 4   Critical

- Corruption at highest levels of national police and judicial systems, endemic extortion rather than bribery
- Top-level police enter drug trade, protect it, and authorize political assassinations
- Financing of journalists and magazines by drug lords; narco-journalists become known and remain in place

Level 5   Advanced

- Compliance of ministries, in addition to judiciary and police, with organized crime
- A president surrounded by compromised officials
- Possible complicity of the presidency itself; e.g., the president may be charged as *capo di tutti capi* and public not be surprised

of both the presidency and the parliament, the predominant ruling elite has emerged from the former communist ruling class. "By February, 1994," Handelman says, "the majority of senior cabinet posts in the Yeltsin government was occupied by former communist officials with deep ties to powerful state industrial and agricultural interests. Russia was well on its way to a form of state capitalism in which former communists played the commanding roles." Former communist officials are not only senior cabinet ministers, bank presidents, CEOs, and board members of corporations, they are, in the words of the Soviet dissident Lev Timofeyev, "bound hand and foot . . . to the apparat, the military-industrial complex, and the [former] KGB."[1]

The hold on private financial resources by party elites and nomen-klaturas began in February 1990. At that time, the Communist Party's governing central committee revoked the privileges the party maintained under Article 6 of the Soviet constitution, wherein it was the only legal political organization. Shortly thereafter, large amounts of money were transferred to one of the many private banks established by the party. According to Handelman's sources, "several Communist-established 'private' banks in Russia accepted huge dollar deposits from Panamanian and Colombian drug dealers, converted them to rubles, and then recon-verted them to dollars, transferring the money overseas again in return for a hefty commission." The newspaper following Russian crime, *Kriminalnaya Khronika*, stated that "the Soviet Union was operating as a colossal launderette."[2] The party security structure of the former Soviet Union set itself up to operate in the international financial system as a criminal money-laundering operation. It was only a matter of time before this transnational enterprise merged with Russia's organized crime cartels and cooperated with those of other nations.

As Russia turned to electoral politics, elements of the former Soviet ruling party fused with organized crime. The economic basis for this fusion developed prior to the transition. Vadim Bakatin, minister of internal affairs in the Gorbachev government until 1990, maintained that

> bureaucrats and mobsters not only shared a common interest in blocking the creation of a competitive open market, but had joined forces in terrorizing independent businessmen as well. . . . The foundation of today's organized crime was the shadow economy, but the roof was our own bureaucratic system. . . . Our bureaucrats,

police, procurators, judges, even the KGB, were merging with the underground world. It was a critical change in the development of crime in our country.[3]

The criminal-bureaucratic fusion was not accidental. Government authorities had been cooperating with black marketeers as early as the 1960s. According to the studies of Aleksandr Gurov, top Communist operatives had been collaborating with the trade mafia since 1974. As Gurov said, "It began under Khrushchev and developed under Brezhnev. But the Gorbachev era was the period when organized crime really became powerful."[4]

No one predicted how much of this informal capitalist activity would fuse with organized crime and the global narcotics industry during the transition from the Soviet Union to a democratizing Russia. According to Handelman,

> The Eurasian shift in the global trade came to fuel a substantial part of post-Soviet Russia's prosperity. "We estimate that 40 percent of the movement of capital in Russia is now linked with narcotics," said Col. Valentin Roshchin, who led the Moscow Police's Anti-Drug Squad until he was promoted to a senior post in the criminal-investigation division in 1993. "Organized criminals abroad have discovered how easy it is to launder drug profits through businesses and banks here.[5]

A study by Olga Kryshtanovskaya, head of the Department of Elite Studies at the Russian Academy of Sciences, found that more than 60 percent of Russia's wealthiest millionaires were former members of Russia's communist elite. She estimated that Russia's new millionaires had an average individual net worth of $19 million and that their wealth was increasing steadily in Russia's privatization process because of their positions within the power structure.[6]

Among the new millionaires were such people as Sergei Rodionov, who was head of the banking department of the Soviet Finance Ministry in the communist era. He was able to use his position to become chairman of one of Russia's largest commercial banks. According to her study, Kryshtanovskaya said, "There are hundreds of examples of this, but it hasn't become widely known. There is a popular myth that only criminals and thieves have become millionaires. I think that's wrong. It's the people who could easily infiltrate the new system because of their connections in the old system, who have become rich."[7]

The elite of an authoritarian system are in the best position to become wealthy during a transition and thereby perpetuate a disproportionate degree of power in a system that is electorally democratic. Claire Sterling writes, "In 1991, the year of the communists' fall, the All-Union Research Institute of the Soviet Interior Ministry estimated that half the income of an average government functionary was coming from bribes, compared to 'only 30 percent' before 1985."[8]

According to Sterling, the Soviet prosecutor general stated that from a third to a half of all heads of cooperatives in the USSR were probably embezzling funds.[9] In 1991, Boris Yeltsin said, "Organized crime is destroying the economy, interfering in politics, undermining the public moral, intimidating individual citizens and the entire Russian nation. . . . our country in now considered in the power of the mafia."[10]

Sterling indicates that the corruption of the ruling elite and of civil society's mafias are symbiotic activities. They divide among them the plunder of a privatizing authoritarian state. "The Yeltsin government is selling state enterprises amounting to ninety-two billion rubles," Sterling quoted the top social economist and leader of the first parliamentary antimafia commission in Russian history as saying in 1994. "Organized crime is putting fifty billion rubles through the banking system. So the mafia can buy up more than half."[11]

Becoming well known for their violence, Russian gangsters have gunned down bankers for refusing to pay extortion money, grant loans, or illegally transfer hard currency abroad. Moscow police estimate that organized crime groups control more than 40 of Moscow's 260 banks. International money-laundering schemes, counterfeiting, and an array of financial fraud are widespread in Russia's underregulated, undercapitalized, and technologically backward banks. The economy's criminalization is so pervasive that there is often a fine line between street hoodlums, corrupt bureaucrats, and entrepreneurs. Allegations of corruption within the government have become widespread.

Nonetheless, there are some analysts who believe that the mafia threat is inflated and the evidence imprecise. Some of those who think the threat is exaggerated are concerned that the charges of corruption will be used to slow down, stop, or even reverse the privatization process. In one study, for example, despite recognizing that criminal structures may control over "80 percent of all economic entities," the authors argue that "even if the estimate is correct, the numbers do not bear out the charge that the entire privatization process was criminalized."[12] That the corruption problem may not be as widespread or as threatening as some Russian sources report should not be allowed to prompt a false sense of security regarding the narcostatization of the Russian regime. A corrupt authoritarian system adapting to democratic procedures may be particularly vulnerable to a political-criminal alliance within democratic forms.

The vestiges of the planned economy's centralized command structure create fertile ground for gangsters and government officials to work together.[13] It is difficult to determine to what extent this corruption applies to the immediate group surrounding President Yeltsin. A number of top Russian businessmen formed an alliance to back Yeltsin's reelection in 1996 and placed two of its members—Vladimir Potanin and Boris Berezovsky—in key government positions. This group, which funded Yeltsin's reelection drive, includes Vladimir Gussinsky, head of the powerful Most banking and media group; Mikhail Khodorkovsky, the head of a financial and oil empire; and the heads of the Alfa and Stolichny Banks. According to Berezovsky, the six enterprises this so-called group of seven heads control about 50 percent of the economy. One member of the group fits the pattern of the state and free enterprise symbiosis. Potanin was the former head of the Oneximbank and became first deputy prime minister for the economy. Members of this oligarchic group "not only have significant roles in the cabinet and the Kremlin, they also control Russia's two top television networks, a popular radio station, and a growing number of national newspapers—assets they are happy to use to advance their agenda."[14]

When Berezovsky was fired as deputy secretary of the Kremlin's Security Council in November 1997, it was billed by Yeltsin's reform ministers as an effort to break the power of Russia's new oligarchy. The reformers, deputy prime ministers Anatoly Chubais and Boris Nenotsou, claimed they would no longer tolerate "the old rules of backroom deals and insider privatization of state companies in which the oligarchs often gained lucrative state-owned businesses for a small price."[15]

The old communist system was premised on a cosmopolitan utopia: a "new man"; pleasurable work; to each according to his or her needs, from each according to his or her ability; and a vanished state. The legitimacy of the transition in post–Communist Russia is based on democratic principles, although it occurs in circumstances of the criminalization of both the national and international environments. Criminalization is likely to produce a crisis of legitimacy for the Russian regime. The government is unable to regulate the financial institutions that launder money, control the criminal organizations that ship cocaine and other narcotics through the country, or eradicate the opium and other domestic narcotics produced naturally in the fertile valleys of Kazakhstan and Kyrgyzstan and synthetically in laboratories.

"Few sectors of Russian society have been left untouched by the narcotics trade, Stephen Handelman says.

> Directors of military-industrial plants provide facilities for the clandestine laboratories that make synthetic drugs and trucks for shipping them. Private bankers accept deposits from known drug profiteers without asking difficult questions; commercial managers eagerly take their investments. Meanwhile, narco-bizness is attracting some of the best research minds of the younger generation.[16]

In addition, there is evidence that the Russian army has also become involved in the shadow economy. Elements were involved in black market activities before the Russian forces left Germany in August of 1994. There is growing concern in the West that, in conjunction with the old Soviet nomenklatura, the military has become involved in arms sales—another means for laundering money. The scale of the corruption in the new Russian state is nearly inconceivable. "In 1993, more than forty-six thousand officials from all levels of government in Russia were brought to trial on charges relating to corruption and abuse of office," according to Aleksei Ilyushenko, a government prosecutor.[17]

The case of Russia implies that the old authoritarian elite may return to power and rule the country in conjunction with organized crime and the international financial system. If that elite fuses with the corrupt military establishment, then the new Russian state may become as fearful to its neighbors and the world as was the former communist state. In such a criminal capitalist state, the electoral system ratifies the permanence in power of these former communists to create a corrupt anocratic state threatening to its neighbors and the global system, while still, unfortunately, being considered by many a "democratic" regime.

According to the Index of Narcostatization Indicators, the development of narcostatization in Russia had reached level 4, the critical stage, as this book goes to press. But it is possible that the privatization process, if it increases the prospects for legitimate economic activity, will help reduce the criminalization of the Russian state.[18]

THE PERUVIAN ANOMALY

Narcotics trafficking threatens not only countries with recent democratic transitions but also those with a longer tradition of elections. The Latin American countries examined here demonstrate how corruption jeopardizes their democratic credentials. Venezuela began its experiment with democracy in 1958 and both Bolivia and Peru turned to elected governments in the 1980s.[19]

From the beginning of Peru's transition to democracy with the election of Pres. Fernando Belaunde Terry (1980–85), narcotics trafficking threatened to make the regime an anocracy. By controlling the industry, a small group of narcotics traffickers controlled much of the country. For instance, the Paredes family was described by a DEA Centac analyst as "the biggest cocaine smuggling organization in Peru and possibly the world." The Paredes were part of an established oligarchy that "controlled not only the roots of the cocaine industry but, to a large extent, the country itself."[20]

Corruption charges tainted many of the security agencies of the Peruvian government. Widespread corruption in the police force and even within a cabinet ministry was revealed when the Reynaldo Rodriguez López drug organization was accidentally busted in mid-1985. An explosion led a Peruvian SWAT team, rather than the corrupt investigative police (PIP), to respond to an emergency call. The team uncovered a criminal organization that occupied an entire city block and had a direct telephone line to the minister of the interior's private secretary, Luis López Vergara. According to one investigator, "Reynaldo Rodríguez López simultaneously was an adviser to the Director of the Peruvian Investigations Police (PIP) and maintained an office at PIP headquarters."[21]

Economic factors and the alleged corruption of top ministers in the Belaunde government discredited his party, Acción Popular (AP), which lost the next election, in 1985, to its principal rival, the Aprista party (PAP), and then lost to Pres. Alberto Fujimori's Cambio 90 party in 1990 and again in 1995. After charges of corruption discredited the Apristas to an even larger extent, many Peruvians welcomed Fujimori's April 5, 1992, "autocoup," which disbanded Congress in hopes of eliminating corrupt political elites and parties.

Narcotics, terrorism, and government corruption had played a destabilizing role in Peru in the 1980s. President Alán García (1985–90) faced charges of corruption that included questionable ties to BCCI. BCCI figured in García's banking policies during his term in office, and on August 16, 1991, the Peruvian House of Representatives accused García of "looting the country of as much as $50 million and moving the money through the Bank of Credit offices into foreign bank accounts." This sum was identified because it had been passed on to Panamanian bank accounts in the name of the president's wife via BCCI. García, who became a multimillionaire during his term in office, had an official annual salary of $18,000. According to a report of the U.S. House Committee on Banking, Finance, and Urban Affairs, "the full extent of García's personal fortune is still unclear, but the source of his wealth is mainly plundered assets of the national treasury, especially skimmed-off funds deposited in BCCI, paid back interest on Peruvian interest deposits, and payment for 'special services' rendered to BCCI and its special customers." The report further explains how the nation's reserves were deposited in BCCI, how officials were bribed to carry out the transfers, and how BCCI assisted García in flouting the IMF.[22]

Peter Truell and Larry Gurwin give another account of García's corruption in their book on BCCI. In July 1985, before taking office, García secretly canceled an arms deal Peru had made with the French in 1982. A new agreement was allegedly crafted during a preinaugural trip he took to France. Under the previous agreement Peru was to purchase twenty-six Mirage 2000 jet fighters, costing $12 million to $14 million each. Under the 1985 contract, Peru would buy only twelve planes for the same amount, leaving the surplus planes to be sold to Morocco at $30 million a piece. Huge profits were made from this deal and deposited in BCCI.[23]

Despite having four consecutively elected governments, Peru is still considered to be in transition to democracy, and it serves as a good example of how a beleaguered government in the transition phase places the antinarcotics trafficking fight as a lower priority to eradicating insurgency and fostering economic development. At the Andean Drug Summit in Cartagena, Colombia, in 1990, Pres. George Bush acquiesced to pressure from Peru and focused the Andean strategy on interdiction rather than crop eradication. The Andean strategy also focused on alternative development programs and on U.S. responsibility for curbing domestic demand.

President Fujimori has been successful both in fostering economic development and in his attack on insurgency. Under Fujimori's initiative, coca farmers are no longer considered criminals, and he has prohibited the aerial spraying of coca fields with herbicides. Nonetheless, Fujimori is concerned with the growing presence of Colombian drug cartel operations in Peru and views the transnational mafia as a threat to the state. In his speech to the Peruvian Congress in early 1991, he said, "Peru is on the way to becoming a totally narco-terrorist country in which the ideas for which we fight will no longer be important, the only goal will be the illegal profits of groups and factions with a complete lack of morals and altruism, and there will be minimum conditions for social coexistence."[24] Subsequent events, however, indicate his lack of resolve to act against producers.

In July 1991, Peru and the United States concluded three bilateral accords governing U.S. antinarcotics assistance. Throughout the negotiations Fujimori stressed that programs eradicating the coca fields were directly related to the size of U.S. financial support, denoting his unwillingness to crush the producers. Much of the intellectual direction of Fujimori's economic program came from Hernando de Soto, president of the Institute of Democracy and Liberty in Lima. De Soto resigned his position as advisor to the president because of Fujimori's unwillingness to attack police and military corruption or to subvert the fifth column within his government that allied bureaucrats and drug traffickers. De Soto's resignation was a confirmation of the breakdown in the government's war on drugs and cooperation with the United States.[25]

President Fujimori strained ties with the United States even further on April 5, 1992, when, in a daring maneuver, he closed down the Peruvian Congress and the nation's judiciary and suspended the Constitution. He justified these actions by claiming that these institutions were harming his fight against terrorism and drug trafficking. The United States was further concerned that Vladimiro Montesinos, the alleged mastermind behind the coup and one of Fujimori's chief advisors and de facto intelligence chief, had previously in his law practice defended Colombian and Peruvian drug traffickers.[26] Still the United States continued to assist the antinarcotics program in Peru. DEA administrator Judge Bonner said it was something that "should be done in our best interest [if] not in the best interest of the Peruvian government."[27]

On September 12, 1992, five months after disbanding Congress, Fujimori captured Abimael Guzmán, head of the notorious Sendero Luminoso terrorist group, which had a working relationship with drug traffickers. But even with Guzmán's capture, drug trafficking continued, with approximately 640 tons of cocaine being shipped out of Peru that year. Only 8 of those tons were seized by police. The U.S. government in effect admitted defeat in the interdiction program when it slashed the staff and budget of the narcotics program and sharply reduced DEA personnel, the defense budget, and the State Department's Bureau of International Narcotics Matters. The Fujimori government concurred with the Clinton administration's reductions and publicly stated that the American-Peruvian drug policy was a failure.

The failure in Peru was due far more to internal political considerations than to U.S. policy. At the end of 1992, an active group of officers organized a countercoup against Fujimori. There were actually two clandestine opposition groups: Commanders, Majors, and Captains (COMACA) and Sleepy Lion. But both groups were weakened by Guzmán's capture and were penetrated by Montesino's National Intelligence Service (SIN), the state agency in charge of national security. Fujimori's crackdown on the two groups triggered a conflict within the army, which provided further information on the extent of military involvement in drug trafficking. In part to protect themselves from Fujimori and SIN, COMACA and Sleepy Lion began leaking to the press information on military involvement in the drug trade in early 1994. Their accusations implicated military commanders in the Upper Huallaga Valley, the commander of the army's air force, and the army's commander-in-chief, Gen. Nicolás Hermoza.[28]

After initial denials, overwhelming evidence forced General Hermoza to admit that more than a hundred army officers were linked to the drug trade. The investigation was limited to officers who were not part of Hermoza's inner circle, but the damage was so extensive that Fujimori removed the military from antidrug operations in 1995.[29] Peter Andreas quoted a senior DEA official in assessing the role played by the military in Peru's drug industry: "In Peru, the world's largest producer of coca (the raw material of cocaine), major coca-processing facilities and airstrips in the Upper Huallaga Valley are located near military facilities to provide them with greater protection," the official said. Andreas continued:

> We know as a fact that the Peruvian Army gets payments for letting traffickers use airstrips," says U.S. Special Forces commander Colonel Robert Jacobelly. For example, the military reportedly charges traffickers up to $15,000 per flight to use the airport at Uchiza, a small town in the valley. Two to four drug flights reportedly left the Upper Huallaga Valley for Colombia every day in 1992—yet only five flights were intercepted that year. At times, military personnel have even directly blocked drug-enforcement efforts. For example, Peruvian Navy commanders operating along the Ucayali River have reportedly not let U.S. drug-enforcement agents enter coca-producing areas. There have also been repeated cases of military personnel firing at helicopters carrying U.S. DEA agents and Peruvian anti-drug police.[30]

The narcotics problem in Peru facilitates the maintenance of elite rule despite contestation and full participation of the citizenry. Elements of authoritarian elitism within Peru's procedural democracy have several interrelated components. One is the existence of the coca lobby that represents interests of coca cultivators in the Upper Huallaga Valley and Cuzco. The coca lobby includes elected officials and human rights groups seeking to protect growers from abuse by the police and military. This diverse lobby is a political force that all candidates seeking to represent the region or running for national office must take into account. Another element in the narcostatization process that assists elite rule in Peru is the government's inability to maintain a consistent eradication and interdiction program. In the fall of 1995, reports of success in the interdiction program in Peru fueled fears of the rise of insurgency because of campesino discontent, but the removal of the military at the end of the year eased those concerns.

There is the paradox of the neoliberal reform agenda where the government privatizes state-owned enterprises and promotes the acquisition of property by national entrepreneurs. To the degree the new wealthy are fueled by criminal profits, they are able to acquire an ascending presence in the nation's economy. Fujimori privatized 173 of the 183 state-run companies that existed in 1990. The only major concerns that have not been privatized are the state oil companies, a large mining company, and the ports.[31] The ascendancy of the new wealthy suggests that a criminal oligarchy may be allying itself with a corrupt statism in Peru. Reports of military corruption come from many sources. One source writes that military protection of the drug trade costs traffickers $20,000 per shipment.[32] If this is the case, Peru's transition to electoral democracy has in fact created an anocratic state that is far from purging corruption from its institutions, electoral process, and civil society. According to the Index of Narcostatization Indicators, Peru may be at level 4, the critical stage, of narcostatization.

There is some evidence that Peru under Fujimori is trying to reverse its rise in the narcostate index. Since 1993, the Fujimori government has reduced coca cultivation by as much as 40 percent according to some estimates. Nonetheless, the prococa lobby in Peru has grown, and it receives considerable support from outside interests. The Andean Commission of Jurists (CAJ) works for drug legalization in Peru and has ties with the Lindesmith Center and Human Rights Watch/Americas. Ricardo Soberon, a representative of CAJ, participated at a conference hosted by Acción Andina (AA), George Washington University, the Institute for Policy Studies (IPS), the Transnational Institute (TNJ), and the Washington Office on Latin America (WOLA) on June 11, 1998. AA portrays itself as providing a platform on which groups and researchers from the Andean region dedicated to ending the war on drugs can work together. IPS and TNJ promoted the Drugs and Democracy project, which was set up to attack the militarization of antidrug policies. These anti–drug war coalitions could make the cultivation reduction efforts temporary and prevent Peru from reversing its narcostatization trend.

THE POLITICS OF PRODUCTION IN BOLIVIA

Similar to the case of Peru, Bolivia faces increasing narcostatization. Despite full participation of the citizenry and contested elections, the government is subject to unaccountable and corrupt elites. Like Peru,

Bolivia has a significant coca lobby. It is estimated that in Bolivia there are approximately seventy thousand to eighty thousand growers in a population of 6.5 million people. Bolivia has a National Coca Producers Association and a National Coordinating Committee of Coca Producers. The growers hold national congresses and have the support of Bolivia's largest workers' organization, the 1.3–million member Congress of Bolivian Workers (COB). According to one study, approximately eighty thousand tons of coca leaf produced by Bolivian peasants are under the control of some thirty to forty Bolivian drug trafficking organizations. The same source estimates that Bolivian enforcement agencies "are able to interdict only 1 to 2 percent of these illicit products whose sales pump between $200 and $370 million into the Bolivian economy."[33]

As in Peru, numerous elected representatives from the region and national candidates solicit the support of growers. Although there are differences among the various components of the coca lobby, on balance it opposes U.S. policies of eradication in Bolivia. According to statistics and as substantiated by government policy, it is in the economic and political interest of the Bolivian elite to support coca producers.

The United States recognizes the reluctance of the Bolivian government to wage an unconditional attack on coca crops. In its International Narcotics Control Strategy Report of 1993, the U.S. Department of State noted that Bolivia "continues to refrain from employing measures of force" to protect coca eradication. The lack of political will was primarily attributed to the opposition of the coca lobby.[34]

Narcostatization began in Bolivia following an economic boom during the regime of Gen. Hugo Banzer Suárez (1971–78). This period of prosperity was financed by heavy borrowing from abroad, which increased Bolivian debt from $671 million to $2.5 billion. The expansion in foreign debt was financed from tin and oil earnings. This period of prosperity ended in the late 1970s and early 1980s when interest rates rose dramatically and a worldwide recession began. As oil and tin prices collapsed and capital fled, the country fell into an economic depression. Between 1978 and 1982, Bolivia had nine heads of state, but its nadir occurred with the July 17, 1980, coup d'etat headed by Gen. Luis García Meza.[35]

With the García Meza coup, links between the military high command and Bolivia's drug trafficking came to light. It soon became apparent that Bolivia would seek to maintain itself by relying on the cocaine traffic. The production of coca leaves had risen from 5,800 to 16,811 tons a year between 1971 and 1977. These nearly 17,000 tons of coca leaves made possible the manufacture of 62 tons of cocaine, which earned the Bolivian sellers $300 million. In contrast, the country earned $220 million from tin exports and $67 million from petroleum exports. Thus, by 1977, Bolivia was earning far more from cocaine than from tin and petroleum combined.[36]

Investigations revealed the military government was deeply involved in cocaine trafficking with the Bolivian mafia. As Peter Andreas has observed,

> Corruption within the Bolivian military is particularly entrenched because of the lack of accountability to civilian authority. As one former Planning Minister noted, "when you have a corrupt chief of police, you fire him. When you have a corrupt chief of the army, he fires you." Not surprisingly, Bolivians from across the political spectrum have been skeptical of using the military as drug warriors. "To bring in the army [for drug control] would be the best way to promote drug trafficking in Bolivia," notes one development worker from Cochabamba.[37]

The Bolivian military was forced out of power in October 1982 and was replaced by the Hernán Siles Zuazo–led Democratic and Popular Unity party (UDP), which had won the 1980 elections, before being brought down by the García Meza coup. The Siles Zuazo government signed a drug-control agreement with the United States in 1983 to set up the Mobile Unit of Rural Patrols (UMOPAR), which operated as a paramilitary force to fight drug trafficking. The Siles Zuazo statist economic policies, however, created hyperinflation and badly undermined popular support for the regime.

The serious economic situation led Siles Zuazo to call for early elections in 1985. He was succeeded by Victor Paz Estenssoro of the National Revolutionary Movement (MNR). Although he was also long associated with statist economic policies, Paz Estenssoro made a 180-degree turn in the face of his country's total economic bankruptcy. Confronted with hyperinflation of 15,000 percent a year and a GDP that had declined for five consecutive years, Paz Estenssoro began privatizing some of Bolivia's parastatal, or state-owned, companies, but drug money continued to stabilize the nation's finances. In the period from September 1985 to just before the 1989 elections, short-term dollar deposits in the

Bolivian Central Bank increased from $28 million to $700 million.[38] Much of this money was linked to the drug trade and to the corruption of the country's financial institutions:

> In Bolivia, between $500 and $800 million is generated annually from the illicit industry—a significant amount, considering that the country's combined legal exports generate only about $300 million a year. As part of the economic-stabilization program initiated in 1985, the Paz Estenssoro government instituted a number of measures that have facilitated the absorption of these drug revenues into the financial system, such as loosening the disclosure requirements of the Central Bank and declaring a tax amnesty on repatriated capital. New laws prohibited official inquiries into the origins of all wealth brought into Bolivia, and tellers at the Central Bank were not allowed to question the source of dollar deposits. The government also created a foreign-exchange auction, called the bolsin, which allowed the Central Bank to compete with the parallel foreign-exchange market for drug dollars.
>
> These financial policies have boosted Bolivia's foreign-exchange reserves, which in turn have helped to stabilize the currency and to curb inflation. According to Rolando Morales, the former president of the Bolivian association of economists, the influx of drug dollars is "the only way we've been able to balance the balance of payments.[39]

Even with drug money, the economic turnabout was slow. Although hyperinflation was restrained, the country's GDP did not grow. MNR candidate Gonzalo Sánchez de Lozada gained the first plurality in the 1989 elections but lost in Congress to Jaime Paz Zamora of the Left Revolutionary Movement (MIR), who had the support of Gen. Hugo Banzer Suárez, the other major candidate. (Banzer himself would regain the presidency in 1997.)

Paz Zamora's regime was not successful in eradicating illegal coca crops. Only 3 percent of illegal coca cultivation was destroyed in 1992. This is a remarkably poor record when it is recalled that in 1989 President Bush earmarked $2.2 billion for the eradication of cocaine production in Bolivia, Peru, and Colombia. For its efforts, Bolivia received more than $200 million in 1992 alone.[40]

Further damaging the credentials of the Paz Zamora regime's anti-narcotics reputation was the appointment of Col. Rico Toro as head of the special antinarcotics forces (FELCN). Toro was head of army intelligence during the García Meza period and had been indicted in Florida on drug trafficking charges. He finally resigned after a long delay related to support he received from General Banzer. Other Paz Zamora appointees—his national police commander, Gen. Felipe Carvajal, and his interior minister, Guillermo Capobianco—were identified as involved in drug trafficking. U.S. government sources also connected Paz Zamora to Isaac Oso Chavarría, chief of the Santa Cruz drug cartel. When the Bolivian Supreme Court delayed the extradition of Rico Toro, the U.S. Embassy in La Paz asserted that collusion existed between the court and the colonel.[41]

High-level institutional government involvement in drug trafficking includes the Bolivian navy. It has protected or been involved in drug trafficking since at least the early 1970s.[42] One former Bolivian naval officer, Humberto Gil Suárez, is the founder of the Mamore cartel, which produces and exports high-grade cocaine and has ties to the Cali cartel of Colombia.[43] The overall picture is one of institutional support of drug trafficking in the permanent bureaucracies of the government, with elected officials either supporting the traffickers or helpless to do anything about it. (Paz Zamora's narcotics interests have yet to be fully investigated.[44])

The election of Gonzalo Sánchez de Lozada to the presidency in 1993 raised hopes that he would combat the corruption problem. However, narcostatization in Bolivia is so far advanced that even an honest and well-intentioned president would be unable to reduce its control over the country's political and economic policies without a drastic confrontation with corrupt elites, traffickers, and campesino interests. General Banzer's return to power as president in 1997, following Sánchez de Lozada, opens new questions for Bolivia's future with respect to its drug policy. According to the Index of Narcostatization Indicators, Bolivia has reached level 4, the critical stage of narcostatization, and even shows evidence of some elements of level 5, the advanced stage.

There is also evidence, however, that under Gen. Hugo Banzer Suárez Bolivia is committed to a major reduction in coca production. Banzer, who took office in August 1997, issued a report in early 1998 calling for a five-year plan to move the country out from under the drug trafficking industry. The report, *With Dignity*, announced that the drug trade was a threat to national security, and if the threat was not met Bolivian society might be permanently divided.

Nonetheless, to achieve any success, a substantial prolegalization lobby backed by powerful international interests has to be overcome. The principal domestic group in this lobboy is the Evo Morales–led Andean Council of Coca Leaf Producers (CAPHC). Behind CAPHC, as in the case of the Andean Commission of Jurists (ACJ), lie numerous nongovernmental organizations (NGOs) backed in part by the ubiquitous George Soros and, surprisingly for some, the European Commission, the executive branch of the European Union.

During the summer of 1994, fifteen NGOs representing eleven European countries met in Brussels to support a project labeled "Coca 95." Financed in part by the European Commission, Coca 95 aimed to curtail coca eradication programs and to remove coca from the 1961 UN Single Convention of prescribed drugs. The project was continued under the name Coca 97/98 and is run by the Antwerp, Belgium–based NGO, European NGO Council on Drugs and Development (ENCOD). Personnel helping this NGO have links to the Drug Policy Foundation's International Anti-Prohibitionist League.[45] The domestic and foreign support of drug legalization may cause the Banzer program to fail and thereby help prevent the reversal of the narcostatization process in Bolivia.

VENEZUELA'S DEMOCRACY IN CRISIS

Until the late 1950s, Venezuela had never had the experience of one democratic government succeeding another. But the successful military uprising of 1958, which had the cooperation of the country's principal political parties, led Venezuela to become one of the more stable democracies of Latin America. The country then attained one of the most important indicators of a consolidated democracy as competitive parties succeeded each other in office.

The Acción Democrática (AP) party led by Pres. Romulo Betancourt (1959–64) used the country's rich oil holdings and foreign exchange earnings to modernize the economy and improve the standard of living. But as oil revenues declined, it was drug trade and money laundering that maintained the Venezuelan economy in the 1980s. During this time the Sicilian mafia, represented mainly by the Cuntrera brothers, was deeply rooted in Venezuela. They set up a heroin and cocaine alliance with the Colombian cartels operating on a global scale. By 1982, an estimated four-fifths of the cocaine shipped into the United States and Europe traveled through Venezuela, and an estimated $2 billion in narcotics profits was recycled there.

Long considered one of Latin America's consolidated democracies, Venezuela was plunged into a prolonged and deep political and economic crisis at the end of 1991. Mass protests, two failed military coups in 1992, constant cabinet changes, and the impeachment of the president in 1993, followed by an ongoing economic crisis since 1994, have combined to threaten the continuation of democracy in that country.

The extensive corruption infecting the Venezuelan political elites and the country's financial establishment contributed to the lack of popular support for the president and led to an attempted coup in 1992. The *New York Times* reported, "no reliable polls have been made public since the coup, but in one measure of the politician's dangerous isolation from the people, no leader has dared to call a mass demonstration in support of democracy."[46]

Explanations for the impeachment of Pres. Carlos Andrés Pérez (1974–79 and 1989–93) in 1993 cited his failure to gain support for his neoliberal reforms from his own party—Acción Democrática (AD), the first party to see its candidates elected in Venezuela. Pérez had excluded party professionals from his cabinet and had relied excessively on independent technocrats to execute the needed neoliberal reforms. Thus, the politicians of his own party could not know the degree to which the country had become dependent on organized crime and narcotics trafficking, and they rallied around Pérez's predecessor, Jaime Lusinchi, to oppose him.

AD's opposition to Pérez provided an opportunity for the military to move against him and nearly overturn the government. Political opponents inside and outside his party did not realize that by charging him with corruption they would expose the country's dependence on narcotics revenues to maintain the statist policies Pérez was trying to change. But they soon came to realize that greater privatization was necessary or the country would continue to be dependent on narcotics to compensate for lost petroleum profits. Income from Venezuela's oil exports had increased briefly in the last five months of 1990 because of

Iraq's invasion of Kuwait. However, much of this windfall was spent on social programs and was not replenished after the end of the Gulf War in 1991.

No matter how long a country has been in the democratic consolidation phase, that phase can be reversed by a variety of processes and events. In the case of Venezuela, a pattern of corruption at the highest levels of government became increasingly visible as the country embarked on the privatization of its inefficient state enterprises. Although privatization was beneficial for the long-term economic health of the country and for the empowerment of the country's civic culture, the visibility of corruption during privatization provoked serious criticisms of the sale of state enterprises. Privatization exposed the obvious corruption in the Pérez administration.

The crisis had begun a few weeks after Pérez took office as president of Venezuela in 1989. He called Thor Halvorssen into his office and asked him to serve as antidrug czar in his administration. Halvorssen had served in Pérez's first administration as vice president and as president of the state-owned telephone company. Upon his appointment as drug czar, he was instructed to "tell the Americans that [the Pérez regime] will be a term known for its commitment in the drug war."[47] Halvorssen says he provided Pérez with many reports on the money laundering and drug trafficking occurring in Venezuela but the president no longer welcomed them. Halvorssen subsequently gained the support of Sen. Cristobal Fernandez Dalo and was appointed special overseas investigator for the Venezuelan Senate's Anti-Money-Laundering Commission.[48] Among the banks Halvorssen investigated was the Banco Latino. "It seemed inconceivable to me," Halvorssen reported, "that this bank could move the enormous amounts of money that it did without being involved in some kind of money-laundering scheme. I alerted the U.S. Federal Reserve and the New York District Attorney's Office of my suspicions. I believed the bank was being used in a Ponzi scheme that sooner or later would have to fall."[49]

While working with Manhattan district attorney Robert Morgenthau, Halvorssen "discovered more than $19 million that President Pérez and his mistress, Cecilia Matos, had squirreled away in secret accounts."[50] President Pérez was impeached in May of 1993. Then, in September 1993, Halvorssen received from an informant what he considered to be incontrovertible evidence of money laundering in Venezuelan banks. The most damaging evidence concerned Banco Latino, the country's second largest bank. After informing Venezuela's minister of interior of this fact, Halvorssen became increasingly concerned about attempts on his life. In October of 1993 he was arrested on trumped-up charges as the mastermind of a series of bombings in Caracas. Even so, he was able to push an investigation of the Cuntrera brothers and have them extradited to Italy and in 1994 Carlos Pérez himself was indicted for money laundering.

This case precipitated the collapse of Banco Latino and involved many of the country's largest and most prestigious banks. More than seventeen closed as a result of the financial panic that followed the government's eighty-three-day closing of Banco Latino in 1994. In all, the Venezuelan courts issued arrest warrants for 322 bankers and businessmen.[51]

In addition to the ongoing saga of financial corruption in Venezuela is the April 1996 Miami arrest of Caracas financier Orlando Castro, who was indicted by Morgenthau on charges that he "defrauded a Puerto Rican bank he controlled by funneling money to his troubled Venezuelan bank." Venezuelan bankers in the United States began to fear extradition and twelve of them pooled their resources and hired New York lawyer Theodore Sorensen, the former advisor to President Kennedy, to make their case with the U.S. State Department against extradition. Other Venezuelan bankers were so concerned they moved to Great Britain, which does not have an extradition treaty with Venezuela.[52]

In 1994 when Rafael Caldera was elected to the presidency, he promised a reversal of privatization. Because of the growing dependence of Venezuela's ruling elite on narcotics revenues, the danger of reversing privatization would expand even further government dependency on narcotics revenues. Narcotics income allows the government to afford inefficiencies. Where drug trafficking is covertly a government-protected activity, the governing party may consider the continued protection of drug trafficking essential to its economic viability. Government involvement in drug trafficking, however, provides a basis for blackmail. Any president who moves contrary to the elite's interests can easily be forced out of office on narcotics corruption charges. The vulnerability of the president to narcotics charges makes his economic decisions subject to the interests of criminal wealth. This situation results in the creation of a narcodemocracy, where the ruling elite is able to stay in power through a mutual dependency with criminal interests.

The disgust the Venezuelan people have had with the corruption of their government led to the election of Hugo Chávez to the presidency on December 6, 1998. The rise of the populist leader who led the failed February 1992 coup against the Pérez government is a clear indication of the people's aversion to the anocratic order. Their decision does not challenge constitutionalism; instead it denounces corruption, because the people perceive the state to be merely a facade for unaccountable ruling interests.

According to the Index of Narcostatization Indicators, Venezuela may have reached level 5, the advanced stage. Consequently, the election of Chávez demonstrated the conflict between a corrupted drmocracy and the existential demands of the population for genuine representation.

NARCOSTATIZATION AND ACCOUNTABILITY

As these examples illustrate, narcostatization may occur at any time in a country's transition to a democracy or after an apparent or presumed democratic consolidation. In the transformation of the former Soviet Union to the Russian state, the merging of criminal and political elites began before elections were held. In the cases of both Peru and Bolivia, corruption showed up in the first elected transition regimes. In the case of Venezuela, deep corruption in an apparently consolidated democracy led to the impeachment of a president and the rise to the presidency of a populist challenge to anocracy.

Anocratic governments arise when democratic forms have been deeply compromised by criminal organizations. Disguised by democratic forms, anocratic governments do not achieve the purposes of the democratic structure and do not produce accountability or effectively check corrupt political elites. A common form of an unaccountable anocratic regime is the narcodemocracy.

A civil society that seeks to make democratic leaders accountable is critical to the democratic regime. In the emerging narcodemocracies or the more inclusive anocratic regimes, where large segments of the population are economically dependent on the narcotics business, society is less likely to hold elites accountable for protecting and profiting from drug trafficking.

CHAPTER 8

PRETRANSITION REGIMES AND ORGANIZED CRIME: MEXICO

The democratization process is internationally heralded as transforming the state. However, the problems posed by the ostensibly democratizing state are exemplified best by Mexico. Extensive evidence suggests that even with all the formal attributes of democracy, its elected government may only be a facade for the reality of a narcodemocracy. Donald Ferrarone, a retired special agent of the DEA's Houston office, testified before the U.S. Senate Foreign Relations Committee in October 1997 that "every indicator now and over the last 20 years reveals the government of Mexico consistently works together with the major drug-trafficking families, seeing to it that the drugs . . . are offloaded securely, protected, shipped cross-country under convoy, stored and safely transported to our border."[1]

Ironically, Mexico's electoral system has been highly praised in the United States and other countries. President Ernesto Zedillo Ponce de León, elected in 1994, has shown an unusual tolerance for political opposition. On July 6, 1997, Mexicans elected the five hundred-member federal Chamber of Deputies in which for the first time the official party did not hold a majority of the seats. In addition, the elected mayor of Mexico City, Cuauhtémoc Cárdenas, came from an opposition party, the left-wing Party of the Democratic Revolution (PRD), and several new governors were elected from the center-right opposition party, the National Action Party (PAN). PAN candidates won in the important states of Nuevo León and Querétaro. There were, however, widespread charges of fraud and vote buying in the small, oil-producing state of Campeche on the Gulf Coast. Even though the electoral process seems to be improving, the criminalization of the Mexican system is so far advanced that it needs additional institutional safeguards against corruption to avoid being considered a narcodemocracy.

As in the former Soviet Union, narcostatization has proceeded among the ruling elite in Mexico so that many have positioned themselves to remain in power with the help of the mafias. Even if the electoral system becomes fully competitive, the institutions separate from presidential dominance, and the civil society free of state control, the degree of corruption of both state and society implies ruling elites will remain unaccountable and civil society demoralized.

THE ANOCRATIZATION OF THE AUTOCRATIC STATE

Electoral procedures are easily made a facade behind which the corrupt elites of the authoritarian regimes retain their power. The August 21, 1994, Mexican presidential elections gave some indication of how long and uncertain the prospect of a democratic transition can be in a one-party state. Mexico's single-party system has shown a remarkable capacity to adjust to challenges, crises, and threats to its continuing domination of the nation.

Founded in 1929 to cope with the assassination of a presidential candidate, Alvaro Obregón Salido, the Mexican Institutional Revolutionary Party (PRI)[2] survived many challenges to its hegemony. The roots of the crisis in the 1990s may be traced to 1968, just prior to the Olympic Games, when Luis Alvarez Echeverría, at that time minister of the interior, crushed a left-wing-inspired student uprising. When he became president in 1970, Echeverría moved Mexico to the left to restore his standing with reformist opinion. In October 1973, the Arab oil embargo radically raised Mexican petroleum revenues, causing a currency windfall that allowed Echeverría to increase public spending and helped elevate his popularity. The rise in revenues also permitted Echeverría to borrow vast sums at favorable rates from international financial institutions.

This deficit-financed public spending continued under Pres. José López Portillo (1976–82), and by the early 1980s the Mexican debt was becoming unmanageable. By the end of López Portillo's administration,

Mexico's capacity to service its debt had collapsed. Blaming the crisis on the private banks, López Portillo nationalized them.

Under Pres. Miguel de la Madrid (1982–88), competitive economic pressures for reversing the previous administration's policies increased. The professional financial managers, the technocrats, began taking over the leadership of the PRI and the management of the country's financial problems. This alienated the PRI's old guard left, and a large group defected to form a new party prior to the 1988 elections. Their candidate was Cuauhtémoc Cárdenas, the scion of Lázaro Cárdenas, the presidential icon of the left-wing PRI. Cárdenas was a powerful challenger to de la Madrid's chosen successor, Carlos Salinas de Gortari. According to official tabulations, Salinas won with a bare 50 percent majority. Cárdenas held 37 percent of the vote, and the conservative party (PAN) trailed in third place. Many observers believed this election was fraudulent and that Cárdenas was the rightful winner.

The new president embarked on bold and innovative programs. He cooperated with Pres. George Bush's Enterprise for the Americas Initiative (EAI) and favored the North American Free Trade Agreement (NAFTA). He privatized major Mexican state-owned enterprises, supported electoral reforms, repaired relations with the Roman Catholic Church, and permitted the operation of private Catholic schools. His political and economic reforms further alienated the old guard of the PRI and led to the formation of a powerful opposition group within the party identified in the Mexican press as "the dinosaurs." Salinas's group, called "técnicos" or "modernizers," belonged mostly to a younger generation educated in the United States.

A deep ideological split had developed between the old- and new-style politicians in the mid-1980s. The modernizers promoted a restructuring of the system. The dinosaurs resisted modifications of the Constitution that permitted privatization, NAFTA, a competitive political system, the legal acknowledgment of the church, and the reestablishment of relations with the Vatican.

Among Salinas's most important efforts was his reform of the electoral system. In a study officially sponsored by Mexico's private Business Coordinating Council, Theodore Sorensen of Paul, Weiss, Rifkind, Wharton & Garrison, a New York law firm, evaluated Mexico's new electoral system in order to remove fears of fraud and the possible deligitimization of Mexico's presidency. Sorensen concluded that the 1994 election "satisfied practically all the principles, norms and established criteria of international law and practice."[3]

Opposition to Salinas's policies was nevertheless fierce. Several events exposed organized resistance from the dinosaurs and their supporters. The 1993 assassination of Juan Jesús Posadas, the cardinal of Guadalajara; the well-orchestrated January 1, 1994, Chiapas rebellion followed by the kidnapping of Alfredo Harp Helú; and the assassination of presidential candidate Luis Donaldo Colosio on March 24, 1994, signaled to many a coordinated opposition to reform. Mexican analysts felt Colosio's assassination was particularly significant. Because of what he stood for and because he was Salinas's designated successor, many Mexicans believed his assassination was arranged by the left-wing old guard of the PRI.

After Colosio's death, Salinas chose Ernesto Zedillo to be his successor to the presidency. At the time it was not clear whether Zedillo would continue Colosio's democratization agenda or be reconciled with the PRI left. The PAN presidential candidate, Diego Fernandez, pounded Zedillo and Cárdenas in the presidential debates. For the first time since 1929, polls indicated that a PAN candidate had a chance to win. Zedillo's response to this was twofold: On the one hand he claimed he was Colosio's heir, while on the other he appointed some of the key leaders of the PRI left who had been bitterly opposed to Colosio to positions in his campaign and later in his cabinet.

THE COLOSIO ASSASSINATION

Why was Colosio assassinated? One possible reason was the Gulf cartel's belief that his policies would affect them negatively. It was well known that Colosio intended to attack the principal Mexican drug cartels and get to the bottom of other narcopolitical assassinations. The Gulf cartel's leaders were incensed by Colosio's refusal to meet with Humberto García Abrego, brother of the cartel boss. Colosio was assassinated two days after he declined the cartel's invitation.[4]

There are precedents in Latin America of uncooperative presidential candidates being killed by drug traffickers. In Colombia, the Liberal Party candidate, Luis Carlos Galán, was assassinated in August 1989, halfway through his campaign. Galán was one of the few political leaders in Colombia who had refused to bow to the wishes of the drug lords.

Journalists have linked Colosio's assassination to a narcopolitical nexus inside the Mexican political system. The candidate's security detail was allegedly implicated in his murder. Jorge Vergara Verdejo, a coordinator for Colosio's campaign routes, and Jorge Antonio Sánchez Ortega, an advisor to Salinas, are both connected to Marcela Bodenstedt, the Gulf cartel's principal liaison to the government.[5] Romiro García Reyes, Colosio's chief of security, had questionable ties to then-secretary of communications and transportation (SCT) Emilio Gamboa Patrón and Salinas. Another member of the security team, Fernando de la Sota, was part of a secret intelligence group, CO47, that was trained by the CIA to deal with and investigate insurgency groups in Mexico. Among the skills they learned from the CIA was how to incite groups of people to fanaticism and how to create screens to hide responsibility for assassinations.

According to Eduardo Valle, a former member of the Mexican attorney general's office, who was assigned the task of investigating narcotics trafficking and corruption, there are three possible scenarios for Colosio's assassination. First, Mario Aburto Martínez, the accused assassin, acted alone. This theory is highly implausible. A videotape of the assassination shows the people in charge of guarding Colosio actually clearing the way so Aburto Martínez could get close to him. The second theory is that there was a plot by PRI activists from the state of Baja California who had local grievances against the federal PRI. This is not convincing because none of these men were even nearby when Colosio was killed. The third theory is that federal or state officials, or both, acted in alliance with narcotics interests. This is the view most widely held because narcopoliticians and narcotraffickers had a combined interest in terminating Luis Donaldo Colosio's bid for the presidency.[6]

The First Gunman

In the fall of 1994, the Mexican government declared that Colosio's assassination was the act of a lone gunman, Mario Aburto Martínez. Aburto was convicted and sentenced to forty-five years in prison. Polls showed most Mexicans doubted that the investigation had revealed the facts and believed that elements of the government were involved in the killing. Prosecutors had ignored crucial evidence—they did not account, for instance, for the fact that Colosio had bullet holes on both sides of his body and that the videotape showed Colosio's bodyguards clearing the way for the assassin. "One of the main discrepancies in previous government investigations," the *Washington Post* reported, "was the fact that Colosio was shot twice at point-blank range from opposite sides, with the bullets traveling in widely different trajectories."[7] Prosecutors claimed that Aburto's confession did not exonerate the six other men who trapped Colosio, making him an easy target. Defense lawyers, however, maintained that the evidence against the six men accused of complicity was inconclusive.[8]

In an unprecedented move upon taking office on December 1, 1994, Zedillo appointed Antonio Lozano García, a member of the PAN opposition party, attorney general. Lozano proceeded to reopen the prematurely closed investigation, promising to unmask the authors of the assassination.

The Second Gunman

On February 25, 1995, federal agents arrested a twenty-eight-year old former member of the PRI and charged him as the second gunman in the Colosio murder. Othon Velásquez Cortés was arrested on the basis of testimony by three witnesses, the videotape, and evidence gathered by the third special prosecutor assigned to the case, Pablo Chapa Bezanilla. Cortés was an assistant to the general in charge of Colosio's security detail.[9] Consistent with his security duties, Cortés carried papers allowing him unrestricted access to Tijuana International Airport. At the time of the assassination, the Tijuana airport was run by Roberto Alcide Beltrones, brother of the governor of Sonora, Manlio Fabio Beltrones. Governor Beltrones was the protégé of Fernando Gutiérrez Barrios, minister of the interior in Salinas's cabinet until 1993. Salinas had named Gutiérrez Barrios, a longtime personal friend of Fidel Castro,[10] director general of Federal Roads and Bridges (CPFI) in December 1982 and Roberto Alcide Beltrones his advisor for operations in the northeast. Alcide had thereupon established an extensive network, including the assignation of police officers to his brother's security detail.

Alcide's position ended abruptly in 1989 with the election of PAN candidate, Ernesto Ruffo, to the governorship of Baja California. With the support of SCT secretary Emilio Gamboa Patrón, Alcide was then appointed administrator of customs (IMSS) in Tijuana. His chief was

Jesús Armando López Ferreiro, a commander of CPFI. Alcide was associated with the regional IMSS through Raúl Zorrilla Cosio, a known protector of drug traffickers. Zorrilla attempted to arrange the meeting between a representative of the Gulf cartel and Colosio two days before his assassination.[11]

Colosio was murdered in Lomas Taurinas, close by the Tijuana airport. Alcide was already under suspicion in 1993 after Cardinal Juan Jesús Posadas Ocampo was killed near the Guadalajara airport. The drug traffickers accused of murdering the cardinal were allowed to escape through the Tijuana airport hours after the assassination. This investigation also came to a premature end when the government concluded the cardinal's death was the result of an accident.

Governor Beltrones's director of security, Jaime López Ferreiro, was allowed to interrogate Colosio's first assassin outside of federal police custody, "at a house in an outlying neighborhood."[12] The claim that Aburto had acted alone arose during this interrogation, although he had denied it previously. In August 1996, Othon Velásquez Cortés was freed by a judge who declared there was insufficient evidence to keep him in jail. This led to the firing of the third special prosecutor in the Colosio investigation. But several questions continue to agitate Mexican journalists and the public: Who were the masterminds behind the Colosio assassination? Why were government officials who might have been involved in an assassination plot allowed to interview suspects? Were the drug connections of corrupt officials explored? Did judicial authorities properly analyze the evidence?

THE MAFIA PROBLEM

From 1929, when the PRI was organized, until 1994 there were no assassinations of either a sitting Mexican president or a candidate of the party. The organization of the party was designed precisely to end the bloody conflicts over the succession crises that followed the Mexican revolution, which had been responsible for the deaths of former presidents Madero, Carranza, and Obregón. With Colosio's death, instability in the succession of leadership returned. The principal reason was the corruption of the state and the unwillingness of the ruling class to change to a more competitive and open political system. Modern-day conflict within the ruling class is ultimately linked to the criminalization of the Mexican state.

Analysts like Brian Crozier consider Mexico to be the principal object for control by international mafia. Like Russia, Mexico is an example of the criminalization of a state in transition from autocracy to democracy. According to Crozier's analysis, the Russian mafia has taken advantage of the economic privatization of the former Soviet Union to the extent that Russia now resembles Colombia, where, he says, "the state has almost ceased to exist." He does not consider Mexico to have reached this extreme yet, but some regions of Mexico are close to seeing a merger of the state and mafia.[13]

Important public officials have charged elements of the Mexican leadership with intermingling with narcotraffickers. Indeed, some of the ruling elite have been allied with top mafia figures since the Echeverría administration.[14] Former president López Portillo was designated president after Echeverría's first choice, Mario Moya Palencia, Echeverría's minister of the interior, was revealed to be associated with Alberto Sicilia Falcón, Mexico's top drug lord of the 1970s. It was discovered, one observer has said, "that Gobernación head Moya Palencia was a frequent user of Sicilia's Lear jet. It was also rumored that Moya had presented Sicilia Falcón with the official Gobernación Special Agent credentials that he carried."[15]

Although Moya was disappointed to lose his position as the presidential candidate, he continued to cooperate with and serve the PRI's ruling elite as manager of Mexico's Tourist Development Fund in the López Portillo administration. López's successor, de la Madrid, who assumed office in 1982, appointed Moya ambassador to the United Nations. Moya's protégé, Manuel Ibarra Herrera, was named head of the Mexican Federal Judicial Police, and a cousin of Ibarra Herrera was named head of INTERPOL. Peter Lupsha claimed that having Manuel Ibarra Herrera head the Mexican federal judicial police was "both curious and regrettable." Ibarra's brother, Antonio, Lupsha said, "was involved in drug money laundering through his currency exchange house in Tijuana. Another relative, Victoria Adato de Ibarra, who had just been appointed the government's chief prosecutor for the Federal District, was linked by the DEA in Colombia to that country's cocaine traffickers."[16]

Mexico's equivalent to the FBI, the Dirección Federal de Seguridad (DFS), was dissolved in 1985 amid charges of corruption. Its director, José

Antonio Zorrilla, it was said, protected the drug traffickers who kidnapped, tortured, and killed U.S. DEA agent Enrique "Kiki" Camarena. Some held the minister of interior, Manuel Bartlett Diaz, responsible for the crimes committed by the DFS, since its director, Zorrilla, answered directly to Bartlett Diaz. But Bartlett deflected the charges: Zorrilla, he said, "actually was loyal to a former intelligence czar."[17]

President Echeverría's brother-in-law, businessman Rubén Zuno Arce, was among the key police and political figures associated with drug traffickers. In the summer of 1990 a Los Angeles federal court convicted Zuno for involvement in the Camarena case.[18]

THE SALINAS ADMINISTRATION

By the time Salinas became president in 1988 there was a long history of coalitions between corrupt officials and mafia dons at the highest levels of the Mexican government. Affiliations of the three previous presidents were widely considered to be highly questionable, and Salinas was surrounded by many of the same compromised figures from the very beginning of his administration.

In a 1989 Senate Foreign Relations Committee hearing, U.S. senators charged several high-ranking members of the Salinas administration with having criminal connections to the Mexican mafia. Basing their information on the files of U.S. law enforcement and intelligence agencies, the committee implicated fourteen government officials—including the attorney general; the secretaries of the interior, national defense, public education, and fisheries; the Mexico City chief of police; and other investigators and drug enforcement officials. Even the chief of the anti-narcotics police unit was implicated.

Several members of the Salinas government were publicly charged with having ties to the Gulf cartel. Oscar Malherbe was the main liaison between the Gulf and Ciudad Juárez cartels and the Cali cartel. An agent of Malherbe, Marcela Bodenstedt, was involved with two key figures of the Salinas administration, José Córdoba Montoya, Salinas's cabinet chief, and Carlos Hank González, Salinas's minister of agriculture.[19] Hank González, connected with the old guard of the Mexican political system, was a member of a group known as "Ahora o Nunca" (Now or Never), which opposes the liberalization of the Mexican political system.

After Colosio's assassination, Hank González supported the new president, Ernesto Zedillo Ponce de León. A prominent Mexico City editor called Hank Gonzalez "the biggest money launderer in Mexico."[20]

Mexican drug lords have used Boeing 727s and French-made Caravelle jets to carry six tons or more of cocaine on a single flight into the United States out of northern Mexico. Some of the Boeings are used by the Mexican airline Taesa, which was founded in 1988 by Carlos Hank Rohn, the eldest son and business manager of Hank González. Carlos Hank Rohn was secretary of agriculture and water resources in the Salinas administration. He reportedly sold his 51 percent interest in the airline to his partners, but it is questionable whether the family ties were really cut.[21]

Salinas's SCT secretary, Emilio Gamboa Patrón, was also reportedly connected to Malherbe and the drug cartels through Marcela Bodenstedt.[22] This is an important connection because the SCT controls roads, ports, planes, telecommunications, cellular telephones, airspace, radars, pilots, transport companies, and the federal police in charge of roads and bridges. Gamboa Patrón is a member of the powerful *familia feliz* ("happy family"), a group of de la Madrid associates and a major branch of the modernizers whose reputations have been tarnished by narcotics associations.[23] Gamboa Patrón worked in de la Madrid's administration as private secretary to the president and became head of the national lottery in the Zedillo administration.

Kaveh Moussavi, IBM's representative to Mexico, reported that he sold faulty radars to the SCT during the tenure of Gamboa Patrón's predecessor, Andrés Caso Lombardo. The radars contained gaps that effectively allowed planes to get through airspace undetected.[24] Moussavi claimed the radars were installed intentionally to allow planes carrying narcotics to take off and land unobserved in various areas. Moussavi's accusation was the catalyst causing Lombardo's removal from office.

Another Salinas minister, Fernando Gutiérrez Barrios, minister of the interior until 1993, was closely associated with individuals who were convicted of serving narcotics interests in Mexico, including former president Luis Alvarez Echeverría. Gutiérrez Barrios's wife was Echeverría's private secretary, and he had close connections to José Antonio Zorrilla, the former head of the disbanded DFS, who is serving a thirty-five-year sentence as the author of the 1984 assassination of Mexican journalist Manuel Buendia. Buendia had been investigating narcotics involvement in the upper reaches of the Mexican government.[25]

El Buho

Eduardo Valle Espinoza (nicknamed El Buho, or "The Owl") proved an important source of inside information on Mexican government ties to international and domestic drug traffickers. Valle served as an advisor to Mexico's attorney general under Salinas. In addition to his experience inside the government, Valle served as president of Mexico's Association of Journalists and was a member of the executive committee of Mexico's Socialist Party (Partido Mexicano Socialista). After Colosio's assassination in 1994, Valle resigned from his position in the attorney general's office and placed himself in self-imposed exile in the United States.

Valle had first become disenchanted with pro-Cuban apologists after Castro became involved in narcotics activities in the early 1980s. "Since the Guillot Lara narco-trafficking affair (where in 1982, guerrillas, Colombian narco-traffickers, Gutiérrez Barrios and Castro were mixed together)." Valle wrote, "it was known that the Cuban government was profoundly involved in the drug question."[26]

Eduardo Valle's argument that Mexico is a narcodemocracy is supported by the statement of Pedro Aspe Armella, Salinas's former secretary of finance, who said the narcotics traffickers had penetrated practically every level of Mexico' security forces. "The narcotics traffickers have penetrated not only the federal government, but the state government and municipalities," Armella has been quoted as saying. "It has penetrated the legislative, executive and judicial powers of the country. . . . [It is] the most powerful economic organization in the world today, the world's most important multi-national organization." The narcotics connections, Armella claimed, have penetrated "all of the structures of power of Mexico, to the point that, without any euphemisms, the country does what the narco-traffickers want."[27]

The de la Madrid "Happy Family"

President de la Madrid, like his predecessors, had campaigned in 1982 on an anticorruption platform. His slogan was "Moral Renovation." However, Stephen Morris claimed that the era of de la Madrid was "el sexenio de la impunidad," marked by the protection of "syndical caciques, speculators, narcos, police, and electoral fraud."[28] Mexicans charge that elements of the *familia feliz* have operated in a symbiotic relationship with governmental institutions and a transnational criminal enterprise. Emilio Gamboa Patrón's position in the Salinas administration, while still connected with the de la Madrid family, exemplified how a major government agency can protect and facilitate narcotics trafficking.

Carlos Cabal Peniche, a wealthy Mexican businessman and member of the *familia feliz*, was also connected to drug traffickers. Cabal Peniche spent more than $1.5 billion in less than two years in an effort to buy two of the largest food companies in the United States, Promosi and Del Monte Fresh Produce. He took loans from Easterbrook Company (linked to BCCI) to construct his Cabal Group and then used the Cabal Group to finance investments in bananas in the state of Tabasco and in other commodities in the southeastern states of Mexico. In addition to purchasing major worldwide food distributing firms, Cabal bought the Banco de Sédulas Hipotecarias and combined it with the Banco Cremi to form the Banco Unión. This put him in a position to finance his own enormous distribution network.[29] By the early '90s Cabal Peniche had completed his famous $70 million business tower on land owned by Carlos Hank González in Tabasco, a notorious area for money laundering and drug trafficking. Principal shareholders in the Cabal Group included Federico de la Madrid, son of the former president, and President Salinas's brother-in-law.

While visiting Mexico in September 1994, treasury secretary Lloyd Bentsen announced U.S.-Mexico collaboration to control money laundering at the national, state, and municipal levels. His visit was motivated by concern for twelve cases of money laundering implicating important and respected financiers, including the Cabal Group. Cabal Peniche fled the country in 1994 with an estimated $700 million. After a worldwide manhunt, Cabal Peniche was arrested in Australia, where he was living disguised as a wealthy Italian merchant.

The de la Madrid family is allegedly involved not only in the protection and facilitation of drug trafficking but also in the laundering of illegal drug profits. They are widely perceived as soft on corruption, and during their period outside the government, they have laundered and invested money obtained by narcotraffickers.[30] Other charges against the family include laundering funds obtained from kidnappings.[31]

The kidnapping in early 1994 of Alfredo Harp Helu, a wealthy businessman, illustrates possible political-elite involvement in money laundering. Individuals in the government came under suspicion when $26 million to $30 million in marked ransom money was discovered in Pemex, the state-owned petroleum company. Deputy attorney general Mario Ruíz Massieu detained two Pemex officials several days before his brother, José Francisco Ruíz Massieu, secretary-general of the PRI, was assassinated.

Emerging from the history of corruption in Mexico is evidence that present and past members of the ruling class have associated with and facilitated the domestic and worldwide drug trafficking cartels. It no longer seems incredible that a fused ruling elite and mafia would have the power to assassinate a presidential candidate. Furthermore, a ruling elite and mafia coalition would easily have enough power to prevent the country from exposing the true instigators of the crime.[32]

THE RUÍZ MASSIEU ASSASSINATION

José Francisco Ruíz Massieu, secretary-general of the PRI, was a forty-eight-year old congressman and ex-governor who was expected to become the PRI majority leader in December 1994. He was a leading candidate for the ministry of the interior position in the Zedillo administration. But, on September 28, 1994, Ruíz Massieu was assassinated upon leaving a reunion with 287 newly elected deputies to Congress. The assailant, Daniel Aguilar Trevino, was seized at the scene when his automatic pistol jammed after firing the single shot that killed Ruíz Massieu. According to the *Wall Street Journal*, "The fact that the gunman reportedly used an Uzi weapon raised speculation that drug gangs, which use such weapons, might have been behind the killing. . . . Mr. Ruíz Massieu's brother, Mario, Mexico's deputy attorney general, has been vigorously prosecuting drug traffickers."[33]

On October 6, 1994, Mario Ruíz Massieu imputed a political motive for his brother's murder. He charged that narcotraffickers were working together with a group of resentful politicians.[34] The authors of the crime were allegedly deputies and senators from the state of Tamaulipas, the home base of the Gulf cartel. According to official reports, the deputies and senators were "seeking to change the direction of the country, restoring to key positions those who had been displaced and to use whatever means were necessary to do so."[35] Deputy Manuel Muñóz Rocha, who had disappeared immediately following the assassination, was identified as the mastermind behind Ruíz Massieu's slaying.

Muñóz Rocha was closely associated with Carlos Hank González and belonged to his political group.[36] As president of the Commission of Water Resources of the House of Deputies, Muñóz Rocha cooperated with the secretary of agriculture and water resources. According to Eduardo Valle, "When this man, Muñóz Rocha, reached the Commission it signified that he was a man [who held the] confidence of Carlos Hank . . . and with Hank you must investigate the Group Hermes and Jorge Hank Rohn (Hank González' son) and his relations with Marcelino Guerrero, the husband of Marcela Rosaura Bodenstedt."[37]

Initially, the PRI and the government denied the existence of any conspiracy against Ruíz Massieu, but their facade soon fell. Mario Ruíz Massieu charged, "It is obvious the Deputy Muñóz Rocha did not act alone, but obeyed directions of higher political figures."[38] The investigation led to Raúl Salinas, the brother of the president, and he was formally charged as the intellectual author of Francisco Ruíz Massieu's assassination.[39] As the investigation reached the highest names in the revolutionary family, Mario Ruíz Massieu received instructions from the office of the president, Los Pinos, to slow down the investigation and stop speaking to the media without prior approval from the president's press chief.[40] Ruíz Massieu later said he no longer believed there was a top-level conspiracy and fled to the United States, where he was detained while Mexico attempted to extradite him for further investigation.

At his March 1997 trial in Houston, Mario Ruíz Massieu was accused of accepting cash from some of the county's most notorious drug dealers and depositing it in a Texas bank account. Assistant U.S. Attorney Susan Kempner told jurors in her opening remarks, "You'll learn about suitcases of money on planes belonging to the Mexican attorney general's office."[41]

Raúl Salinas was arrested for ordering the assassination of the secretary-general—a powerful example of the extent of corruption in the Mexican ruling elite. In the course of their investigation, Salinas prosecutors uncovered extraordinary financial dealings. The magnitude of these dealings led to another charge of corruption on the grounds of "inexplicable enrichment." Mexican prosecutors identified $120 million in foreign bank accounts in addition to investments in real estate and other assets. Investigators came across secret Salinas accounts in

Switzerland and the Cayman Islands and calculated Salinas's total fortune at more than $300 million. Raúl Salinas made $190,000 in his annual salary as a civil servant.[42]

THE ZEDILLO ADMINISTRATION

In campaigning for the presidency Zedillo had promised a balance of power among the state's legislative, presidential, and judicial authorities and a crackdown on narcotrafficking. Upon taking office in 1994 he announced a policy, strongly resisted by the old-guard PRI, to make the PRI independent of the presidency and put it on a level playing field with the other major parties. Response to this policy was swift. *Interacciones*, a weekly publication, declared a crisis of confidence in the new president. The weekly, owned by Interacciones Financial Group, whose president is Carlos Hank Rohn, stated, "We think one of the most important issues is the failure of Pres. Zedillo to demonstrate the political capacity to control a political situation that grows more turbulent each day." Four days later, Zedillo devalued the peso, which then fell far below the proposed 15 percent devaluation. Coparmex, a private sector business group, alleged that "the confidence crisis was performed from inside Mexico and with very well-targeted political intentions." The discrediting of Zedillo in his area of expertise, the economy, was aimed at slowing down privatization and increasing dependency on the old-guard PRI.

In March 1995, the United States approved a multibillion dollar rescue package for Mexico. The U.S. Treasury, together with the IMF, provided Mexico with a loan that did not require congressional approval. The U.S. Congress did not support the bailout, in part because of growing concern over Mexico's inadequate antinarcotics effort. In an attempt to head off criticism of its drug program, Mexico pledged to crack down on smugglers entering Arizona through irrigation tunnels and step up its campaign against the cartels. These promises were difficult to achieve, what with the drug traffickers' embedded position within the political system, and Mexican government crackdowns have by and large been aimed at those elements of the trafficking system that do not enjoy political protection.

Despite efforts to reduce drug trafficking, Mexican control of the U.S. cocaine market continues to grow. A senior DEA official reported that Mexican traffickers have been "rolling trucks into New York."[43] This move into the U.S. cocaine market was pioneered by Amado Carrillo Fuentes. With his death, a struggle between Colombians and Mexicans for the New York market may be expected.

◆ ◆ ◆

The case of Mexico demonstrates how an anocratizing authoritarian state produces instability. A democratization process that retains in power the corrupt elites who had previously ruled in an autocracy is not likely to discourage support for insurgency. Mexico has reached level 4, the critical stage, in the Index of Narcostatization Indicators (table 2, chapter 7). Although it was previously at the advanced stage of narcostatization, it may have retreated from this extreme with Zedillo's 1994 election and the congressional elections of 1997.[44]

CHAPTER 9

CONSOLIDATED REGIMES AND ORGANIZED CRIME: COLOMBIA

Colombia is heading in the same direction as Mexico, but from a different starting point, as illustrated in table 3. Colombia is an example of an allegedly stable democracy that is in the process of becoming an anocratic state through narcostatization. An examination of the narcostatization of Colombia shows the corruption of its ruling class and the extent to which the government is dependent on the economic power of the drug mafias. The details of this process illustrate how a country that is considered to be a consolidated democracy supports instead a facade of democratic procedures that cover the reality of unaccountable, corrupt elite rule.[1]

THE COLOMBIAN PRESIDENCY

The Colombian 1982 presidential elections provided the first test case in presidential corruption. An estimated $1 million to $3 million in drug money supported the campaigns of candidates sympathetic to narcotics interests.[2] Ernesto Samper, who would become president himself a dozen years later, acted as the national coordinator for Alfonso López Michaelsen's failed candidacy, which was allegedly financed in part by drug money.[3] Samper's own unsuccessful 1989 campaign was also allegedly paid for in part with Cali narcotics funds. In return for cartel support, Samper supposedly promised that whether he was elected or not, he would do "everything he could to get rid of extradition."[4]

TABLE 3.

NARCOSTATIZATION IN MEXICO AND COLOMBIA

Mexico: Democratizing Anocratic State	Colombia: Anocratizing Democratic State
1. A democratic electoral system is in place.	1. A democratic electoral system is in place.
2. The governing party rules with the cooperation of narcochieftains.	2. The governing party gains power with the assistance of drug cartels.
3. Opposition parties are not infected—and were not in power except in the provinces until the 1997 elections. The opposition-controlled Congres resists narcoinfection.	3. Opposition parties show signs of narcodependence.
4. Major federal institutions are complicit with organized crime.	4. Major federal institutions are complicit with organized crime.
5. Congress is ineffective in investigating and checking government, yet with the July 7, 1997, congressional elections, the possibility of checks does exist.	5. Congress is ineffective and infiltrated.
6. The state is susceptible to external pressure for some repression of organized crime.	6. The state is susceptible to external pressure for some repression of organized crime.

Samper was already known to be soft on narcotics in 1980, when, as the head of the National Association of Financial Institutions, he endorsed the legalization of marijuana, arguing that legalization would attract millions of dollars in revenues.[5] Furthermore, Ana Carrigan reports, "In 1989, an informant from the Drug Enforcement Agency (DEA) claimed to have witnessed a meeting between Samper and Cali leaders Rodríguez Orejuela and José Santacruz Londono, from which the future president allegedly walked away with several briefcases stuffed with $300,000 in cash."[6]

When Samper ran again for the presidency in 1993, the assistant secretary for International Narcotics Matters (INM), Robert Gelbard, said the United States knew Samper had received money from narcotics traffickers. In 1994 the CIA and Colombian police taped a discussion about Cali cartel donations to the Samper campaign. After losing the 1994 presidential election, the Conservative Party candidate, Andrés Pastrana, published taped conversations between one of the Cali cartel dons and a journalist in which the contributions to President-elect Samper's campaign were discussed. Samper denied the charges, but his denials were questioned when his campaign treasurer, Santiago Medina, was arrested in July 1995 on charges of elicit enrichment. Medina implicated Samper's campaign director, Fernando Botero, as compelling him to accept campaign contributions from the Cali cartel. Medina said Samper approved all his actions in advance.[7]

Medina's testimony led to Fernando Botero's resignation as defense minister on August 2, 1995. The same testimony put Samper under pressure to resign the presidency, but he refused. Under the Colombian Constitution, the president has immunity for actions taken before and during his term in office. By law, only the Senate can impeach or convict the president.

To ease pressure from the United States, Samper cracked down on the Cali cartel. Under the strain, Cali cartel leader Gilberto Rodríguez Orejuela proposed to surrender to the Colombian justice system and face trial. The deal specified that, in exchange for their surrender, the Rodríguez Orejuela brothers would submit only to the new set of Colombian laws, which made extradition unconstitutional. Newly elected President Samper wrote to *Time* magazine that he considered it more important to dismantle the cartels than to incarcerate their leaders. In response, the *Time* reporter concluded that "if Colombian authorities were to accept the details of the offer Rodriguez displayed. . . , the drug lords would walk away with little jail time and their fortunes intact."[8]

It is not surprising, therefore, that in March of 1996 the United States withdrew President Samper's visa and decertified the country for not cooperating in combating drug trafficking. The Colombian government protested strongly, and anti–U.S. sentiment ran high not only in the government but also among the general population.

On June 12, 1996, in a vote of 111 to 43, the Colombian Congress absolved Samper of all drug charges. The United States had expected the case for impeachment to be upheld, and the vote made repeal of Colombia's decertification unlikely. A spokesman for the U.S. Department of State, Nicholas Burns, announced that "governments that reward corruption and allow trafficker influence to penetrate to the highest levels of authority will have difficult relations with the United States."[9]

THE COLOMBIAN CONGRESS

The office of the prosecutor general in Colombia has been more independent than any directly appointed presidential office. Prosecutor General Alfonso Valdivieso, who was chosen by the Supreme Court from a list of three names presented by President Samper, could only be removed from office by the House of Representatives Committee of Accusations. An investigation conducted by the chief prosecutor turned up serious charges against members of the Colombian Congress. Valdivieso has investigated members of Congress for cooperating with and receiving money from the drug cartels. Valdivieso also investigated Samper's attorney general and controller general, directly appointed by Samper, for illicit enrichment.

"Illicit enrichment" has been the principal charge for incarcerating the leaders of criminal and political enterprises, but the Columbian Senate attempted to decriminalize this activity by making illicit enrichment a misdemeanor that could be charged only after a commission of a felony. Since the leaders were not personally involved in the manufacture and sale of narcotics, this change in law would make it extremely difficult to capture or charge them. The Colombian House of Representatives refused to cooperate with the Senate in making these changes. Nonetheless, the House Committee of Accusations may be compromised. When Samper asked for a congressional investigation of his receipt of Cali cartel largesse, the House Committee exonerated him in mid-December 1995 in a 14-1 vote. The Senate and the House's generally favorable reception of President Samper made it unlikely the Congress would ever check his activities. According to a 1996 staff report of the U.S. Foreign Relations Committee,

> If the Accusations Committee decides there is a cause to investigate the President, the decision will have to be voted on, first by the full House, then by the Senate, both of which are controlled by legislators either loyal to the President or under investigation for illicit enrichment. The President preserves his immunity (for actions taken before and during his term in office) until the Senate considers charges.[10]

THE COLOMBIAN JUDICIARY AND SECURITY FORCES

The Colombian courts historically have not been severe either in meting out prison sentences or in demanding asset forfeitures of convicted drug lords. Even when drug lords are sent to jail, they receive very light sentences and their business empires remain intact. The Cali cartel is not beheaded when its chiefs are sent to jail because they continue to run their organizations from prison. Life in jail is luxurious and there have been several escapes that were clearly arranged from the inside, such as Pablo Escobar's famous stroll out of prison in 1993. Since the reform of the Colombian Constitution in 1991, Colombia's cartel chieftains cannot be extradited to the United States, where they would be prevented from running their narcotics businesses.

The police and army have also experienced extensive corruption. Although the Samper government bowed to U.S. pressure in appointing Gen. José Serrano (who was viewed as an acceptable appointee by the DEA) chief of the Colombian police, there still was considerable corruption. Raids of cartel hideouts have turned up long lists of police receiving payments from drug traffickers. Army officers are frequently employed by the cartels and there is substantial evidence that cartels purchase weapons and sophisticated electronic gear from military officers. Some members of the military high command have been compromised by corruption and are facing much more difficult relations with the United States as a result.

Nonetheless, Valdivieso has had some substantial successes against political corruption from his independent judicial office:

By May 1996, one government minister and the Attorney General were behind bars. The Minister of the Interior, the Foreign Secretary and the Minister of Communications were charged with complicity in the cover-up of drug-mafia contributions to the Samper campaign. Eight Congress members have also been arrested, while a further 170—out of 230—are under investigation for drug corruption. The Comptroller General and several army generals were reportedly denied visas to the United States allegedly for drug-related activities. The Commander-in-Chief of the army was forced, under U.S. pressure, to retire.[11]

Despite all the difficulties with the Colombian military, on December 2, 1998, the United States and Colombia established a bilateral military task force "to create a special army unit which will support the police in Colombia in counter-narcotics operations."[12]

ECONOMIC, SOCIAL, AND POLITICAL PROBLEMS

Besides the serious problems with Colombia's political and institutional superstructure, the underlying economic structure has been substantially altered. The country has had a long history of land struggles, with campesinos invading large tracts of property and being subsequently evicted by landholders. Over the years, immense amounts of land were purchased from the landed gentry by the newly rich chieftains of the drug mafias. The new landholders, who are estimated to control over 40 percent of the best acreage in Colombia, clash with the Marxist insurgencies and various campesino groups for control.

Part of the corruption of Colombia's armed forces has come from their on-and-off-again alliances with mafia-financed groups in the clash with communist insurgencies. With the growing tension with the United States, there are some signs that the old mafia-political alliances and the communist insurgent elements are becoming united. When the terrorist organization "Dignity for Colombia" kidnapped the brother of former president Cesar Gaviria in April 1996, the group was perceived to be an alliance of Cali cartel hitmen, corrupt elements of the police and military establishment, and former guerrillas tied to Fidel Castro. Former president Gaviria, serving as secretary-general of the Organization of

American States in Washington, D.C., met with Fidel Castro in order to obtain his brother's release.

The formal democratic procedures of the Colombian regime not only cover a growing fissure in Colombian society but also camouflage the vulnerabilities of the institutional order itself. Colombia has experienced various periods of breakdown of its contested electoral system. From 1958 to 1974 the presidency alternated between parties on the basis of an agreement.

The 1996 U.S. decertification of Colombia represents the official U.S. view that corruption has transformed the country into a narcodemocracy. Signs of narcostatization in Colombia are that its Congress no longer holds the executive branch accountable, that the judiciary and police are corrupt, and that the executive is compromised by accepting drug cartel money. In addition, legitimate economic activity of the civil society is jeopardized, and society is demoralized by violence and distrustful of its ability to hold its leaders accountable.

THE TRANSNATIONALIZATION OF THE COLOMBIAN MAFIA

Transnationalization of the Colombian mafia originated in the mid-1960s when the first drug traffickers initiated their operations on a small scale in U.S. territory. After the boom in illegal drug consumption, the Colombian leaders experienced considerable increases in earnings and discovered the immensely lucrative possibilities of drug trafficking. From that moment the powerful webs of the Medellin and Cali cartels were spun and they became the primary producers and distributors of cocaine in the world. In order to obtain maximum political and economic power, the Medellin cartel, with Pablo Escobar Gaviria at the helm, entered into a bloody fight against the Colombian government, bribing and assassinating police, judges, magistrates, journalists, and even presidential candidates.[13]

The Medellin cartel was responsible for the assassinations of Justice Minister Rodrigo Lara Bonilla in 1984 and Attorney General Carlos Mauro Hoyos in 1988. In 1989 the cartel declared war on the government and killed at least 550 people in a bombing campaign. The government essentially capitulated through lax jail sentences for Pablo Escobar and the Ochoa brothers. After his escape from jail, Pablo Escobar was killed in a recapture effort in 1993.[14]

The Cali cartel cooperated with the Colombian government in the war against the Medellin cartel. In the 1980s the Medellin cartel hired Israeli mercenaries to train its private army. In response, the Cali cartel hired an estimated dozen British and South African mercenaries to execute leaders of the Medellin mob.[15] In addition, the Cali group provided intelligence to government forces seeking to eliminate Escobar. As a result of its cooperation with the government, Cali replaced Medellin as the principal supplier of cocaine out of South America. In 1989, the Medellin cartel had controlled an estimated 75 percent of the world's supply of cocaine, but by 1993, they controlled only 40 percent.[16] In 1994, the Cali cartel was estimated to be moving as much as 85 percent of the twelve hundred tons of cocaine shipped out of South America that year.[17] The Cali cartel was now one of the two dominant cocaine mafias in Colombia run by several chieftains. The older group of godfathers were led by Miguel and Gilberto Rodríguez Orejuela and Iván and Julio Fabio Urdinola. Juan Carlos Ortíz and Juan Carlos Ramírez led the replacement group.[18]

The Sicilian mafia and Colombia's Medellin cartel joined forces in October 1987 on the island of Aruba. The top leaders of the world mafias met again in Rome in 1992. By that time, all the great crime syndicates had come together for meetings to parcel out global territorial responsibilities. Representatives of the Medellin and Cali cartels led by Orlando Cediel Ospina-Vargas, alias Tony Duran, met with the foremost powerful families of the Sicilian mafia.[19] Tony Duran went to Italy on behalf of all the cocaine cartels in Colombia. He dealt with the mafia's *capo di tutti capi*, Salvatore "Toto" Riina of the ruling Corleone clan. Among their agreements was the Sicilian assumption of all the laundering of European cocaine profits for the Colombians.

Approximately a quarter of all the money in circulation in the world is in the process of being laundered. This incredible amount of liquid capital is available for purchasing huge corporations, for manipulating financial markets, and even for buying island countries such as Aruba, which is considered the first independent state owned by the mafia.[20]

COLOMBIANIZATION

The situation in Colombia has led to the coining of the term "colombianization," which defines a social situation generated by narcotraffickers.

Colombianization brings the disintegration of institutions—political, economic and social—and a permanent state of violent crimes such as political assassinations, executions, and human rights violations.[21]

"Colombianization" needs to be distinguished from "narcostatization." Colombianization applies to the massive growth of violence within society. It is quite possible to have narcostatization without colombianization. It is feasible, therefore, for Mexico to become a narcostate without going through the colombianization process. Most of the violence in Mexico has been between trafficking groups, not against society, although some officials have been targeted. The Mexican elite, unlike the Colombian elite, was corrupted long before narcotics trafficking became endemic. Consequently, there was not as much resistance from the upper echelons of the state and society to the trafficking cartels in Mexico as in Colombia. As a result, the degree of violence in Colombian society has far exceeded that in Mexico and most other countries. For example, the 1996 murder rate in Medellin was 228 per 100,000 people, compared with the highest murder rate in the United States—70 per 100,000 people in Washington, D.C.[22]

More than thirty thousand people were murdered in Colombia, the violence capital of the world, in 1995 alone. A terrible side effect of organized crime is the general rise in random violence in tandem with organized violence. This climate of unfettered brutality deeply undermines community trust and contributes to the further erosion of community confidence in the government. The population ceases to believe that it will be able to hold its government officials accountable as they too become part of the organized disturbance.

The Colombian elites learned several key lessons from the prolonged violence following the assassination of Jorge Gaitán in 1948, the virtual civil war from 1948 to 1958, the Gustavo Rojas Pinilla coup in 1953, and the National Front experiment from 1958 to 1974. They learned that a long period of objective economic and social development followed by a short period of sharp reversal is likely to lead to nearly uncontrolled revolutionary violence. This "J-curve" hypothesis explains the conditions leading up to and including the ten days of rioting that followed Gaitán's assassination in April 1948. With the ending of the depression in the 1930s there was a long and gradual improvement for urban workers in Colombia, but this growth collapsed in an inflationary spiral at the end of World War II.

Horrific violence continued from 1948 until the early 1970s. The merging of organized crime with the top Colombian elites, according to Colombia's left-wing publication, *Mensajes*, began in 1974. There had been a steady economic rise but the country faced a sharp decline with the Arab oil embargoes following the 1973 Arab-Israeli conflict. The ruling elites, fearing a repetition of violence as predicted by the J-curve hypothesis, decided to allow the drug trade—first in marijuana and later in cocaine—to flourish in order to head off an economic crisis. This reliance on drug revenues allowed Colombia to escape a balance of payments crisis brought about by the high cost of oil, but it started the subterranean cooperation between Colombia's ruling families and the drug traffickers.[23]

Though the Cali cartel keeps a relatively low profile in bribing police and government officials to support its interests, much of the Colombian population is now terrorized, and legitimate businesses must cooperate with the cartels or be driven into bankruptcy. Because the cartels are able to absorb enormous losses in order to make their money legitimate, they easily undercut honest competitors, and some legitimate businesses end up serving as fronts for cartels in order to survive. The U.S. Senate Foreign Relations Committee looked into the situation and reported that

> Since kingpins can afford to operate companies at a loss, legitimate businessmen cannot compete and are forced into bankruptcy. One U.S. based fruit concentrate importer, for example, was forced out of business because a cartel operated fruit concentrate company flooded the U.S. market with a cheaper Colombian product. Many such "legitimate" Colombian companies export products to the United States, laundering money and in many cases, transporting drugs into the U.S. in shipments of legal products.[24]

Colombianization clearly represents the massive decay of Colombian civil society.

THE ANOCRATIZATION OF A CONSOLIDATED DEMOCRACY

Colombia's corrupt political elites maintain themselves in power despite the supposedly competitive nature of the political system. As John A.

Peeler observed, "The old system of elite domination through liberal democratic institutions is still in place and working, but the society is moving beyond its control. In effect, the Colombian democratic regime is going through a process of deconsolidation."[25]

According to the definition of democracy developed earlier, elites in power must be checked by other institutions and must be accountable to the electorate. In Colombia the regime is based on elite dominance reinforced by a thinly disguised alliance with the immensely wealthy and powerful organized drug cartels. The February 1996 U.S. recommendation for decertification specifies the corruption of the Colombian presidency and the self-protection of the political class. It calls Colombia's political system "a restricted democracy that has been corrupted not just by drug traffickers, but by the power the political class has had for the past 30 years."[26]

William Olson, the former deputy assistant secretary of state for narcotics, noted that "The scale of penetration and corruption which reaches into every facet of life and the highest reaches of government, is staggering . . . so staggering that it is hard to grasp either by those who stand outside Colombia or those caught in the problems of Colombia."[27] Olson maintained that the government pitted one cartel against another: "The Cali cartel used Escobar's troubles to their advantage. They provided information to the government to help track Escobar down."[28]

Criminal activity has not declined, despite the 1993 demise of Pablo Escobar, the last leader of the Medellin cartel, and the arrest of Gilberto and Miguel Rodríguez Orejuela, the leaders of the Cali cartel. The Cali cartel and the rising Valle del Cauca cartel have continued to supply massive amounts of drugs to international markets without interruption. According to a staff report of the U.S. Senate Foreign Relations Committee,

> The lesser known, but equally dangerous members of the Valle del Cauca cartel work with Cali traffickers when it suits their business interests. In all of the excitement surrounding the Cali cartel kingpins' captures and surrenders in Colombia, little attention has been given to this powerful cartel which even controls the airstrips used by the Cali cartel. One of the Valle traffickers, Luis Alfredo Grajales, was indicted last year in the Southern Florida District Attorney's landmark "Operation Cornerstone" case. In 1991, ship-

ments by his family's fruit company were found to be laced with cocaine.

One of the jailed traffickers, Henry Loaiza, is a key figure in this cartel. He became a celebrity in his town, buying the poor with free bus tickets and sponsoring beauty pageants; showering the children with candy; and even supporting the church with donations for building repairs. His alias, "the Scorpion," however, belies a less kindly disposition. Possibly acting under Cali kingpin Ivan Urdinola's orders, Loaiza reportedly killed 107 unionists with chain saws and dumped them in the Cauca river. After a local priest complained, his decapitated and dismembered body was found in the same river. "The Scorpion" also allegedly was responsible for the assassination of the Intelligence Director of the DAS, Colombia's domestic intelligence organization, in retaliation for arresting Loaiza's lover.[29]

In turn, the DEA estimated that, in 1994, "the Cali mafia produced more than 700 metric tons of cocaine, and that proceeds from the mafia's operations in the U.S. exceeded $7 billion—that's more than 8 times the size of DEA's annual budget. And this figure does not include the billions of dollars that stay in the hands of retail drug dealers in the U.S. or that are derived from the Cali mafia operations in Europe."[30] The cartel is believed to control 30 percent of the country's best farmland and a major share of the Colombian stock market. Joe Toft, the former DEA chief who retired in 1994 after seven years in Colombia, maintains that narcodollars rent between 50 and 75 percent of the Congress and control an unknown number of police prosecutors and soldiers.[31]

NARCOSTATIZATION AND ANOCRATIZATION TRENDS

The extent of the narcostatization of the Colombian regime has led the U.S. government to conclude that both the executive and legislative branches of the Colombian government are fundamentally compromised by the drug cartels. The implications of this for Colombia's democracy are grave. It means its electoral system is no longer accountable, its institutions no longer provide checks and balances on government corruption, and its civil society is demoralized. The state's institutions are unable to either resist the encroachment of criminal economic activity, an activity protected by the state, or to hold its representatives accountable while in office. Colombia's allegedly consolidated democracy has been deconsolidated. The country has moved toward becoming an anocratic or pseudodemocratic state where democratic forms and institutions are a facade. The fusion of the ruling elite and mafia in Colombia, as in Mexico, has meant that the elite are able to maintain power against the wishes of the people and the uncorrupted elements of the state. The compromised ruling elite push the state further along the path of unaccountability.

When Colombia held presidential elections on May 31, 1998, Horacio Serpa Uribe, the Liberal Party candidate handpicked by Ernesto Samper, won the first round by a narrow margin. He told supporters at a campaign rally May 23 that if elected his administration would promote a peace process. That process would include negotiations without any conditions with the narcoguerrilla armies of FARC and the National Liberation Army (ELN). He would remove the army from contested areas if that would facilitate negotiations and he would reduce the military and allow guerrillas to join. The result of the June 21, 1998, runoff election between liberal Horacio Serpa and conservative Andrés Pastrana, who took office in August 1998, was surprising to many observers. Like Serpa, Pastrana proposed a negotiated solution to the guerrilla insurgency and agreed to turn over a large part of the country to the FARC, which, along with the ELN, finances itself by taxing the drug trade and protecting cocaine labs and airstrips. Pastrana met leaders of the FARC in July and agreed to demilitarize an area comprising more than sixteen thousand square miles. Reports from the area have the FARC ruling without any resistance from the government and the insurgents wishing to create an independent republic.[32]

The case of Colombia demonstrates the instability of an anocratizing democratic state. By 1998, Colombia had reached level 5, the advanced stage in the Index of Narcostatization Indicators. Many of its ministries and enforcement agencies (some willingly, others not) have been compliant with organized crime, although since the election of Andrés Pastrana the presidency itself is no longer perceived to be complicit with the drug cartels. Nonetheless, the gravity of the insurgency problem makes the task of reversing narcostatization difficult.

PART IV

Drug Culture, Conflict, and Order

CHAPTER 10

CULTURAL UNDERPINNINGS OF MODERN DRUG CONSUMPTION

Countercultural values are the underlying support for the globalization of drug consumption. According to Samuel P. Huntington, "The great divisions among humankind and the dominating source of conflict will be cultural. Nation states will remain the most powerful actors in world affairs, but the principal conflicts of global politics will occur between nations and groups of different civilizations. The clash of civilizations will dominate global politics. The fault lines between civilizations will be the battle lines of the future." Huntington's thesis stresses the differences between civilizations as the principal basis for conflict in the post–cold war world. He sees civilizations as differentiated

> from each other by history, language, culture, tradition and, most important, religion. The people of different civilizations have different views on the relations between God and man, the individual and the group, the citizen and the state, parents and children, husband and wife, as well as differing views of the relative importance of rights and responsibilities, liberty and authority, equality and hierarchy. These differences are the product of centuries. They will not soon disappear. They are far more fundamental than differences among political ideologies and political regimes.[1]

The problem with the development of the counterculture in the West is that the West itself consists now of two civilizations. One of those civilizations is based on the Judeo-Christian tradition—and Huntington recognizes religion as the most fundamental component of a civilization—and the other is based on a scientistic, hedonistic value system accepted by alternative elites and a large sector of the population. Although other civilizations have historically clashed with the Christian Western tradition, in the twentieth century the non-Christian world clashes with the Western counterculture just as that counterculture clashes with Western traditionalism.

The clash between the West's secular culture and other traditional cultures has become globalized because of the revolution in communication. Since the late 1960s American popular culture has been infused with the values of Western counterculture. This culture is spread to the world's traditionalist civilizations through film, television, electronic communications such as the Internet, and the nearly half a million foreign students who study each year in the United States. Many nations consider the West their cultural enemy but find it nearly impossible to prevent cultural penetration from the West.

Cultural conflicts exist within civilizations and not just between them. The West faces a conflict within itself. The clash between traditionalists and the countercultural movement takes shape increasingly around that movement's support for drug consumption.

THE DECAY OF CIVIL SOCIETY

The demand for drugs is the basis for maintaining the profits of the drug cartels. Since the underlying support for this demand is the drug culture, that culture is fundamental in maintaining the narcotics threat to democracy. Culture supports consumption and consumption supports drug trafficking, which in turn threatens democracy.

The interconnections of organized crime, governments, and the international financial system synergistically produce narcostatization. The narcostatization process in turn produces the contemporary anocratic state for both democratizing autocracies and consolidated democracies. One effect of the narcostate is to increase the possibilities of inter- and intrastate conflict and insurgency. Indeed, the chief characteristic of warfare under the influence of globalization and narcotics trafficking may be that of an insurgency against a national government rather than an armed conflict between states, reinforcing the anarchical nature of the international environment and the likelihood that political elites will protect drug trafficking.

The impact of narcotics on both domestic regimes and the international system is a massive problem in itself. However, the problem of narcostatization is further aggravated by the underlying worldwide cultural supports for narcotics consumption. As Machiavelli and Tocqueville argue, a moral society is critical to the functioning of the democratic regime. Their discussions of freedom and the liberty-preserving regime stress the necessity of a moral civil society. Machiavelli saw the necessity of moral civic virtue for the establishment of a good regime and the maintenance of freedom. He believed that when civic virtue is lost, rulers rely on fraud, deception, and naked force to retain their power. A moral society that is able to criticize and remove public officials from office is absolutely essential, he said, for a self-governing democracy. The moral consensus holding a public together is a fundamental condition for democracy.

Tocqueville's analysis is similar. For him, the freedom and independence of human beings in society was essential to an accountable republic. Without religion, the stability of political society was destroyed and the public threatened with anarchy or despotism. Tocqueville criticized French thinkers of the eighteenth century for practicing a form of self-idolatry and for not having the essential spiritual modesty necessary to sustain a republic. Neither Machiavelli nor Tocqueville specified any particular religion as the basis of a free and stable society, beyond identifying that the early Roman and American republics were each supported by religion.

In contrast, today's drug-consuming society would overthrow traditional morality and put in its place an alternative value system. The origins of the modern alternative American culture date to the middle nineteenth century when a few intellectuals were first seized with the possibility of an alternative morality. Their heirs today, scientists influenced by the discoveries and innovations of the intervening years, support the transformation of traditional moral societies. The social interpretations of Charles Darwin have had an especially materialistic impact on modern moral culture. The predominant interpretation of Darwin's evolutionary theory—translated to the social realm—was that random natural forces accounted for the origin of life, with no divine guidance or intervention. This revolution of materialism created a new orthodoxy, which precluded the discussion of intelligent design of the natural world. The social interpreters of Darwin applied this materialistic view to society with revolutionary implications for traditional moral premises.[2]

With Darwin's premise of the evolutionary process of life came the idea that science could improve human beings. The elementary assumption of evolution was spontaneous generation and the improvement of species over time. Social Darwinists asked, if beings could be physically improved, then why could they not also be mentally improved? Evolution was the required assumption for humanists who adapted the concept of survival of the fittest to the human species. The human controllers' objective was to elevate the level of human awareness and improve consciousness, and they raised the question of whether or not drugs could be used for this purpose.

T. H. Huxley, as the propagator of Darwinian evolutionary thesis, had intuitively rejected the "creation hypothesis," but he had no feasible alternative until Darwin's *Origin of the Species* provided one. It was then that Huxley became a proponent of the Darwinian explanation and an opponent of Christian dogmas.[3] He was concerned with what ethical structure could be inserted to fill the void left by the removal of "revealed" religion and to guide men's purposes in a world understood in Darwinian terms.

Aldous Huxley, the grandson of T. H., was deeply interested in the evolution of consciousness. In 1952 he read an article on psychological medicine in the *Heggert Journal*. That article, by Humphrey Osmond, inspired his interest in using drugs to experiment with human consciousness. He had previously been interested in the ceremonies and rites of primitive people to reach other levels of experience. Among the rites that interested him were those of American Indians who extracted fluids from the peyotl cactus to produce hallucinations.

In 1953, when Osmond attended the American Psychiatric Association meeting in Los Angeles, Aldous Huxley invited him to explore drug use with him. Osmond provided mescaline and Huxley and his wife agreed to self-experimentation. Osmond described the experiment: "It slowly etched away the patina of conceptual thinking; the doors of perception were cleansed, and Aldous perceived things with less interference from his enormous rationalizing brain."[4]

Ascending to the use of psychedelic materials such as LSD, Huxley experimented twice a year from 1953 into the 1960s, partly to reach a higher level of consciousness and partly to explore the links between mind and matter. He recounted his experiments with what has been called "chemical epistemology" in two books, *The Doors of Perception* and *Heaven and Hell*. He considered both books to be interim reports of his experiences. His conclusions he stated in his autobiography, *Life*, writing that chemical changes of the mind provide a genuine religious experience: "These new mind changers," Huxley said, "will tend in the long run to deepen the spiritual life of the communities in which they are available."[5]

Aldous Huxley's brother Julian initially focused exclusively on the biological sciences. In the 1920s he worked with H. D. Wells on *The Science of Life* and gradually shifted to the study of human nature and world order. As a student, Wells had heard T. H. Huxley lecture and had imbibed from Huxley his concern with constructing new ethical formulas. Now he served as the link between T. H. Huxley and his grandsons, Julian and Aldous.

Julian Huxley changed his primary interest in the biological sciences to a concern with ethics during his tenure at Rice University in 1914. While on a trip to a library in Colorado Springs he read an essay by Lord John Morley who had written that "the next great task of science will be to create a religion for humanity."[6] From this point Huxley began to forge his scientific humanist beliefs and to promote his thesis of religion without revelation. His concern for a religion of humanity became the basis of his intellectual cooperation with Wells.

Julian Huxley's cooperation with Wells served as a bridge to his brother's mystic interests. The key was Wells's twelve year search for a secular religious basis for a "single world commonweal" that would control the moral, biological, and economic forces that historically led to war. Julian Huxley worked with Wells on developing a worldwide movement to overcome existing religions and governments, economic nationalism, and racial and ethnic hostilities. Wells's book, *The Open Conspiracy*, published in 1928, called for individuals and groups to cooperate together on six broad principles:

1. The complete assertion, practical as well as theoretical, of the provisional nature of existing governments and of acquiescence to them

2. The resolve to minimize by all available means the conflicts of these governments, their militant use of individuals and

property, and their interferences with the establishment of a world economic system

3. The determination to replace private local or national ownership and production with a responsible world directorate serving the common ends of the race

4. The practical recognition of the necessity for world biological controls, for example, of population and disease

5. The support of a minimum standard of individual freedom and welfare in the world

6. The supreme duty of subordinating the personal life to the creation of a world directorate capable of these tasks and to the general advancement of human knowledge, capacity and power[7]

Wells and the Huxleys were pioneers of the globalist ideology, which is not to be confused with the concept of globalization. Globalization is a trend of the international system to bring people closer together through mass communication, transportation, trade, technology, and finance. Globalism, an ideology brilliantly reflected in Wells's *The Open Conspiracy*, calls for overcoming nationalism, creating a world government, and developing a rational religion to supplant the various world religions. As one analyst of Wells's work observed, Wells established the "structural frame" of his life as the propagation of a worldwide "Open Conspiracy" to "rescue human society from the net of tradition in which it is entangled and to reconstruct it upon planetary lives."[8]

Julian and Aldous Huxley joined together in search of a secular religious ethic to inspire humankind, one not based on revelation. They believed that humans may be controlled by "unreason which alone [has] power to rule the minds of men."[9] The use of narcotics was one method for inducing an "unreasoned belief." Julian came to believe that evolution had crossed the line separating mind and matter and this belief led him to an investigation of the paranormal. By the 1950s he was investigating extrasensory perception and was developing an interest in Aldous's mind-altering experiments.

The paths of the two brothers converged as "scientist and mystic began to find common ground in that border land between mind and matter."[10] They came to believe that even if evolution had initially been spontaneous, the evolution of human consciousness could be brought under human control. Julian Huxley believed the scientific method should be brought into social and economic organizations and religion. It was the brothers' mutual vision that humans could be transformed as an end product of the evolutionary process. Evolution was not just a theory about the origin of life, but a fact that could serve as the foundation of ethics and the future order.

In this way, the social-political thinking of Wells and the Huxley brothers came together on Darwinian, narcotic, and social-utopian premises. Aldous Huxley, in *Brave New World Revisited*, claimed that his *Brave New World* was far more prescient of the future than was George Orwell's *1984*. "It now looks as though the odds were more in favor of something like *Brave New World* than of something like *1984*," he claimed.[11] He foresaw a narcotics revolution that would make people love their servitude and lose any desire to rebel against their controllers: "The systematic drugging of individuals for the benefit of the State (and incidentally, of course, for their own delight)," he wrote,

> was a main plank in the policy of the World Controllers. The daily soma ration was an insurance against personal maladjustment, social unrest and the spread of subversive ideas. Religion, Karl Marx declared, is the opium of the people. In the Brave New World this situation was reversed. Opium, or rather soma, was the people's religion. Like religion, the drug had power to console and compensate, it called up visions of another, better world, it offered hope, strengthened faith and promoted charity.[12]

Aldous Huxley died in 1963, but Timothy Leary carried on his idea that mental evolution could be shaped through experimentation with narcotics, but while Huxley thought drug consumption should be limited to elites, Leary wanted to make it available to the masses:

> Our hypotheses were simple. History seemed to show that our human species has always eagerly accepted any new technology that gave them more power to receive and transmit information. Our experiment sought to demonstrate that it is in our nature to want to expand consciousness, change our brains, open up to new experiences. Radio, television, transistors, and psychoactive drugs are all instruments for widening the range of input experience.

According to Leary, the struggle to change consciousness was a basic tenet of the counterculture and was as important to the values of the counterculture as the fight against the Vietnam War and racism.[13]

Leary went to Harvard in January 1960 with a funded project to change the neurochemical processes of the brain. Leary called his new science "neurologic." Believing that the human being has several "minds," he attempted to induce brain changes by experimenting with psychedelic therapy on prison inmates. He later alleged that his methods cut the prison return rate by 90 percent.[14]

In 1963 Leary left Harvard and became, as he says, "without knowing it," a shaman. He studied the Hindu Vedanta, the Buddhist Tantra, and Taoist techniques for understanding the flow of energies. He was especially interested in the role psychedelic plants had played in the religious histories of Egypt, Persia, India, China, and Greece. He set up the Castalia Foundation, where musicians experimented with electric sounds and lights to replicate the drugged experience.

According to Leary, the real revolution of the early 1960s was neurological, but it provoked a backlash in 1966 when Congress criminalized LSD and other drugs. He conceded that there were some costs to the collapse of authority that came from the understanding that the nervous system creates its own reality, but he believed that the conscious control of the nervous system, a live-and-let-live tolerance of difference, open sexual expression, and the revelation of "Higher Intelligence" within natural processes "will produce a new philosophy of Scientific Paganism" that "will assume physical immortality provided by scientists and encouraged by those intelligent enough to want to live forever."[15]

There is, perhaps, a certain irony here about both the sources and outcome of the drug culture. There is considerable evidence that the origin of the mass basis to the drug culture came from CIA scientists who sought to control behavior with drugs. The initial code name for the CIA's mind-control efforts was Bluebird, and later Artichoke. According to John Marks, "Men from the Office of Security's ARTICHOKE program were struggling—as had OSS before them—to find a truth drug or hypnotic method that would aid in interrogation. Concurrently, the Technical Services Staff (TSS) was investigating in much greater depth the whole area of applying chemical and biological warfare (CBW) to covert operations."[16] In the early 1950s the government's mind-control program came under the direction of Dr. Sidney Gottlieb, who ran it under the codename MK-Ultra. The project's purpose was "to investigate whether and how it was possible to modify an individual's behavior by covert means."[17]

The intelligence community was interested not only in mind control of an individual, the so-called Manchurian candidate, it was also interested in mind control of large populations. Under the direction of Gen. William Creasy, the army ran a program that targeted mass groups. Ken Kesey, one of the most famous propagandists of drugs in the 1960s, was a volunteer in a government-sponsored drug program. While a graduate student at Stanford University he volunteered for drug experiments at the Veterans Hospital in Menlo Park. Soon he and his Merry Pranksters were involved in the Berkeley Free Speech Movement (FSM) and had joined the activist elements of the antiwar campaign. Although the bonding of drugs to the antiwar movement may have been unintentional on the part of government experimenters, they did in fact prove that drugs could effect large mass movements.

Significantly, the growth of the scientific culture and its merger with the counterculture provided a favorable climate in the United States for promoting drug use and experimentation. The scientific elite concerned with drug philosophy saw itself on the cutting edge of scientific and behavioral experimentation, though society may not have recognized the officially sanctioned experimental bases for the radical increase in drug consumption in the late decades of the twentieth century.

Culture and Narcotics

Commercial and economic interests have further strengthened the cultural bases of drug use and experimentation. The entertainment industry exploits the challenges to rules so attractive to youth. The music of the counterculture incorporates a positive attitude toward chemical alteration of the mind. The counterculture combines music and drugs to negate the established order and to offer a radical alternative based on "pleasure, pacifism, non-nationalism and a non-religious spirituality."[18]

Carl Raschke's book, *Painted Black*, lists frequent examples of convergence between rock music, drug abuse, occultism, Satanism, and crime.[19] Allan Bloom stresses the important effect of rock music on the young in *The Closing of the American Mind*.[20] Robert Pielke in *You Say You*

Want a Revolution: Rock Music in American Culture describes explicitly how rock music challenges and transforms cultural values with regard to work, race, sex, and the Judeo-Christian traditions.[21] Robert Pattison traces the pantheistic sources of modern rock music to nineteenth-century poets. He demonstrates how rock music has promoted drug consumption since the 1960s, citing how three of the most popular groups—the Beatles, the Rolling Stones, and Led Zeppelin—exploited cult imagery and promoted drug use. By the 1990s, bands promoting drug consumption had sold more than 60 million albums.[22]

In 1996, the vice president of MusiCares, an outreach program, brought together more than four hundred members of the music industry to discuss the drug problem among the artists. A manager of one of the bands said the industry's response was hypocritical: "The reality is, none of the record companies are going to let go of a platinum artist because they're on drugs. And if they would take a position saying 'We don't want to do business with you,' then there's 20 other record companies that would do it in a second."[23]

The film industry has also contributed to the glamorization of narcotics consumption. Early on, movies warned about degradation through drug use. The 1950 Frank Sinatra movie, *The Man with the Golden Arm*, revealed the destruction of a jazz musician who became addicted to heroin. In contrast, popular movies in the 1990s have increasingly portrayed drugs in a nonjudgmental way. *Pulp Fiction* and *Trainspotting*, featuring a tour of Scotland's heroin junkies, received excellent reviews, and the latter was called "a pop culture cyclone."[24]

Vast markets exploiting counterculture images and the consumption of drugs have attracted economic entrepreneurs such as Paul Allen, the cofounder of Microsoft, who sees the exploitation of drugs as leading to greater profits in cyberspace technology. Allen's marketing report disclosed that "Shocking parents, family, friends and community is often a part of this group's self-definition process. They will want a record of the most socially unacceptable image of themselves to freak out their parents. . . . The majority of them will be drunk, stoned, tripping, or otherwise chemically altered."[25]

The extent to which the counterculture has become acceptable to the U.S. mainstream press is revealed in the 1997 obituaries for Allen Ginsberg and William S. Burroughs, the Beat generation's leading poet and novelist, respectively. Ginsberg, the author of *Howl* (1956), and Burroughs, the author of *Naked Lunch* (1959), were heralded as geniuses, satirists, and reformers in these obituaries. No mention is made of the pornographic content of their work or that both authors were drug abusers. The *New York Times* obituary for Burroughs reported that he had experimented in sex with men, women, and children. The traditional media and literary establishment's treatment of Ginsberg and Burroughs illustrates the public's acceptance of narcotics consumption, pornography, and obscenity.

In short, an unplanned synergy exists between culture and narcotics. Technological entrepreneurs, musicians, and antitraditional philosophers have combined to promote a drug-consuming culture. Parallel to the rise of the promoters of the drug culture is the undermining of the traditional culture. Remarkably, the U.S. Supreme Court has played a prominent role in this.

LAW AND CULTURE

The Supreme Court has undermined the traditional safeguards against the most revolutionary alternative cultural values in the American political system by issuing decisions that erode public support for the religious and metaphysical values basic to the nation's traditional civic culture. Before the 1940s, the Court decided less than a dozen cases involving religion and the First Amendment wall of separation. Since the 1940s, the number of First Amendment cases involving religion freedoms has grown rapidly, and a materialistic premise to the Court's decisions has become increasingly evident. For example, the 1963 Supreme Court decisions outlawing Bible reading and the recitation of the Lord's Prayer in public schools overturned more than a century and a half of accepted practice. The Supreme Court's restraints on "revealed" religion have also made it illegal to post the Ten Commandments on public school buildings [*Stone v. Graham*, 449 U.S. 30 (1980)]; unconstitutional for the state to allow public school children an occasion for prayer [*Wallace v. Jaffree*, 472 U.S. 38 (1985)]; and prevented a Catholic display of the crèche on the staircase of the Allegheny County Courthouse [*ACLU v. Allegheny County*, 492 U.S. 573 (1989)]. *Lemon v.*

Kurtzman, 403 U.S. 602 (1970) provided a firm basis for enforcing a secularized culture in the United States. By that decision, the Supreme Court voided a Pennsylvania bill passed in 1968 that permitted non–public school children to use service contracts with the state. The Pennsylvania act was designed to help educate children in parochial schools by providing assistance in mathematics, foreign languages, physical science, and physical education. Though there was no provision for direct assistance to any religious activity in the parochial schools, the Supreme Court relied on the interpretation of Professor Paul Freund who argued in a *Harvard Law Review* article that "political divisions along religious lines was one of the principal evils against which the First Amendment was meant to protect."[26] The Court ruled that because the passing of the Pennsylvania legislation entailed considerable political activity, it involved political divisiveness along religious lines, and consequently was prohibited by the First Amendment. This decision was an innovative revision by the Supreme Court of what was formerly considered normal political activity.

Though in the 1990s the Supreme Court reversed some of its opposition to revealed religion, permitting parents, for instance, to exclude their children from public schools on religious grounds, a majority of the Court's decisions have provided an effective legal instrument to foster the secularization of the U.S. civic culture. A survey in the summer of 1995 by Colombia University's Center for Addiction and Substance Abuse found that a major predictor of a child's potential drug use was whether or not the child's family was religious. By excluding religion from the public sphere and barring public assistance to the secular activities of religious schools, the Supreme Court of the United States may have undermined the civil institutions most likely to protect children from drug abuse.

The consequences of drug consumption for society have become increasingly serious. The struggle to check the narcotics trade has gone through cycles of rise and decline. In the context of increased consumption, the greater part of society continues to oppose drug use. However, there is a growing and vocal minority that argues legalization is the best way to deal with the problem. Members of the political, economic, and cultural elites who advocate drug legalization, or the ending of the "prohibitionist regime," provide substantial economic support to groups seeking to end the ban on drugs.

Arguments For and Against Legalization

There are many arguments supporting the legalization of narcotics in the United States. The first is that the United States is and has been losing the battle against drug trafficking.[27] This argument is based on the premise that the United States has waged an all-out effort against drugs, but given the complexity of the problem and the narrowness of the model on which the drug war has been fought, the full scope of the drug problem has never truly been diagnosed or engaged.

A second argument for legalization is that prohibition is a violation of human rights. In this view, if drug use is a crime, it is a victimless one: "As long as an individual's behavior does not adversely affect others, then he ought to be free to do as he chooses."[28] However, as the statistics given in chapter 11 will demonstrate, drug use causes criminal behavior to increase and endangers the safety of the non-drug-using population.

Another aspect of the human rights argument is that individual rights have been violated in the war against drugs, including "the elimination of an accused's right to pretrial release for most charges under the drug laws; heightened restrictions on post-conviction bail; and invasions into the attorney-client relationship through criminal forfeiture."[29] According to Robert Sweet, legalization would further civil liberties by ending police searches, road blocks, and random analyses in the workplace. However, this argument is faulty since road blocks exist for alcohol, which is currently a legal drug, and must continue for safety reasons. In addition, searches and random analyses in the workplace would necessarily remain for airline pilots, bus drivers, and other professions that require mental clarity during working hours.

Kenneth Roth, executive director of Human Rights Watch, argues, "human dignity means the freedom, the autonomy to use drugs." This is an interesting statement since the inability to control one's personal behavior historically has been considered a loss of human dignity. Concurrent with the right to use drugs, of course, is the right to receive health care in order to offset the consequences of such a decision. The bulk of the cost would be borne by the non-drug-using population who would pay for the consequences of the legal use of a damaging product.[30]

A third argument for legalization is that the war on drugs, not actual drug use, causes violence and crime. This argument is based on the assumption that the deaths and violence associated with drugs are caused by people struggling to get drugs and to protect their terrain in the distribution of drugs. However, studies show that more crime is committed by people on drugs than in any other circumstance. A Temple University study linking crime and heroin addiction reveals "237 addicts committed more than 500,000 crimes during an eleven-year period (192 per addict per year)."[31]

A fourth argument for legalization is that the drug war is substantially a racist conflict. In this view, since many immigrant and ethnic groups are distributors of narcotics in the United States, a war against narcotics is ostensibly a war against ethnic or racially distinct elements. However, immigrant groups and ethnic and racial minorities are also the most victimized by the purveyors of drug use.

Additional arguments for legalization are that it would decrease crime in the inner cities, eliminate criminal mafias, reduce the prison population, and help combat diseases such as AIDS by allowing the state to provide clean needles to drug users. However, statistics reveal that since most crimes are committed while under the influence of drugs, increased availability and consequent expanded drug use would serve to increase, not decrease, crime. Research has also indicated that the distribution of clean needles may reduce the spread of AIDS, but there is no assurance that drug abusers will utilize them. Furthermore, the message implicit in the distribution of needles may appear to encourage their use.

A qualified argument for controlling narcotics combines legalization with education. Rensselaer W. Lee argues that the legalization of drugs— combined with a drug use education campaign—deserves serious consideration. He expresses concern that the number of drug users might expand, but he thinks the benefits, on balance, would be significant. One of the benefits would be financial because money spent on the drug war would decrease and revenues would increase from the taxing of drug producers and consumers. A further gain would come from the decreased costs of drugs, which would in turn lower profits, reduce the incentive to corrupt police and judges, and undermine gang wars in the cities. Lee suggests that legalization might also be beneficial to U.S.-Latin American relations by reducing U.S. pressure on these countries. Nonetheless, Lee concedes that new problems such as increased consumption would arise and offset expected gains.[32]

SUPPORT FOR LEGALIZATION

A large number of organizations, foundations, groups, and prominent individuals have supported drug legalization over the years. During the 1970s, the Ford Foundation funded the Drug Abuse Council, which recommended decriminalization. Gabriel G. Nahas reported that "The trustees of the Ford Foundation endorsed the creation of the Drug Abuse Council with a $7.5 million grant. Three other foundations, Carnegie, Kaiser, and Commonwealth, pledged an additional $2.5 million. Further funds came from the Equitable Life Assurance Society, the United Methodist Church, the City of Phoenix, and the United States State Department."[33] Later, the Ford Foundation provided funds to the Drug Policy Foundation (DPF) for the purpose of seeking an alternative to the criminalization of narcotics. The DPF is the most influential foundation seeking alternatives to criminalization. Headquartered in Washington, D.C., it has received substantial funds from Chicago commodities broker Richard J. Dennis and international financier George Soros, who contributed $10 million through his Open Society Institute (OSI). OSI administers programs in both research and public education to provide alternatives to law enforcement in dealing with drugs. David Geffen, president of Geffen Records, has also contributed to the DPF.[34] Arnold S. Trebach, president of the DPF, boasts that the foundation's membership has grown to over seventeen thousand and "may be the best funded drug policy reform organization in history."[35]

At the November 1994 Eighth Annual Conference of the Drug Policy Foundation, Trebach announced that the foundation's main objective was "harm reductions," claiming that the prohibitionist attitude will destroy democracy. "I do not see a threat from drug users; I see a threat from drug warriors," he said.[36] The defeat of the "prohibitionist mentality" was the crux of Trebach's argument and those of other speakers such as David Condliffe, the executive director of the DPF and former drug czar of New York City, and Ira Glasser of the American Civil Liberties Union (ACLU).[37] Also supporting legalization are the National Organization for the Reform of Marijuana Laws (NORML), which has been bankrolled by the Playboy Foundation, and the militant homosexual organization ACT-UP.[38]

At the 1998 DPF conference, Dale Gieringer of NORML characterized that year's U.S. congressional and state elections as opening up an era of new opportunities. California attorney general Bill Locke was recognized as prolegalization and California's Mendocino County was identified as a center for the war against the U.S. government's drug policy and as the future "Amsterdam of the West Coast." The passing of the initiatives legalizing medical use of marijuana in Alaska, Arizona, Oregon, and Washington was heralded as a great victory. Nonetheless, drug czar Barry McCaffrey warned that there was no change in federal law regarding the possession and distribution of marijuana, despite the results in the four western states.

The most important mainstream organization, from a libertarian perspective, supporting drug legalization is the Cato Institute, which is backed by Kansas oil millionaire Charles Koch and such major multinationals as Coca-Cola, Citibank, Shell Oil, Philip Morris, and Toyota.[39] Cato Institute's president, Ed Crane, and vice president, David Boaz, both sit on the DPF's board of advisors, and the Cato Institute's journal, *Reason*, runs DPF ads encouraging legalization. Boaz claims that the day will come when there will be a sufficient number of legalization supporters to bring about decriminalization.[40]

Many proponents of the antiprohibitionist position recommend a gradual approach to achieving legalization. Stephen B. Duke, a professor at Yale Law School, has long been a critic of drug prohibition. His book with Albert C. Gross, *America's Longest War*, describes the use and partial decriminalization of marijuana in the 1960s as integral to the social protests that "contributed greatly to progress and civil rights and put an end to the Vietnam War." Duke and Gross contend that "Drug prohibition is motivated in part by a fear of the resurrection of the essence of the 60s which was revolution."[41]

Ethan Nadelmann's Lindesmith Center in New York City is a think tank devoted to legalization, funded in part by George Soros. *International Organization* published Nadelmann's critique of what he calls "transnational moral entrepreneurs" who have supported global prohibitionist regimes.[42] Nadelmann, who predicts that drug prohibition will fail because it is essentially unenforceable, was an advisor to Mathea Falco, assistant secretary of state for international narcotics matters in the Carter administration. Later, in the early 1990s, Falco was appointed to head the Drug Strategies Institute (DSI) in Washington, D.C., which supports education and treatment for narcotics. In that position, she advocated turning more of the drug war over to international agencies and removing it from the U.S. government. "World opinion and resources channeled through the United Nations often have more impact than bilateral pressure because they are more politically acceptable," she claimed.[43]

Falco counted herself among the international relations experts who did not consider drug trafficking a national security threat. Joseph J. Romm endorsed this view: "Drug trafficking should not be seen as the cause of domestic drug consumption and its concomitant problems," Romm asserts, "and, therefore, it should not be viewed as a significant threat to national security."[44]

During the week of June 7, 1998, the UN General Assembly held a special session on the world drug problem. The 150 participating nations promised to work together to reduce the demand for illegal drugs over the next five years. They also promised to phase out the cultivation of opium and the coca leaf, to expose money launderers, to tighten controls on precursor chemicals, and to cooperate on the extradition of traffickers.

The first day of the special session, five hundred people signed a letter alleging that "the global war on drugs is now causing more harm than drug abuse itself" and asserted that punitive prohibitions should be dropped in favor of approaches based on "common sense, public health, and human rights." Among the prominent signers were former secretary of state George Shultz, former White House general counsel Lloyd Cutler, and former Stanford University president Donald Kennedy. George Soros was reported to have enlisted them in his "legalization crusade."[45]

CONSEQUENCES OF DRUG CONSUMPTION

The year 1992 brought a reversal in the twelve-year decline in drug use by American teenagers.[46] Then statistics released in August 1996 revealed that teen drug abuse had risen 105 percent between 1992 and 1995 and increased 33 percent from 1994 to 1995. From 1994 to 1995, monthly use of LSD had risen 54 percent, cocaine use 166 percent, and marijuana use 37 percent.[47]

The 1996 National Household Survey on Drug Abuse found that 7.1 percent of youths aged twelve to seventeen reported using marijuana in the previous month, compared with 8.2 percent in 1995. The survey also showed an overall drug use increase in the eighteen- to twenty-five-year-old group—from 13.3 percent in 1994 to 15.6 percent in 1996.[48]

National reports on drugs, crime, and the judicial system and Bureau of Justice statistics demonstrate a close link between drug use and crime. According to data released in 1986, 26 percent of violent offenders in state prisons, inmates who were under the influence of drugs at the time of their offense, victimized someone who was also using drugs at the time of the crime. The Bureau of Justice reports that prisoners were under the influence of drugs at the time of their offense for 28.2 percent of violent offenses, 35.4 percent of property offenses, 36.9 percent of drug offenses, and 18 percent of public order offenses. When these general categories are broken down into specific crimes committed while under the influence of drugs, it is found that homicide can be laid 27.7 percent of the time to drug abuse; rape, 24.5 percent of the time; other sexual assault, 17 percent; robbery, 37.5 percent; assault, 22.9 percent; other violent crimes, 23.6 percent; burglary, 39.7 percent; larceny/theft, 37.7 percent; motor vehicle theft, 27.8 percent; fraud, 27.9 percent; stolen property, 24.5 percent; other crimes, 24.7 percent; drug possession, 37.8 percent; drug trafficking, 36.2 percent; other drug crimes, 43.4 percent; weapons offenses, 18.8 percent; and other public order offenses, 17.8 percent.[49]

These crime statistics reveal that drug-related crimes do not diminish with legalization.[50] This contrasts with the human rights argument that legalization would reduce crime. People under the influence of drugs are undeniably dangerous to others. In fact, if legalization increased the use of drugs, it would lead to a further increase in drug-related crimes. As the severity of crimes committed by drug users rises, so too does the legitimacy of the restrictions imposed.

Since permitting drug use does not eliminate crime, it becomes all the more important to find an alternative means of combating the problem. What emerges from this debate is the realization that neither legalization nor punishment is the ultimate solution to this problem. Imprisonment is an insufficient remedy, since as the jail population increases, inmates must be released to alleviate overcrowding. Between 1980 and 1991, populations of local jails increased 103 percent—from 209,582 to 426,479 inmates. At the same time, state and federal prison populations increased nearly 150 percent—from 329,821 to 823,414 inmates.[51] The number of drug offenders in federal prisons grew from 25 percent of inmates in 1980 to 61 percent in 1993. In state prisons the number increased from 9 percent in 1986 to 21 percent in 1991.

Although a substantial amount of the narcotics offenses involve persons who commit crimes in order to get money to buy drugs, a far higher percentage of crimes are committed by people under the influence of drugs. In 1991, 17.1 percent of all offenses by state prison inmates were committed to get drugs. This compares with 31.1 percent of all offenses committed while the offender was under the influence of drugs.[52] A "Monitoring the Future" study indicated a slight overall decline in illicit drug use for 1998. However, the survey also showed that "nearly a quarter of eighth-graders and about half of all high school seniors said they had tried marijuana—figures that are much higher than a few years ago."[53]

CONSEQUENCES OF LEGALIZATION

One of the most serious consequences of legalization is the danger of an increased rate of addiction among the general population. This happened in China after the British won the opium wars in 1860. After that country was forced to accept and legalize opium, nearly one-third of the Chinese population became addicted.[54]

Carried to its logical conclusion, when drug consumption is made legally acceptable for the adult population the costs to society are increased rather than decreased. The creation of an entire legal structure and new set of rules becomes unavoidable. It becomes necessary to establish, for example, the legally acceptable amount one may use while in the workplace or in public. If the economic and social costs of legalization are not to be overwhelming, then as in the case of alcohol, laws must be made regarding how much can be consumed before one becomes criminally or civilly liable for one's actions. Among the questions to be answered are:

1. When is one criminally liable for what occurs while under the influence of drugs when driving, at work, at home, etc.?
2. Does society have a responsibility to provide welfare to families of breadwinners unable to work because of an addiction to legal drugs?

3. What will be the regulations determining how much drug residue may be allowed in the systems of airline pilots, train engineers, police, bus drivers, doctors, nurses, etc., when performing their duties?
4. Will society still be permitted to impose mandatory drug testing on people performing duties while using a legal drug for which the consequences of abuse are not known? If so, will not testing necessarily be far more extensive than when the drug is illegal?

An expected consequence of legalization would be a far more intrusive government, with a massive number of new laws, rules, and regulations that would be considerably more elaborate and harder to enforce than absolute prohibition. Further, with legalized consumption, it must be decided to what extent society will finance the health costs for those suffering the consequences of addiction.[55]

There are high social costs to illegal use: crime, corruption, and the expenses attached to maintaining security forces, courts, and jails. The costs of legal use would include all of these plus more, including increased health care expenses and the social responsibility of providing products that pass Food and Drug Administration (FDA) standards. With the government involved in certifying the quality of legal drugs, it would presumably have the moral obligation to provide workers' compensation for those unable to work because of drug abuse. The government would also be required to provide drugs for those already addicted and health care for those who contract drug-related illnesses such as AIDs. Some legalization advocates assume that AIDS will no longer be transmitted when "clean" needles are provided by the government. However, the possibility remains that addicts will not share the government's concern with the cleanliness of the needles they use to satisfy their habit.

Laws against usage by children and teenagers and people responsible for handling public transportation and heavy equipment—pilots, railroad engineers, and bus drivers—as well as persons in critical positions of responsibility—police, firefighters, doctors, and nurses—would remain. Federal jurisdiction would increase as testing for drug use by these critical personnel would of necessity be mandatory.

And finally, legalization would not abolish the illegal market.

NARCOSOCIALISM

The consequences of legalization could well be the creation of a privileged but addicted class of people supported by society at large.[56] Aldous Huxley's prediction would then come true:

> That a dictator could, if he so desired, make use of these drugs for political purposes is obvious. He could ensure himself against political unrest by changing the chemistry of his subject's brains and so making them content with their servile condition. He could use tranquilizers to calm the excited, stimulants to arouse enthusiasm in the indifferent, halluciants to distract the attention of the wretched from their miseries. But how, it may be asked, will the dictator get his subjects to take the pills that will make them think, feel and behave in the ways he finds desirable? In all probability it will be enough merely to make the pills available.[57]

Of course, the justification for making drugs available in the democratic or anocratic society would be based on social welfare, human rights, and society's inability to prevent crime. The simplistic solution to solving a problem is to pronounce that it is no longer a problem.

A democratic or anocratic society that provides and pays for its citizens' addictions would no longer be a simple democracy or anocracy. Legalization would create a new social order, not a narcodemocracy, but a narcosocialist democracy. Narcosocialism is a government-sponsored system that manipulates the population's attitudes and health by what would inevitably be a ruling class, or in Huxley's words, "controllers." Under this regime, the fictional world Huxley described so aptly becomes possible. "Pharmacists," he said, "would be instructed to change their tune with every change of circumstances. In times of national crisis it would be their business to push the sale of stimulants. Between crises, too much alertness and energy . . . might prove embarrassing . . . [and] the masses would be urged to buy tranquilizers and vision-producers."[58]

As a leftist analyst wrote in the 1970s, "One disgraceful form of oppression was the prohibition of drugs, and this too must be fought against. Sexual liberation, freedom from work, from academic discipline and restrictions of all kinds, universal and total liberation —all this was the essence of Communism."[59] The ideal was that of the student rebellions of the 1960s. This was the classic realization of utopia for an alienated segment of the population. Narcosocialism would be the logical result of the Western cultural revolution.

While it is necessary to explore the arguments for legalization and determine the extent and range of its popular support, legalization remains a false solution because not all drugs can be legalized nor can legalization check the growth in consumption. Legalization would produce an addicted, nonworking, drug-consuming class whose care would be foisted on the rest of society. Moreover, legalization would increase the likelihood of the creation of an unaccountable political regime in charge of pharmaceutically managing a dependent society.

CHAPTER 11

ANARCHY, NARCOSTATIZATION, AND WORLD ORDER

The principal debate in international relations theory at present is between the various schools of realism and liberalism. The premises of this debate are inadequate for dealing with the problem of narcostatization, which impacts on both realist views of state behavior and liberal views of transnational regimes. Narcotics trafficking fundamentally affects the state, the state system, and the transnational cooperative regimes. Its impact is noticeable on the democratic peace thesis and the transnational regimes' responsibility to control money laundering.

UNDERMINING DEMOCRATIC PEACE

The hypothesis that democracies do not fight democracies is called the "democratic peace thesis."[1] As Bruce Russett has observed:

> First, democratically organized political systems in general operate under restraints that make them more peaceful in their relations with other democracies. Democracies are not necessarily peaceful, however, in their relations with other kinds of political systems. Second, in the modern international system, democracies are less likely to use lethal violence toward other democracies than toward autocratically governed states or than autocratically governed states are toward each other. Furthermore, there are no clear-cut

cases of sovereign stable democracies waging war with each other in the modern international system. Third, the relationship of relative peace among democracies is importantly a result of some features of democracy, rather than being caused exclusively by economic or geopolitical characteristics correlated with democracy. Exactly what those features are is a matter of theoretical debate.[2]

Russett uses Dahl's definition of democracy or polyarchy, which, he writes, "is . . . a voting franchise for a substantial fraction of citizens, a government brought to power in contested elections, and an executive either popularly elected or responsible to an elected legislature, often also with requirements for civil liberties such as free speech."[3]

Russett derives his democratic peace thesis from the assumption that regimes that base their policy formation on democratic principles will resolve disputes among themselves without force. Democratic peace, he says, results from "the culture, perceptions, and practices that permit compromise and the peaceful resolution of conflicts without the threat of violence within countries." These apply "across national boundaries toward other democratic countries."[4] Assuming this argument is true, there must be some agreement as to the definition of a democratic regime. And, this definition must address the inclination to war of states that appear to be democracies but that in reality fall short.

Democratization, despite the existence of an electoral process, may be a facade for elites to continue in power without actual accountability. Through narcostatization, then, the democratization process is subverted into anocratization. Figure 5 shows how the democratization of a narco-authoritarian state in Mexico led to a narcoanocratic state, while the narcostatization of a democratic state in Colombia led to the same result.

CONFLICT AS A NORM OF ANOCRACIES

Narcostatization forces a reevaluation of the concept of conflict as explained by the democratic peace thesis. A war between democratic states, according to the democratic peace thesis definition of war, requires a minimum of one thousand battle fatalities, excludes covert actions, requires a public declaration of war, must be between sovereign states internationally recognized, and excludes colonial wars fought for the

MEXICO

Democratization of an authoritarian state
+ critical-to-advanced narcostatization
= Narcoanocratic state

COLOMBIA

Democratic state
+ serious-to-critical narcostatization
= Narcodemocratic state

Narcodemocratic state
+ advanced narcostatization
= Narcoanocratic state

FIGURE 5. Narcostatization and the Reversal of Democratization in Mexico and Colombia: Steps Toward the Narcoanocratic State

acquisition of territory inhabited by "primitive" people who have no recognized state. If these conditions are not met, then a war—even where conflict is present—does not exist, by democratic peace thesis standards.[5]

If the alleged democratization processes are in fact anocratization processes, then the prospect that the international environment is producing the conditions for democratic peace is remote. Various forms of conflict are likely to be endemic within and between states in a predominantly anocratic and autocratic state system, and the limits that are put on the definition of war in the democratic peace thesis need not be adhered to when dealing with anocratic conflict.

If the democratic state environment remains an essentially unrealized condition, then it is necessary to return to the traditional mode of dealing with conflict. The traditional state of affairs stresses the ever-present danger of war and the desirability of prevailing with as few casualties as possible. From the perspective of traditional theorists, large casualties are an indication of the failure of politics.

Notable among the theorists of this traditional understanding of conflict are Sun Tzu, Carl von Clausewitz, and Antonio Gramsci. Sun Tzu claims that the acme of political skill is winning without fighting.[6] He stresses defeating an enemy's strategy, disrupting an adversary's alliances, and fighting an enemy's army only when the prospect of victory is certain. Clausewitz maintains that war is politics by other means: "War in itself does not suspend political intercourse or change it into something entirely different." He argues that policy permeates "all military operations, and, in so far as their violent nature will admit, it will have a continuous influence on them."[7] Gramsci views war as replacing one hegemony with another in society without the use of violence except at the moment when the attacking side judges the situation to be favorable. He writes, "The most important observation to be made about any concrete analysis of the relations of force is the following: that such analyses cannot and must not be ends in themselves (unless the intention is merely to write a chapter of past history), but acquire significance only if they serve to justify a particular practical activity, or initiative of will."[8]

From the perspective of these classic authors, high casualty rates indicate a failure of the political agenda and of conflict management. State policy, in their view, should focus on prevailing in a naturally conflictual situation, and not on the relatively rare circumstances where states perceive each other as benign democracies.

Russett writes that U.S. post–cold war policy should be "designed to consolidate the new acceptability of free institutions around the world." In his 1994 State of the Union address, President Clinton justified the U.S. policy of promoting democracy on the basis that democracies do not fight each other. Earlier, in September 1993, U.S. National Security advisor Anthony Lake characterized U.S. policy "as seeking an 'enlargement' of the zone of democracy and free markets in the world."[9] Following the U.S. military intervention in Haiti, Lake underscored U.S. support for installing democracies because democracies "tend not to abuse their citizens' rights or wage war on one another."[10]

Statistical analysis demonstrates a correlation between stable democracies and peace, yet there is a distinct correlation between war and states in transition to democracy.[11] Mansfield and Snyder found that states in the transition process are more likely to go to war than those which are not in transition:

A change from anocracy to democracy increased the probability of any type of war by roughly 15 to 100 percent, and of interstate war by roughly 35 to 115 percent, compared to a state that remained anocratic. . . . A change from autocracy to anocracy increased the probability of war by about 70 percent compared to states that remained autocratic, based on the openness of executive recruitment, whereas it slightly decreased the likelihood of war.[12]

The reason autocratization and democratization increase the chances of war is that "threatened elites from the collapsing autocratic regime, many of whom have parochial interests in war and empire, use nationalist appeals to compete for mass allies with each other and with new elites." Democratic procedures do not reflect the lack of accountable elites in the political system. According to Mansfield and Snyder, "At least in some cases, the link between autocratization and war reflects the success of a ruling elite in using nationalist formulas developed during the period of democratization to cloak itself in populist legitimacy, while dismantling the substance of democracy."[13]

The democratic peace thesis may only be expected to hold in well-institutionalized democracies, these authors state: "In newly democratized states without strong parties, independent courts, a free press and untainted electoral procedures, there is no reason to expect that mass politics will produce the same impact on foreign policy as it does [in] mature democracies." However, in cases of the narcostatization of regimes that are allegedly procedural democracies, "even the elites who are doing well in the transition have a stake in making the transition a controlled, partial one, where profiteering is not too fettered by democratic scrutiny or rule of law."[14]

Evidence of the narcostatization process accords with a thesis that elites in a transition process are attracted to organized crime and to the protection of narcotics trafficking in order to retain power.

Drug Trafficking and State Conflict

If there are in reality far fewer democratic states than the democratization process is heralded to have achieved, then most of these so-called democratic states will perceive all other states as dangerous rivals. They will not operate on the basis that a new democratic peace is in place. Consequently, most states in transition must be treated as rivals of other states. These states will approach the narcotics trafficking problem as a rivalry rather than a cooperative endeavor.

The anarchical rivalry pattern between states is not one of either absolute or relative gain, but a mixture of both gains and losses. The state's decision to pursue either one or both is affected not only by what is occurring in the regime, but also by the power relationship between the states. To understand what decisions a state will make in a situation of expected conflict, it is first necessary to answer the following three questions:

1. Do both State A and State B lose by terminating drug trafficking? (For example, State A loses profits and State B loses debt service.)
2. Can both State A and State B gain by ending drug trafficking? (For example, State A reduces criminality and State B reduces drug addiction.)
3. Assuming that both State A and State B will undergo gains and losses from permitting or ending drug trafficking, which set of gains and losses will they choose?

Past descriptive behavior leads to the expectation that elites in transition will seek profits and cooperate with organized crime. In a stable democracy, however, elites can be expected to accept losses in order to reduce drug addiction in the population. A deductive explanation based on the anarchical structure of the international system would anticipate that both states would seek profits so as to prevent the other state from obtaining relative economic gains. The states would find themselves in a novel "prisoner's dilemma," where both will be worse off at the same time they are better off. While both states gain revenues, they become increasingly criminalized. In this scenario international rivalry will assist the spread of narcostatization.

The spread of international narcostatization and the criminalization of states raise several interesting questions:

• If State A becomes a narcostate, does it change State B's desire to cooperate financially with State A (for example, Colombia and the United States)?
• If State B is a democracy, will it attempt to compel State A to become less of a narcostate and more democratic (for example, the United States vis-à-vis Russia, the Andean region, and Mexico)?

- If, on the other hand, State A, a narcostate, is stronger than State B, will it not attempt to compel narcotics consumption in State B (for example, Great Britain vis-à-vis China in the nineteenth century)?
- If State A, either by itself or in alliance with other states, has equal power with State B, then will the fact that A and its allies are involved in drug trafficking, and therefore becoming economically more competitive, compel State B to become involved even though it officially disapproves of drug trafficking (for example, the United States in the cold war with Vietnam and Nicaragua, and possibly in the post–cold war given the tendencies in Russia and other countries)?

CONFLICT SCENARIOS OF DRUG TRAFFICKING

In the hypothetical conflict scenario of narcotics trafficking between State A, which is a seller of narcotics and a debtor, and State B, which is a purchaser of narcotics and a creditor, is it more or less likely that drug trafficking will continue? It may continue if State A can make profits and service its debts and State B can have its debts serviced with drug money. If State B wishes to curtail the purchase of drugs and State A wishes to continue the sale, State B may resist, but if State A is stronger, then State A may compel State B to acquire drugs despite State B's resistance. Even if it is weaker, State A can facilitate the sale of drugs if it can circumvent economic controls imposed by State B. Drug trafficking continues in this scenario no matter what the relative strengths of the states are when State A is a seller and a debtor and State B is a purchaser and a creditor.

A second hypothetical conflict scenario of narcotics trafficking occurs when both State A and State B are great powers. State A facilitates drug trafficking by production, sale, and money laundering, while State B attempts to curtail production, sale, and money laundering. In this scenario, both states are consumers, but both states seek to reduce their own domestic consumption. What does State B do to check State A's support of narcotics trafficking? State B may have to participate to some degree in drug trafficking in order to penetrate State A's operations and not lose relative economic power vis-à-vis State A. The implications of state rivalry under anarchy suggest that drug trafficking will not be checked until all the states reach the point where their mutual costs are so high that they are induced to cooperate against narcotics trafficking.

This is a modified "prisoner's dilemma": While all states would be better off controlling narcotics trafficking, they will not do so because they do not trust each other. The states are driven to compete in drug trafficking until enough damage is inflicted to force accordance. The problem arises that when they get to this stage the likelihood of most of the states being narcostates is high. These criminal states may be unconcerned that a substantial portion of their population is addicted when the nature of their system is essentially unaccountable. A prediction based on structural realism might be that rational behavior under international anarchy leads to a criminal international relations system where there will be no cooperation after all the states have become narcostates. An international system of narcostates, which has no incentive to cooperate in controlling narcotics trafficking, necessitates the development of a hierarchical state system where the dominant state or states impose an antinarcotics regime.

In fact, the United States has attempted to impose an antinarcotics regime by way of cooperating with the institutions in other countries committed to fighting narcotics. In the *United States–Mexico Bilateral Drug Threat Assessment*, published in May 1997, the United States and Mexico agreed to develop a common strategy. An alliance between U.S. and Mexican governmental institutions was announced and both nations committed themselves to sixteen specific counterdrug goals. These goals included improving their joint capacity to interrupt drug shipments, to combat corruption, to control their common border, and to share information. Under this agreement, Mexico created a special prosecutor's Office for Crimes against Health to replace the National Counter-Drug Institute (INCD), which had been compromised and discredited under Gen. Gutiérrez Rebollo. The Mexicans passed new legislation to expand their investigative and prosecutorial capabilities, developed currency-reporting requirements, and improved their use of the Mutual Legal Assistance Treaty (MLAT) with the United States.[15]

DRUG TRAFFICKING AND INTRASTATE CONFLICT

Besides interstate conflict, narcotics trafficking causes an additional conflict pattern to arise within states. This intrastate conflict occurs between the different drug cartels and their political allies or bosses within a state. One of the characteristic features of organized crime is conflict between cartels. In the United States there is a long history of conflict between the different crime families of Chicago, New York, Detroit, and other big cities, especially during the 1930s.

In Mexico, the conflict has risen to the national level, and the cartels are backed by federal agents and ministries. There have been conflicts between the Amado Carillo–led Ciudad Juárez cartel and the Juan García–led Gulf cartel, where both cartels have had high-level political protectors. Even with Amado Carillo dead and Juan García in a U.S. jail, the rivalry between the cartels continues, as does the struggle for control within the cartels. There has been a conflict between the Arellano Félix brothers–led Tijuana cartel and the Chapa Guzmán–led Guadalajara cartel that has implicated the federal police. There have been conflicts between the Mexican attorney general's Federal Judicial Police and the minister of interior's DFS police. There have even been conflicts between the Mexican police and the Mexican army over drug territory. The same pattern exists in Colombia, where the Cali cartel cooperated with the government to undermine and destroy the Medellin cartel. Narcotics trafficking produces conflict among organized groups within the state, and it generates a logic of conflict between and within states, which increases as the states become narcostates.

NARCOSTATIZATION AND INSURGENCY

The growth of narcostatization in the context of the globalizing drug trade supports the rise of insurgency. The first scenario for the rise of insurgency exists within the context of left-wing revolutionary movements hostile to capitalism. Since the *Communist Manifesto* and the Leninist theory of imperialism, there has been a powerful critique of legal capitalism as exploitive of workers and campesinos. Capitalism is criticized for creating gross inequalities of wealth, particularly in developing countries, but also in developed ones.

Criticism of capitalism has been muted since the fall of communism in eastern Europe and the former Soviet Union, but it has by no means been silenced. In Latin America, it gained renewed force with the North American Free Trade Agreement (NAFTA), which some Mexicans perceived as damaging to small- and medium-sized farming and business interests. A reactionist movement exploded in Chiapas, Mexico, on the first of January 1994, the day NAFTA went into force. The situation in Mexico is aggravated by the increasingly widespread evidence of massive narcostatization that has occurred in the country since the Echeverría presidency.

Support for an antisystem insurgency widens as increasing numbers of people associate the economic distress of the many and the extraordinary wealth of the few with narcostatization. The persistent view that narcostatization occurs not only under an authoritarian government but also under a procedural democracy helps expand the support of insurgency. This was made apparent in Chiapas in 1994 in the negotiating style of Subcomandante Marcos (Sebastian Guillén), the negotiating concessions of the Manuel Camacho team, and the impact that had on Luis Colosio's campaign and, very possibly, his assassination. However the merits of that particular series of events are determined, an increased perception of criminal corruption fuels the support for insurgency. Hostility to Mexican-style democracy, and democracy in general, will continue until the Mexican people realize that the problem lies in narcostatization, not in true democracy.

Camacho and Colosio both recognized that the state must be truly accountable in terms of its selection of public servants and its ongoing checks and balances. Theirs was a critical response to the narcostatization process, calling as they did for its reversal in order to mitigate the appeal of antisystemic insurgencies. If a reversal of narcostatization does not occur, then antisystem revolutionary movements are likely to be rekindled in Mexico and other countries experiencing narcostatization.

Anthony D. Smith has brilliantly identified the reason ethnic nationalisms arise against a modern scientific state. He views ethnic nationalism, or indigenous movements, as an effort to humanize the scientific state run by technocratic elites.[16] These ethnic revolts, rooted in the rural hinterlands, occur in areas besides Mexico. Consider for example,

- Colombia, where the communities of Paez, Guambiano, Coconuco, Totoroe, and Yanacona forced the government to respond to their demands for development projects and to prosecute the perpetrators of the 1991 massacre of twenty indigenous people from Paez.

- Ecuador, where indigenous movements in the eastern provinces have given rise to the Federation of Indigenous Organization of Napo (FOIN) and the Organization of Indigenous People of Pastaza (OPIP). There is also a developing indigenous organization in the highlands. In fact, since the mid-1980s, there has been an organization to unify all of Ecuador's indigenous peoples.
- Peru, where the famous Sendero Luminoso insurgency, although gravely weakened, still exists.
- Chile, where the Mapuches, an organization of about 1 million people, mobilized to protest NAFTA in 1994.
- Three other Latin American states—Brazil, Guatemala, and Bolivia—where significant indigenous movements exist.[17]

This intrastate conflict is fostered in part by the delegitimized narco-state that exhibits indifference toward the problems of ethnic groups within its boundaries. In time, the indigenous groups protest the transformation of their societies by the policies of a state dependent on criminal domestic groups and international interests. Although the problems of the indigenous community long antedate the rise of narcostatization, their aggravation and the delegitimization of the state through corruption can only intensify the seriousness of indigenous revolts.

The worldwide expansion of organized crime, criminal capitalism, and narcostatization provides the most important challenge of the post–cold war era. It challenges traditional understandings of how to ameliorate conflict, eliminate organized criminal forces, and check state criminality and other threats to democracy.

Liberal Theory and an Accountable World Order

The impact of narcotics trafficking on transnational regimes[18] raises the question of whether or not the criminalization of the international monetary system can be controlled. A monetary regime is in place that is based on the cooperation of the central banks of the G-10—twelve major industrial countries—mediated through the Bank of International Settlements. The BIS annual report of 1935 stated the regime's purpose was "to evolve a common body of monetary doctrine and assure the widest possible measure of common agreement on monetary theory, problems and practices."[19] The problem facing the United States is whether it can partially "nest"[20] an anti-money-laundering regime within the current international monetary regime when this country does not have a hegemonic position with respect to the monetary regime.

There are two major tenets to a theory of hegemonic stability. One is that world order is created by a single dominant power and the other is that the maintenance of that order requires the continuation of hegemony. Most theorists believe that these propositions do not apply to the current international system, that there is no hegemonic state. However, many theorists believe that a period of hegemony can assist the development of a cooperative regime and that "after hegemony" the hegemony of a single power is not necessary to keep the system going.[21] A leading proponent of cooperation after hegemony argues that cooperation can take place without hegemony and in particular that "cooperation can under some conditions develop on the basis of complementary interests, and that institutions, broadly defined, affect the patterns of cooperation that emerge."[22]

NONHEGEMONIC MULTILATERAL COOPERATION

So far, this multilateral effort has been only partially successful. In 1961 the United Nations held its first convention on narcotic drugs. It was followed with the 1972 protocol. Then the UN Convention against Illicit Traffic and Narcotic Drugs and Phychotropic Substances was signed in 1988. This was the first official international criminalization of money laundering. It requires the exchange of information and the enforcement of criminal statutes, but it does not require banks to examine the origin of their deposits nor the commercial activity generating these deposits. An additional international agreement compelling due diligence on the part of the banks is necessary to reveal who and what commercial activity is behind deposits. The Bank of International Settlements has accepted the principle that banks should know their customers as a standard for financial oversight. It is in this developing cooperative regime that additional mechanisms for controlling money laundering are nested.

The Financial Action Task Force (FATF) was founded in July 1989 at the Group of Seven Economic Summit in Paris. It includes the European Union, other European nations, and several countries and entities beyond Europe—such as Turkey, Hong Kong, New Zealand, and Singapore—and the Gulf Cooperation Council, which has a total of twenty-six members. The IMF is an observer at FATF meetings. It is necessary to create, in the words of David A. Andelman, "a true multinational bank regulatory body that would function like the Comptroller of the Currency, the Federal Reserve or the Department of Justice to compel examination of the sources of deposits in every nation."[23] The FATF does not meet this requirement.

The principal purpose of FATF was to prevent banking systems and financial institutions from laundering illegal money. In addition, it sought to establish measures that countries could use to combat money laundering. In April 1990, the FATF announced forty recommendations that countries could use for monitoring and reporting suspicious financial activities, but these recommendations to control money laundering lack the force of law.

One of the important recommendations of FATF is to study what measures can be used to detect cash flows between countries. The FATF and the Basel Committee have issued statements prohibiting the criminal use of members' banking systems. Both the FATF and the BIS recognize that once bank managers have been corrupted the safety and soundness of the bank have been undermined. The IMF's link to the anti-money-laundering regime is just beginning. There is a growing concern from some of its analysts that money laundering could lead capital to be invested in areas where there are lower rates of return because of the need to recycle illegal money. There is also concern that the consequence of using noneconomic factors in making investments could confuse policy makers and bank regulators.

Nonetheless, FATF can help individual national systems enforce their own standards, if they so wish. According to Andelman, FATF officials think they will have a global regulatory and enforcement mechanism in place before the end of the century. He believes that when a critical mass of countries has adopted laws consistent with FATF's proposals, it will be possible to penalize banks that do not cooperate. In effect, there will be a black list of nations who will be compelled to make their banks cooperate or else lose access to those that do cooperate. In this regard, Andelman recommends U.S. government policy that would convince countries to make their banks inaccessible to money launderers. This policy of removing money profits from the drug cartels may turn out to be the preferred strategy for combating the cartels and the criminalization of international capitalism.[24]

U.S. BILATERAL COOPERATION

Obviously, the anti-money-laundering multilateral regime is still in a rudimentary form. As a consequence, the United States has been pushing bilateral anti-money-laundering agreements. In the Money Laundering Control Act of 1986, the U.S. Congress made money laundering a federal crime. The objective was to create a formidable legal barrier to drug traffickers transferring illegal profits to legitimate businesses. Through the Mutual Legal Assistance Treaty (MLAT), the United States attacks the bank secrecy laws of countries such as the Cayman Islands, which launders an estimated $3 billion to $10 billion each year. The MLATs are part of a growing number of bilateral agreements by which the United States hopes to obligate other countries to cooperate in criminal investigations and prosecutions. The MLAT with the Cayman Islands calls for mutual assistance in both criminal prosecutions and investigations. MLAT agreements avoid the problem of requiring that the definition of fraud be the same in both jurisdictions.

The ratification of an MLAT allows the United States to bypass the agreeing government's bank secrecy laws. Such an agreement is better than Letters Rogatory, which operate through very slow diplomatic channels. The MLAT also overcomes the methods of "compelled consent," which serve to warn a suspect that he is under investigation. The principal difficulty with an MLAT is that it can do nothing to stop a launderer from shifting to a new secrecy haven that does not have a treaty with the United States. To avoid such loopholes, bilateral agreements need to be interlocked to create a network of obligations. This would require nesting the MLATs in a multilateral agreement.[25]

The new internationalism builds on state-to-state institutional arrangements to control the unregulated global capital markets. Nonetheless, the process of forging these arrangements is among the most difficult tasks for the new internationalism. One direction in which the United States appears to be heading is to embed these bilateral arrangements in regional understandings, though this process is still rudimentary.[26]

UNILATERAL U.S. ANTI-MONEY-LAUNDERING INITIATIVES

In January 1990, Federal Reserve Chairman Alan Greenspan created a senior-level working group to assist the federal government's anti-money-laundering efforts. The working group in turn formed three task forces to cover the areas of cash, fund transfer, and supervision. The Fed has estimated that in 1990 the U.S. share of drug proceeds was $100 billion. More recently the FBI estimated that the amount of money laundered through the United States on a yearly basis from narcotics trafficking as well as from other major crimes was $300 billion.[27]

The Fed cooperates with the money-laundering section of the Department of Justice's Criminal Division to identify potential money-laundering activities in both domestic banks and in foreign banking institutions doing business in the United States. The Fed also works with FATF. Since 1989, it has had a special counsel within the division of Financial Supervision and Regulation to enhance its money-laundering capability. The special counsel has traveled widely abroad to accomplish this mandate.

In late 1991, the Fed created a special committee of bank examiners and set up procedures to view the operation of U.S. banks in foreign jurisdictions that do not have laws and regulations comparable to the Bank Secrecy Act of 1970. A principal focus was to encourage financial institutions to adopt more comprehensive "know your customer" policies designed to protect banks from the illegal penetration of their facilities by money launderers. The Office of Financial Enforcement (OFE) of the U.S. Treasury promulgates all regulations with regard to the Bank Secrecy Act, which requires banks to report all transactions of more than $10,000 a day and compels individuals taking more than $5,000 in cash on international travel to submit currency reports. The Fed works with The OFE to ensure that financial institutions comply with these rules and regulations. The Fed provides the OFE quarterly information on noncompliance by both domestic and foreign financial institutions.

The principal result of the Fed's efforts has been the establishment of a mechanism for tracking currency flows. Areas can be identified for investigation on the basis of abnormalities in cash flows, either because of surplus or deficiencies. The Federal Reserve Bank of Dallas initiated a cash-flow study that established the normal range of cash activities for each of the financial institutions that use Federal Reserve cash services. As a result of law enforcement agencies' cooperation, all the reserve banks report their cash-flow data to a single government agency. This in turn has resulted in an agreement between the Federal Reserve and the Financial Crimes Enforcement Network (FinCEN) of the Department of the Treasury. Each Federal Reserve bank provides FinCEN specific information on cash shipments on a monthly basis. FinCEN uses this information to identify abnormalities by geographic region or financial institution. This information is then passed on to law enforcement officials.

In addition, various initiatives are under way for tracking funds through the "Fedwire" system. One system is a scanning program that uses information on suspected money launderers provided by the FBI and the U.S. Customs Service to track funds transferred through the Fedwire. In 1982, the Fed recommended to the Federal Financial Institutions Examination Council a policy encouraging all financial institutions to identify both the originator and beneficiary of a wire transfer. The Fed has also encouraged record keeping for funds transferred as a result of the provisions of the Annunzio-Wylie Anti-Money-Laundering Act. Nonetheless, the Fed is concerned that overly onerous record-keeping requirements will have serious adverse effects on the competitiveness of U.S. financial institutions.

THE ANNUNCIO-WYLIE ANTI-MONEY-LAUNDERING ACT

The Annuncio-Wylie Anti-Money-Laundering Act was signed on October 29, 1992, as part of the Housing and Community Development Act. The key to the effectiveness of the new law is the "death penalty" provision whereby a bank's charter is revoked if five factors are proved:

1. The management is involved in illicit activity.
2. Management does not cooperate with law enforcement after criminal allegations are filed.

3. There are no policies in place to prevent money-laundering activity.
4. No adjustments are made to prevent further abuse.
5. Closure of the bank does not harm local access to banking services.

In some cases, the death penalty could in fact work to prevent the revocation of the bank's charter and to promote banking cooperation with law enforcement. Though intended to catch money launderers, the Anti-Money-Laundering Act is favorable to banks in that it protects them from customer charges of negligence to the degree the bank cooperates with law enforcement officers.[28]

Model "know-your-customer" programs have three main elements. First, the bank must make a reasonable effort to determine the true identity of all its deposit and loan customers. Second, the bank must make a reasonable effort to know who is using its other services such as wire transfers, cashier's checks, and money orders. Finally, the bank must refuse to conduct business with any individual who does not provide proper identification or any business that does not provide sufficient background information or credentials.

It is recognized that illegal money is tax-free and that the annual revenues from cocaine trafficking are estimated to be $29 billion a year in the United States alone. Capacity for laundering this money appears to outstrip the international criminal justice system because of its ability to conceal money through coffee exports, car dealerships, insurance annuities, construction projects, money exchange, and other such fronts. There is limited capacity to deal with offshore money laundering.

Drug cartels run a four-part business: production, transport, marketing, and laundering. The two riskiest parts of the cartel operations are transporting the drugs and laundering the profits. As a result, mafias assign specialists to these aspects of the enterprise. In October 1992, the DEA learned how traffickers used a five-stage laundering process to disguise the origin of their illegal cash. In a raid on a leading launderer, the DEA, in cooperation with the local police, found records in Franklin Jurado's Luxembourg apartment revealing how he used 115 bank accounts in 16 countries to take illegal money and turn it into usable currency throughout the world. The key step in the process was to get the money when it was at its dirtiest deposited into a banking account. Any territory maintaining bank secrecy was ideal for the initial investment. Jurado's principal bank secrecy havens were the Cayman Islands, the Turks and Caicos, Venezuela, and Panama.

Until 1994, most launderers chose Panama for the initial laundering process. The bank of choice was the Hong Kong Shanghai Bank of Panama. To close it down, the Justice Department froze its correspondent accounts at the Marine Midland Bank in New York, which had long operated in Panama. Money launderers moved to other territories and bought equity in international banks.

Fair Trade and Financial Services Law HR 3248

The 103d U.S. Congress proposed law HR 3248 on fair trade and financial services, which would require the secretary of the treasury to submit to Congress every two years a report identifying countries that do not offer national treatment to U.S. banks or security firms. When a determination is made under this law, U.S. regulatory agencies have discretionary authority to deny applications from financial institutions of such countries to make financial acquisitions or start new activities in the United States. In addition, when such a finding is published in the *Federal Register*, institutions from such countries already operating in the United States cannot start new businesses or conduct business from a new location without obtaining prior approval from the appropriate federal regulators.

A member of the board of governors of the Federal Reserve, John LaWare, opposed this legislation on the grounds there were better ways to encourage other countries to open their markets and that it would discourage foreign investment in the United States. His testimony reveals that the Fed's desire to keep capital flows uninhibited by regulation outweighs its concern with the corruption of the international financial system.

Nonetheless, the idea behind the Fair Trade and Financial Services Act could be adapted to assist the international fight against crime and money laundering. In this case, Congress could require the secretary of the treasury to submit a report identifying those countries that do not cooperate in the investigation of money laundering. The report could also identify those countries unwilling to provide evidence or to extradite people charged with money laundering to the United States. The Fed might be more receptive to this approach on the grounds that it would not harm U.S. financial competitiveness.[29]

The United States cannot have an anti-money-laundering multilateral regime by decree. Nonetheless, numerous cooperative arrangements were set up when the United States was in a hegemonic position after World War II in which such a regime may be partially embedded. Together with other industrial powers and the transnational G-10, the United States has sufficient capability to forge a system of incentives limiting the narcotics trade. The G-10 undergirds the Financial Action Task Force (FATF) of the G-7. This is a model for a responsible coopera- tive regime of central banks in working with democratic regimes to place controls on money laundering. Although the primary responsibility for the neoliberal international monetary order is to maintain stability, it can develop a subsidiary cooperative mechanism for controlling money laundering. The macroeconomic effects of money laundering suggest the need for a cooperative regime involving the United States, its allies, and the global markets to prevent the corruption of central banks and states. Should this anti-money-laundering regime not be successful, the crim- inalization of international capital could result in the further corruption of the states and the global financial system.

On the one hand, a clean and self-regulating global financial system produces accountable transnational public servants, strengthens the resistance of democratic republican institutions to corruption, and main- tains an environment where responsible financial decisions can be made. On the other hand, should the international financial system be contami- nated by criminal money, then transnational public servants will not be accountable, democratic republican institutions will be increasingly vulnerable to corruption, and responsible financial decisions will not be made. This would turn transnational elites into an overworld of unac- countable managers fused with corrupted upperworld and underworld elites in narcostates. A model of desirable and undesirable relationships between states and the international system is provided by table 4.

Despite the lack of American hegemony, the trends toward coopera- tion are evident. Still, it cannot be ruled out that contrary political and economic forces will prevail over these trends. To a certain degree, the logic of the "prisoner's dilemma" and the theory that large groups seeking to provide collective goods have great difficulty in cooperating

TABLE 4.

TWO MODELS OF THE NEOLIBERAL NEW WORLD ORDER: ACCOUNTABLE AND ELITIST

	Democratice Republican System	Ruling Class/Overworld System
State characteristics	Accountable (democratic) state systems Economic elites responsible to system	Unaccountable (anocratic) state systems Oligarchic upperworld elites aligned with underworld ruling class
Transnational characteristics	Transnational regulatory mechanisms sustain accountable (to democratic republican states) system Transnational elites decide on basis of expertise but are accountable to democratic republican states	Transnational system sustains anocratic states and narcostates Self-serving overworld elites are fused with oligarchic upper- and underworld elites

mitigate against believing the G-10 and the central banks will success-fully control money laundering. Perhaps the greatest test facing the United States is whether or not it will be able to sustain, in cooperation with other countries, the necessary financial system to keep money laundering from corrupting both the transnational economy and the states. This test requires the United States to oppose the continuing deregulation of capital flows not only because they threaten currencies and equity markets, but also because money laundering corrupts domestic institutions and international financial operations.[30]

CHAPTER 12

CONCLUSION

THE NEOLIBERAL PARADIGM

Neoliberalism is a phenomenon of the post–cold war era. It has two interconnected features. One is the international rivalry pattern: The United States is obviously the primary power but rising powers and declining and weak states have an interest in narrowing the gap. Another characteristic feature of neoliberalism is the economic system. Finance, trade, and organized crime are globalized phenomena and operate in a de facto integrated system. This integrated economic system has a tendency to create a transnational criminal oligarchy undergirded by state rivalries. Political rivalry facilitates the growth of an unchecked transnational elite—an important part of which is criminal. At the same time, the processes within the states assist the rise, transformation, and persistence of unaccountable rulers despite formal democratic procedures.

It is necessary to recognize that unless the drug war is properly diagnosed an appropriate response is unlikely. The United States is in a unique position to improve the existing system through forging ties between state institutions combating the drug trade. However, to be effective, the United States must consider the paradoxes of neoliberalism and the forces exploiting it, which benefit narcotics trafficking.

The introductory chapter outlined the five principal assumptions on which the war on drugs is based. The first of these is that supply and demand provide the basic force behind narcotics trafficking. The other assumptions are that the principal culprits in drug trafficking are the various ethnic or national criminal gangs; that financial institutions are victimized by technical and administrative limitations, and occasionally by corrupt individuals in failing to check money laundering; that governments are committed to combating drug trafficking but face overwhelming odds; and that the most influential societal forces are committed to combating drugs and to supporting the criminalization of consumption to control demand.

Most of the time, our federal government has devoted its resources to fighting the supply side of the drug problem. Criticisms of the supply focus led the Clinton administration to emphasize demand reduction in the war on drugs. The 1997 ten-year plan called for an explicit recognition that reducing drug demand through prevention and treatment must be the centerpiece of the federal effort. Acceptance of this assumption reflected to some extent a victory for those who labeled the war on drugs a failure. Whether or not that was acknowledged, this assumption represented the beginning of an alleged paradigm shift: The primary aim in the war on drugs was no longer reducing supply but was instead reducing demand. Demand reduction alone does not constitute a paradigm shift, but if the concept of "harm reduction" is used to legalize consumption, then it does represent a paradigm shift, a shift that would make consumption a public health problem and lead to government regulation of drugs—a controlled form of legalization—as the preferred way to deal with narcotics trafficking.

Proponents of the public health focus, who seek to decriminalize drugs such as marijuana, correctly note that success in reducing the supply of narcotics to consumers has been varied and the escalation in enforcement efforts has swollen the nation's prison population. They cite statistics: For the U.S. market alone, thirteen trailer trucks can stash a year's supply of cocaine and a year's supply of heroin from poppies can be grown on just ninety square miles of farmland. Drug offenders compose 60 percent of the federal and 25 percent of the state prison populations.[1]

Whether supply or demand is emphasized, the evidence developed in this book suggests that this method of analyzing oversimplifies the problem. In fact, placing the problem on the demand side does not represent a paradigm shift but just a shift in emphasis within the already dominant paradigm. Emphasis on demand reduction will not stop the drug trade any more than will emphasis on reducing the supply.

The supply-and-demand model does provide some significant insights, but because it does not take into account government protection and the new post–cold war environment, it remains an incomplete analytical tool. The new world era is characterized by (1) the globalization of finance and organized crime, (2) the dominance of the United States and its policy agendas of democratization, and (3) neoliberal open market economics. This new era of neoliberalism provides the paradigm to analyze the real world of narcotics trafficking in the post–cold war. It provides the framework for critiquing the other current assumptions behind the war on drugs and for understanding conflict and discussing democratization.

The study of organized crime in the United States demonstrates that in its development it was a multiethnic national crime syndicate protected by politicians and used by intelligence services and that it cooperated with major financial institutions. The examination of organized crime in other countries reveals a similar pattern of its being inextricably intermeshed with politicians, intelligence services, and financial institutions. It further reveals that national organized crime groups became international and worked out mutual arrangements over marketing, transportation, and profit sharing in various geographical regions. Thus one of the features of neoliberalism was the globalization of organized crime.

The examination of financial institutions exposes the heavy involvement of both criminal and legitimate banks in laundering drug profits. There is substantial evidence that the top officials of some banks consciously support criminal activity. The Banco Ambrosiano and the BCCI cases are illustrative of this. There are other cases where banks appear to have fallen into questionable activity but the specifics are unclear. For example, the case of First National Bank of Boston was never brought to trial, and the case involving Citibank remains unresolved as this book goes to press.

However, there is a deeper reason for perceiving banks as facilitating rather than hindering drug trafficking. Financial institutions have become part of the neoliberal system because state capital controls have been dismantled. The globalization of finance capital has essentially freed capital flows from effective state regulation, and banks are now part of the trafficking structure rather than victims of it. The logic of the neoliberal construct here is that even legitimate American banks have an incentive to launder drug money. They need to compete with other banks that face far less regulation in their own states as well as with those banks and global hedge funds that operate without any regulation whatsoever. In the logic of the neoliberal system, officials in the highly regulated legitimate banks may well choose not to know what goes on in some of their branches.

The relationship of governments to trafficking reveals that their victim status is also overblown. The supposition that they are committed to combating trafficking, as revealed by statistics on drug seizures, arrests, crop eradication, and money-laundering indictments, conceals the fact that these seizures do not stop either production or transport.

Again there is a deeper reason for the failure of governments to break the trafficking pattern. In the old trade imperialism of Great Britain in the seventeenth and eighteenth centuries, government and commerce were completely intermeshed. As Brian Inglis noted, the opium revenues were "an essential part of the fiscal policy of the British government."[2] There were various trade patterns in the old British imperialism. There was the Atlantic triangle, where arms and some manufactured goods were sent to Africa in exchange for slaves sent to America, there to be exchanged for sugar and tobacco to be sent back to Europe. There was the global circle, where American cotton went to England (some in exchange for manufactured goods), English cotton went to India, Indian opium to China, and then Chinese tea was sent back to England. But the new world system is more complex.

In the transformed international system of the post–cold war era, the new American international standards dictate that states should be democratic and good financial citizens in a neoliberal open trade system. However, most of the transitions to democracy have proved to be transitions instead to anocracies or pseudodemocracies. The elite maintain themselves in power in the transitions from bureaucratic oligarchies to oligarchic democracies. They do so behind a facade of contested elections and citizen participation. Democratic procedures are manipulated with money from extensive alliances between the elite and criminal capitalist elements, alliances embedded in the legitimate financial system and subsidized by overworld capitalists.

In addition, the profits from the drug trade allow the peripheral states of the system to service their debts to the major financial institutions, thus reducing the creditor states' interest in questioning the credentials of the debtor states' leaders. The exceptions to this, such as the U.S. decertification of Colombia under President Samper, where the illegality was too great to conceal, do not undermine the generalization that governments can protect traffickers and still remain certified by the United States.

In addition to economic reasons there are also security reasons behind governmental protection of the drug trade. Because of the nature of the international rivalry in the neoliberal system, it is in the interest of the weaker states and the rising challengers to wage a form of warfare against the most dominant state. It is in their interest to undermine the hegemon's power without provoking all-out war or a breach that would harm the challenger's economic development.

The positivist view of war has done a disservice to understanding the conflictual nature of the neoliberal system. This view describes war as conflict between states in which the battle-connected deaths of all the combatants together surpass one thousand. On such a basis, the conclusion can usually be drawn that democracies do not fight each other.

The combination of the spread of formal democracy, the theory of democratic peace, and the positivist theory of war together forge the impression that the post–cold war era is a time of peace. If, however, the neoliberal system requires a form of warfare for weak and challenging states in which the defeat of the hegemon requires a strategy to undermine its culture, society, and authority, then a new nonempirical definition of war is necessary. In the classical understanding of war, an open, armed struggle is a last resort. The objective of war in the normative sense is to prevail with as little fighting and as few battlefield casualties as possible. However, consider that, by the mid-1990s U.S. casualties attributable to narcotics already exceeded those of the Vietnam War. Additional costs have been sustained by the country's culture, society, and state institutions. The consequence is a decline in society's shared norms, increased crime, and more corruption in government.

The cultural transformation in the United States has deep roots. The historical civic culture has been eroding for many decades. Much of the early erosion was not due to the current drug problem but rather to the value changes among America's intellectual and economic elite. This elite, with its naturalistic metaphysic, provided a nest for self-conscious pragmatic and somewhat utopian intellectuals who experimented with and, in some cases, mass-produced, drugs. In addition, organized groups have developed processes to transform the constitutional understanding of the American regime. These groups, which represent everything from materialistic ideologies to cultural movements, have influenced decisions by the U.S. Supreme Court that restrain public expression of revealed religions. Ironically, it is known that followers of revealed religions have been statistically identified as more likely to resist drug consumption.

The clearest evidence of the existence of major societal forces committed to combating drugs and criminalizing consumption comes from those hostile to these forces. In the United States the elements that have been at the forefront in warning against narcotics trafficking, drug consumption, and criminal activity have been the drug-control government establishment, mainstream journalism, and the religious groups. Yet they are indicted for creating a reactionary climate while the evidence developed here demonstrates that the predominant cultural and economic forces and trends have facilitated drug consumption.[3]

GLOBALIZATION

Globalization of financial markets, the corruption of states, and the transnational movement of organized crime suggest the need for new categories of analysis for the post–cold war world. Realist assumptions about unitary state actors and neoliberal beliefs in the peace-producing effects of international markets, multilateral institutions, and democracy are equally inadequate. Globalization as a process means far more than free trade and open markets. It involves the whole tendency of privileging economic efficiency over state interest in noneconomic market goals such as security, monetary stability, and welfare legislation.

Globalism, the ideology associated with unrestrained support for the globalization process, favors unregulated global companies; limits state sovereignty; promotes global public policy or governance in which transnational regimes, NGOs, and the global corporate community rule cooperatively; and claims legitimacy from a civil society made up of crossnational networks of private and state-sponsored organizations. This book suggests that the realities of drug trafficking require new categories of international relations based on a differentiated concept of the state and a recognition of (1) the existence of a denationalized overworld capitalist class, (2) the fusion of organized crime with transnational capitalism, (3) the spread of an antitraditional culture, and (4) the strength of the ideological justification of globalization.

The state system at the end of the twentieth century is under siege from unregulated global capital movements fused with underworld criminality. The state itself is threatened with narcostatization. If the state is to protect its population, it must forge alliances with the institutions of other states having similar views on crime, monetary stability, welfare and environmental standards, and culture. This cooperation must be the new internationalism's response to the globalization process in order to make that process accountable to democratic republican institutions.

THE NEW INTERNATIONALISM

The main resistance to drug trafficking must come from the new internationalism: the network of state institutions in different countries combating regime corruption, money laundering, and criminal cartels. This interstate institutional cooperation will be critical to creating accountability for those global forces seeking autonomy from democratic principles.

The core strategy of demand reduction must clearly aim at the decline of both hard-core and casual users of addictive drugs. These are measurable categories over both the short and long term. Prevention is critical to lowering the number of casual users. Therapeutical and rehabilitation facilities that do not prescribe hard drugs for their patients are essential to reducing the number of hard-core users. For example, Sweden has a particularly effective program for hard-core drug users that might serve as a model for U.S. treatment procedures. In any case, U.S. government policy must openly and insistently object to state distribution of heroin, cocaine, LSD, cannabis, opium, hallucinogens, and designer drugs in the guise of a treatment program. Such programs only expand the addict population, undermine the casual user's hesitation to experiment with hard drugs, and make enforcement of antidrug laws a farce for police and citizens.

Finally, the protection of children and families from drug propaganda supported by the powerful liberalization-legalization lobby and its activists is critical. This requires open and constant public statements from responsible officials that at least equal those that attack tobacco use. It may help to emphasize that cannabis has 50 to 70 percent more cancer-causing chemicals than tobacco smoke; adversely affects the respiratory, cardiovascular, and immune systems; is dependency-provoking; decreases spermatogenesis and sperm mobility; increases abnormal forms of sperm; and develops apathy.[4]

A demand-reduction program aimed at abstinence and linked to a vigorous foreign policy supporting antidrug lobbies would help overcome some of the vulnerabilities that have emerged in the U.S. strategy.

SUMMARY

Three global macrotrends have undergirded the narcotics threat to democracy: the globalization of finance, the dependency of states on narcotics revenues, and the exploding worldwide demand for drugs. Because these trends have not been taken into account, the narcotics problem has been misdiagnosed by those attempting to combat it. Seeing it as predominantly an economic problem, they have misunderstood or ignored the global political and cultural aspects of the narcotics threat and attacked it as if it were simply a problem of supply and demand. Consequently, the focus has been on the producers, shippers, and consumers. While it is true that a major component of the narcotics problem is economic, a struggle against narcotics that excludes political and cultural aspects and the implications of the global financial revolution is not comprehensive enough—and therefore cannot be effective.

The narcotics trafficking organizations, the cartels, are multinational corporations operating in a global political, economic, and cultural system that substantially facilitates their economic activity while officially disapproving of it. To understand the serious threat of the narcotics problem, one must go beyond the facade of governments, economic systems, and cultures and understand the genuine nature of four factors that facilitate narcostatization:

1. The standard definition of democracy ignores the fact that a regime's democratic procedures may conceal antidemocratic realities. The existence of participation and contestation, the most widely used definition for a democratic regime, may in fact be manipulated by elites to maintain themselves in power and thus create a facade of accountability.

2. Governments, despite abundant rhetoric to the contrary, often support narcotics trafficking both for revenue purposes and to subvert

other states. Not all these states are criminal states, but because of the nature of the international rivalry they may perceive it to be in their interest to exploit other states in order to gain relative advantage.

3. Organized crime is not limited to criminal organizations that combat other criminal organizations and legitimate government authorities. The history of the development of organized crime reveals that it operates with the protection of political authorities. Protection of organized crime began at the local, municipal, and regional levels, but with the expansion of state interests and rivalries in the twentieth century, protection has been provided at the national and international levels.

4. The globalization of the international financial system, freed from state control, naturally opposes the regulation on free capital flows. This system, while extremely efficient in moving billions of dollars each day, has provided a remarkably effective mechanism for criminal enterprises to launder illegally obtained money.

These four factors have the capacity to corrupt existing states whether they are in a pretransition, transition, or consolidated stage of democracy. They facilitate the criminalization, or narcostatization, of states whether they are autocracies in the process of democratizing or democracies that have been consolidated. The cases of Russia, the Andean region, Mexico, Colombia, and even the United States suggest that, because of the emergence of macrotrends and other realities of the end of the twentieth century, no state may be immune from the narcostatization process.

Taking into consideration the powerful economic interests that support legalization and regulation, it is possible that the United States might develop a less accountable government and a more dependent population. If narcotics consumption is legalized in this country—and thereby becomes more widespread—there will be increased dependency of the people on the state and decreased accountability of the state to the people, as Aldous Huxley predicted.

The consequences of the narcostatization process for the international system are just as significant, for the process undermines the democratic regime and the theory of democratic peace. States in the process of democratizing have a high propensity to fight. With narcostatization, most of these democratizations become facades for anocratic or narco-democratic states. Democratic peace is unlikely when democratization leads in fact to anocracy. Anocratic states are likely to experience not only interstate, but also intrastate conflict, involving components of the state structure itself and leading ethnic groups to rebel against what they consider to be unjust or illegitimate state structures.

Finally, even though an international effort supporting multilateral cooperation is possible, it is still at an incipient stage of development. Most of the effort to develop a system to control illegal money flows falls on the United States. However, the bilateral and unilateral efforts of the United States are insufficient without a network of state institutions cooperating to combat the problem. It is not a foregone conclusion that the United States, even in alliance with the G-10, will be able to manage the money-laundering problem without bringing in other states in all the world's regions.

In order to control, if not solve, the international drug trafficking problem, inadequate assumptions about the war on drugs need to be replaced with a diagnosis based on the globalization of the neoliberal paradigm. A proper diagnosis is a precondition for progress.

MEDICAL CONSEQUENCES OF DRUG USE: THE UNIVERSITY OF VIRGINIA POLICY ON ILLEGAL DRUGS (1996)

The following is adapted from material given incoming students about the negative effects of the use of drugs.

Marijuana (cannabis): Marijuana has negative physical and mental effects. Physical effects include elevated blood pressure, a dry mouth and throat, bloodshot and swollen eyes, decrease in body temperature, and increased appetite. Frequent and/or longtime users may develop chronic lung disease and suffer damage to the pulmonary system. The use of marijuana is also associated with impairment of short-term memory and comprehension, an altered sense of time, and a reduction in the ability to perform motor skills such as driving a car. Marijuana use produces listlessness, inattention, withdrawal, and apathy. It can also intensify underlying emotional problems and is associated with chronic anxiety, depression, and paranoia.

Hallucinogens: This category includes phencyclidine (PCP, or "angel dust") and amphetamine variants that have mind-altering effects. Perception and cognition are impaired and muscular coordination decreases. Speech is blocked and incoherent. Chronic users of PCP may have memory problems and speech difficulties lasting six months to a year after prolonged daily use. Depression, anxiety, and violent behavior also occur. High psychological dependence on the drug may result in taking large doses of PCP, which can produce convulsions, comas, and heart and lung failure.

Lysergic Acid Kyethylamine (LSD or "acid"): Mescaline and psilocybin (mushrooms) cause illusions, hallucinations, and altered perception of time and space. Physical effects include dilated pupils, elevated body temperature, increased heart rate and blood pressure, decreased appetite, insomnia, and tremors. Psychological reactions include panic, confusion, paranoia, anxiety, and loss of control. Flashbacks, or delayed effects, can occur even after use has ceased.

Cocaine: Cocaine stimulates the central nervous system. Immediate physical effects include dilated pupils and increased blood pressure, heart rate, respiratory rate, and body temperature. Occasional use can cause a stuffy or runny nose, while chronic use may destroy nasal tissues. Following a "high" of extreme happiness and a sense of unending energy is a cocaine "crash," including depression, dullness, intense anger, and paranoia. Injecting cocaine with contaminated equipment can cause AIDS, hepatitis, and other diseases. Tolerance develops rapidly, and psychological and physical dependency can occur. Crack, or "rock," is extremely addictive and produces the most intense cocaine high. The use of cocaine can cause kidney damage, heart attacks, seizures, and strokes due to high blood pressure. Death can occur by cardiac arrest or respiratory failure.

Stimulants: Amphetamines and other stimulants include "ecstasy" and "ice." The physical effects produced are elevated heart and respiratory rates, increased blood pressure, insomnia and loss of appetite. Sweating, headaches, blurred vision, dizziness, and anxiety may also result from use. High dosage can cause rapid or irregular heartbeat, tremors, loss of motor skills, and even physical collapse. Long-term use of higher doses can produce amphetamine psychosis, which includes hallucinations, delusions, and paranoia.

Depressants: Barbituates and benzodiazepines are two of the most commonly used groups of these drugs. Barbituates include phenobarbital, seconal, and amytal; benzodiazepines include ativan, dalmanc, librium, xanax, valium, halcion, and restoril. These drugs are frequently used for medical purposes to relieve anxiety and to induce sleep. Physical and psychological dependence can occur if the drugs are used for longer periods of time at higher doses. Benzodiazepine use can cause slurred speech, disorientation, and lack of coordination. If taken with alcohol, abuse can lead to a coma and possible death.

Narcotics: Narcotics include heroin, methadone, morphine, codeine, and opium. After an initial feeling of euphoria, usage causes drowsiness, nausea, and vomiting. Effects of overdose include slow and shallow breathing, clammy skin, convulsion, coma, and possible death. Physical and psychological dependence is high, and severe withdrawal symptoms include watery eyes, runny nose, loss of appetite, irritability, tremors, panic, cramps, nausea, chills, and sweating. Use of contaminated syringes may cause AIDS and hepatitis.

GLOSSARY

Anocracy: A system wherein a political or ruling class maintains itself in power despite the apparent existence of contested elections and full public participation. States that are neither democratic nor autocratic are labeled "anocracies." An anocratic or pseudodemocratic state has in place formal democratic procedures such as contested elections and institutional structures such as legislatures and independent judiciaries. However, elections do not produce accountability and institutional structures do not reliably check central power.

Authoritarianism: A political system without competitive accountability of rulers to civil society. The form and shape of citizen participation is decided by the rulers. The constitution controls the population, not the rulers.

Autocracy: A political system wherein a sovereign or monarch rules by claim of absolute right; that is, a despot holds independent or self-derived power and absolute supremacy.

Bretton Woods Agreement: A July 1944 international agreement that permitted governments to use exchange controls to curtail capital movements and cooperate in controlling those movements. In order to create a stable world economy, the system permitted governments to pursue national policies while maintaining a monetary world order based on fixed exchange rates. Under this agreement forged at Bretton Woods, New Hampshire, the International Monetary Fund (IMF) was created to supervise the monetary system and to provide assistance to countries experiencing short-term balance-of-payment difficulties. The United States moved off the fixed exchange rate in August 1971, and the gold convertibility of the U.S. dollar was officially dropped in 1973.

Cash Transaction Reports (*CTRs*): Forms required by U.S. law since 1970 to record cash transactions of $10,000 or more. Under the 1986 Bank Secrecy Law, banks are penalized for failure to properly file these reports with the IRS.

Civic culture: The foundation that undergirds participation of the voting population in an electoral system; establishes congruence between political attitudes, beliefs, and understandings; and, in a democratic republic, sustains the standards for holding governors accountable.

Consolidated democracy: A system of government in which the accountability of actors is complete, the public is convinced that the democratic method is appropriate, continuity is certain, and evidence exists that the system is not precarious.

Corruption: The discreet but illegitimate use of money by public officials or private citizens for illegal gains; traditionally considered to be an isolated event of bribery or extortion without pervasive effect on a political system, even when it is chronic in police or other branches of a government's bureaucracy.

Democracy: A system of government in which the supreme power is retained by the people and exercised directly or indirectly through a system of representation; a political system or regime in which the people constitutionally choose the leaders of the state; an inclusive participatory regime based on party alternation or contestation. A democratic republic has plural institutional powers called checks and balances. The purpose of the regime is to avoid tyranny and to produce and enforce, by definition of the people, "good" laws and policies. While in power, elected officials may not act independently of constraints.

Democratic peace: The concept that democracies do not fight democracies, that disputes can be resolved without force. Democratic peace results from the culture, perceptions, and practices that permit compromise and peaceful resolution of conflicts without the threat of inter- or intranational violence.

FATF: Financial Action Task Force, established at the July 1989 Group of Seven (G-7) Economic Summit in Paris. FATF helps individual nations enforce economic standards. FATF officials are developing a global regulatory and enforcement plan to be put in place before the end of the century.

FinCen: Financial Crimes Enforcement Network of the Department of the Treasury, an alliance of law enforcement agencies. The Federal Reserve banks report their cash-flow data and provide specific information on cash shipments to FinCEN on a monthly basis. FinCEN uses this information to identify abnormalities by geographic regions or financial institutions and alerts law enforcement officials.

Group of Ten (G-10): Eleven countries (originally ten) whose central banks act together as lenders of last resort in economic crises.

Harm reduction: The drug policy designed to limit demand for drugs by treating drug consumption primarily as a health problem. Drug consumption is seen as rooted in social and cultural conditions in the supply-and-demand model; the role of governments or international capital is not addressed.

Hegemony: Preponderant influence or authority, especially of a government or state. According to hegemonic stability theory, an open international system is more likely to occur when there is a single dominant power in the international economic system. The new internationalism, in accordance with hegemonic stability theory, argues that parts of different governments when working together can manage international issues, assist the democratization process, and resist anocratization.

International regime: A system of international governance by which "rules, norms, and decision-making procedures" are designed to mitigate the lack of an overarching sovereign to keep and enforce international agreements. It alleviates anarchy in the international system through facilitating negotiation, cooperation, and coordination among participants. When fully institutionalized, it facilitates communication by providing a forum for scheduled and emergency meetings.

J-curve: The basis of a hypothesis that explains the nearly uncontrolled revolutionary violence that tends to arise when a long period of economic and social development is followed by a short period of sharp reversal. See James C. Davies, "Toward a Theory of Revolution," *American Sociological Review*, February 1962, 5–19.

Liberalism: A political ideology that seeks to restrict the power of the state and define a private sphere of society independent of state intrusion. It aims to free civil society from political interference and limit the state's authority.

Logos: The classic "ultimate truth" that the universe exists under a principle of order. The Logos provides reason and true knowledge of the physical world (nature) and human events.

MLAT: The Mutual Legal Assistance Treaty, a bilateral agreement between the United States and another country that provides a legal barrier to transfer of illegal profits to legitimate activities by the drug traffickers.

Narcodemocracy: A state with an electoral system whereby the ruling elite gain and maintain power with the support of the criminal organization of narcotics traffickers.

Narcosocialism: A political system wherein drug use is privileged and supported by society—and health care, welfare, provision of drugs, and criminal rehabilitation become the responsibility of the state.

Narcostate: A state where the criminalization of the political system has reached the point that the highest officials of the government protect and depend on narcotics trafficking organizations.

Narcostatization: The corruption of the political regime as a result of narcotics trafficking; the criminalization of the state. Narcostatization undermines the democratic check on the abuses of power by insulating elected officials from accountability and transforms the authoritarian state into a criminal one.

Neoliberalism: An international relations theory that supports economic cooperation and the spread of democratic governments under the leadership and prodding of the United States. It stresses the importance of international institutions, cooperation, and nonstate actors.

Oligarchy: A form of government in which the power is invested in the well-to-do few, who rule in their own interest and are not accountable to the public.

ONDCP: The Office of National Drug Control Policy, set up under the Anti-Drug Abuse Act of 1988. The director of ONDCP, who is charged with coordinating drug control policy for the nation, is frequently called the "drug czar."

Organized crime: The institutionalization of illicit activity whereby the public demands illegal goods—or legal goods illegally obtained—and a syndicate provides those goods, coerces the competition, and protects its own enterprises. It requires government protection to be successful.

Overworld: Transnational elites who operate outside the control of individual states and who employ enormous financial resources based in tax havens such as the Cayman Islands, the Jersey states, Liechtenstein, and Luxembourg. The overworld's hedge funds and offshore banks have the capability and the propensity to attack foreign currencies and equity markets. Offshore tax havens frequently are used for money laundering.

Polyarchy: A regime that has been "substantially popularized and liberalized," that is, it is "highly inclusive and extensively open to public contestation."

Ponzi scheme: An arrangement whereby banks illegally repay old depositors from new deposits. Such a scheme is sustainable only as long as deposits continue to double or increase beyond the demand of the old depositors.

Procedural democracy: A competition of parties in an electoral system that assumes the process (the actual election) is at the core of its legitimacy.

Scientific political science: According to one political scientist, the "preoccupation with fashioning political models, meticulous attention to 'research design,' use of quantification where possible, concern for leaving a trail that can be followed—'replication'—and caution in conclusions drawn from particular studies of an ever-growing establishment of generalizations."

Statism: The ownership and control of the major sectors of a country's economy by the state.

Transitional democracy: A regime in the process of shifting from authoritarianism to democracy but where the consolidation and continuity of that democracy are still uncertain and the accountability of the political class remains in complete.

NOTES

CHAPTER 1

1. Jessica T. Mathews, "Power Shift," *Foreign Affairs*, January/February 1997, 50–66.

2. Analysts of Soros's economic power claim that it has "less to do with financial acumen than with connections among Europe's super-rich—many of whom have grown even richer through his investment funds. They say he owes his greatest triumphs to intimate sources within a closed circle." Toni Marshall, "Enigmatic Billionaire," *Washington Times*, November 9, 1997, A12.

"Hedge funds" were among the major speculators against Asian currencies in 1997. In October 1998, however, coordinated action by China, Japan, and the United States led to enormous losses for the hedge funds, which were betting on a further yen devaluation. Hedge fund manager Julian Robertson's Tiger Fund reported losses of $17 billion for 1998, losing $2 billion on October 7, 1998, alone.

Some of the offshore banks that participated in the unregulated financial system are Barclays Offshore Banking and HSBC Private Banking, which operate on the Island of Jersey; Caymanx Trust Company, which operates on the Isle of Man; the Royal Bank of Canada, which operates in Trinidad and Tobago; Eurofed Bank Limited in Antigua; and the Bank of Liechtenstein, which is owned by the Prince Hans-Adam II family foundation. Prince Hans-Adam has called for the liberalization of drugs, "even hard drugs." "Liechtenstein," a special international report prepared by the *Washington Times* advertising department, August 17, 1998, 6.

3. Nicholas Roditi, the fund manager, earned $125 million in 1996 in salary from his backers. Laura Jereski and Michael R. Sesit, "Soros Quota Fun Big Shot Is Hired Gun," *Wall Street Journal*, September 16, 1997, C25.

4. Soros has spent $20 million on easing proscriptions on illegal drugs in the United States. Marshall, "Enigmatic Billionaire." Soros's musings on Russia may have precipitated a crisis already in the making, according to Clay Harris and Norma Cohen, "I Think I've Lost It, Says Soros," *Financial Times*, December 8, 1998, 18. The Soros funds may be sold only to non-U.S. investors.

5. Some other definitions of corruption are: "the illegitimate use of public power for private gain"; "all illegal or unethical use of governmental activity as a result of considerations of personal or political gain"; and "the arbitrary use of power." These various definitions have been cited by Stephen D. Morris, *Corruption and Politics in Contemporary Mexico* (Tuscaloosa: University of Alabama Press, 1991), 2

6. Ibid.

7. Ibid., 5–20

8. A beginning at describing this phenomenon is available in the study by Claire H. Sterling, *Thieves' World* (New York: Simon & Schuster, 1994).

9. Beatriz Johnston Hernandez, "Del expediente de un juicio en Texas: Como subprocurador, Coello Trejo recibio 'mas de un millón de dólares' de García Abrego," *Proceso* 934 (September 26, 1994), 19

10. Typical studies of the rise of ethnic conflict are Gidon Gottlieb's *Nation against State* (New York: Council on Foreign Relations Press, 1993) and Michael E. Brown, ed., *Ethnic Conflict and International Security* (Princeton: Princeton University Press, 1993). The principal study with respect to the clash of civilizations is Samuel Huntington, *The Clash of Civilizations?* (New York: Foreign Affairs Reader, 1993). For variations of this theme, where the struggle is perceived as one between modernity and the postmodern society, see James Kurth, "The Real Clash," *National Interest* 37 (Fall 1994), 3–15.

11. Francis Fukuyama, "The End of History," *National Interest* 16, (summer 1989). Undergirding Fukuyama's optimism is his Hegelian belief that human nature is self-created and is the unfolding of a long-term process. Human nature, he says, has changed over the past couple of millennia and "our modern democratic-egalitarian consciousness is in some sense a permanent acquisition, as much a part of our fundamental 'natures' as our need for sleep or our fear of death." Francis Fukuyama, "A Reply to My Critics," *National Interest* 18 (winter 1989), 28.

12. Philip G. Cerny, "Globalization and the Changing Logic of Collective Action," *International Organization* 49, no. 4 (autumn 1995).

13. Douglas W. Payne writes, "No anti-money-laundering policy can succeed while the global financial system, particularly off-shore havens, continues to virtually welcome massive infusions of dirty money." Douglas W. Payne, "Drugs and Dollars: A Global Challenge," *Freedom Review* 27, no. 4, (July-August 1996), 99

14. David Held, "Democracy, the Nation-State, and the Global System," in David Held, ed., *Political Theory Today* (Stanford, Calif.: Stanford University Press, 1991), 199, 203

15. Cerny, "Globalization."

16. John G. Ruggie, "International Regimes, Transactions, and Change: Embedded Liberalism in the Postwar Economic Order," *International Organization* 36, no. 2 (spring 1982), 195–231.

17. The original 10 countries were the United States, Canada, Japan, the Federal Republic of Germany, France, Italy, the United Kingdom, Sweden, the Netherlands, and Belgium. Later, Switzerland joined the group, but the name was not changed.

18. Ethan B. Kapstein, "Shockproof: The End of the Financial Crisis," *Foreign Affairs*, January/February 1996, 3.

19. Theda Skocpol, *Social Revolutions in the Modern World* (New York: Cambridge University Press, 1994), 112.

20. Kenneth N. Waltz, *Theory of International Politics* (New York: McGraw-Hill, 1979), 97.

21. A standard description of the prisoner's dilemma is as follows: "Two suspects are taken into custody and separated. The district attorney is certain that they are guilty of a specific crime, but he does not have adequate evidence to convict them at trial. He points out to each prisoner that each has two alternatives: to confess to the crime the police are sure they have done, or not to confess. If they both do not confess, then the district attorney states he will book them on some very minor trumped-up charge such as petty larceny and illegal possession of a weapon, and they will both receive minor punishment; if they both confess they will be prosecuted, but he will recommend less than the most severe sentence; but if one confesses and the other does not, then the confessor will receive lenient treatment for turning state's evidence whereas the latter will get 'the book' slaped at him. . . . The problem for each prisoner is to decide whether to confess or not." Duncan R. Luce and Haward Raiffa, *Games and Decisions* (New York: Wiley, 1957), 95.

22. Barry McCaffrey, director, ONDCP, "Strengthening International Drug Control Cooperation," Speech given in Miami, Florida, April 25, 1996.

23. Peter Andreas, "U.S.-Mexico: Open Markets, Closed Border," *Foreign Policy* 103 (summer 1996), 66.

24. Public Law 100–690, 102 Stat 4 189.

25. An estimated fifty-seven federal departments and agencies are involved in some way in the drug war.

26. Eva Bertram, Morris Blackman, Kenneth Sharpe, and Peter Andreas, *Drug War Politics* (Berkeley and Los Angeles: University of California Press, 1996).

27. Ibid., 257.

28. Ibid., 12.

29. The United States officially arrived at this position on May 18, 1998, when a federal grand jury in Los Angeles charged three Mexican banks and twenty-six Mexican bankers with laundering millions of dollars in drug profits. The indictment marked the first time Mexican banks as institutions were charged with knowingly helping drug traffickers.

CHAPTER 2

1. Ted Robert Gurr, "Persistence and Change in Political Systems, 1800–1971," *American Political Science Review* 68, 4 (December 1974), 1487. The anocratic state, Gurr wrote in footnote 11, "has minimal functions, an uninstitutionalized pattern of political competition, and executive leaders constantly imperiled by rival leaders."

2. Edward D. Mansfield and Jack Snyder have differentiated democratizing and autocratizing features as follows: "We consider states to be *democratizing* if, during a given period of time, they change from autocracy to either anocracy or democracy, or if they change from anocracy to democracy. Conversely, states are *autocratizing* if they change from democracy to autocracy or anocracy, or from anocracy to autocracy." Edward D. Mansfield and Jack Snyder, "Democratization and the Danger of War," *International Security* 20, no. 1 (Summer 1995), 9. (Italics in original.)

However, the single term "anocratizing" is used here for all processes toward the anocratic state, whether from a democracy or an autocracy. "Democratizing" is used only to describe a process toward democracy, and "autocratizing" a process toward autocracy. Likewise, the term "anocratization" is used here to describe the false democratization process of an autocracy and the reversal process of a consolidated democracy.

3. Since the Declaration of Independence, Americans have considered unaccountable governments tyrannical if they deprive citizens of their life, property, or liberty. According to American principles, government has the right to execute for criminal behavior, to tax, and to incarcerate only if the people are properly represented.

4. Dwight Waldo, *Political Science in America* (Paris: Unesco, 1956), 21–22.

5. Joseph Schumpeter, *Capitalism, Socialism and Democracy* (New York: Harper & Brothers, 1947), 269.

6. Samuel Huntington, *The Third Wave* (Norman: University of Oklahoma Press, 1991), 7.

7. Robert A. Dahl, *Polyarchy: Participation and Opposition* (New Haven, Conn.: Yale University Press, 1971), 6–7.

8. Ibid., 31–32.

9. Huntington, *Third Wave*, 10.

10. Ibid.

11. Schumpeter, *Capitalism*, 250–52.

12. Ibid., 285.

13. Gaetano Mosca, *The Ruling Class* (New York: McGraw-Hill, 1939), 50, 154.

14. Sartori's critique of the antielitist theory may be found in Giovanni Sartori, *The Theory of Democracy Revisited* (New Jersey: Chatham House Publishers, 1987), 156–63.

15. Michael Burton, Richard Gunther, and John Higley, "Introduction: Elite Transformations and Democratic Regimes," in John Higley and Richard

Gunther, eds., *Elites and Democratic consolidation in Latin America and Southern Europe* (Cambridge: Cambridge University Press, 1992), 1.

16. Ibid., 3.

17. Scott Mainwaring, Guillermo O'Donnell, and J. Samuel Valenzuela, eds., *Issues in Democratic Consolidation: The New South American Democracies in Comparative Perspective* (Notre Dame, Ind.: University of Notre Dame Press, 1992), 5.

18. J. Samuel Valenzuela, "Democratic Consolidation in Post-Transitional Settings: Notion, Process, and Facilitating Conditions," in Mainwaring, O'Donnell, and Valenzuela, eds., *Democratic Consolidation*, 62–68.

19. Burton, Gunther, and Hegley, "Elite Transformation," and Valenzuela, "Democratic Consolidation."

20. The very idea of consent becomes problematic as soon as governing elites are seen as being able to insulate themselves from accountability because of global interconnectedness, which gives inordinate economic power to a nation's ruling class. David Held pioneered the theoretical implications of this problem when he wrote, "Nations are heralding democracy at the very moment at which changes in the international order are compromising the viability of the independent democratic nation-state." Held, "Democracy," 197.

21. We shall see later (chapter 7) how corruption in a regime with democratic features leads to an anocracy or pseudodemocratic state.

22. For a further discussion of these issues, see Anthony H. Birch, *The Concepts and Theories of Modern Democracy* (New York: Routledge, 1993). Also useful is William C. Havard, *The Recovery of Political Theory: Limits and Possibilities* (Baton Rouge: Louisiana State University Press, 1984).

23. William Barclay, *The Daily Study Bible Series*, rev. ed. (Philadelphia: Westminster Press, 1975), 35.

24. Niccolo Machiavelli, *The Discourses* (New York: The Modern Library, 1950), 216.

25. Ibid., 146, 147.

26. Ibid., 148, 165, 166.

27. Michael Hereth, *Alexis de Tocqueville: Threats to Freedom in Democracy* (Durham, N.C.: Duke University Press, 1986), 108.

28. Alexis de Tocqueville, *Democracy in America*, vol. 1 (New York: Vintage, 1972), 300.

29. Machiavelli, *Discourses*, 51.

30. Tocqueville, *Democracy*, vol. 2, 22.

CHAPTER 3.

1. David Held, *Models of Democracy* (Stanford, Calif.: Stanford University Press, 1987), 41.

2. Gabriel A. Almond and Sidney Verba, *The Civic Culture: Political Attitudes and Democracy in Five Nations* (Boston: Little, Brown, 1965), 5, 6, 13.

3. Samuel Langdon, "A Sermon Preached at Concord in the State of New Hampshire; before the Honorable General Court at the Annual Election. June 5, 1788," in Ellis Sandoz, ed., *Political Sermons of the American Founding Era: 1730–1805* (Indianapolis: Liberty Press, 1991), 962, 965.

4. Tocqueville, *Democracy*, vol. 1, 44.

5. John Dewey, *A Common Faith* (New Haven, Conn.: Yale University Press 1934), 87.

6. John Dewey, *Experience and Nature* (New York: Norton, 1929), 293–94.

7. Richard Rorty, *Essays on Heidegger and Others* (New York: Cambridge University Press, 1991), 162.

8. C. S. Lewis wrote, "I am very doubtful whether history shows us one example of a man who, having stepped outside traditional morality and attained power, has used that power benevolently. C. S. Lewis, *The Abolition of Man* (New York: Simon and Schuster, 1986), 75.

9. Tocqueville, *Democracy*, vol. II, 21–22.

10. Higley and Gunther, eds., *Elites and Democratic Consolidation*, 14.

11. John A. Peeler, "Elite Settlements and Democratic consolidation: Colombia, Costa Rica, and Venezuela," in Higley and Gunther eds., *Elites and Democratic Consolidation*, 104.

12. Alan Knight, "Mexico's Elite Settlement: Conjuncture and Consequences," in Higley and Gunther, eds., *Elites and Democratic Consolidation*, 135.

13. It is interesting to note that students are becoming increasingly aware of the elitist nature of procedural democracy. Robert L. Allen in *Open Doors: The Life and Work of Joseph Schumpeter*, 2 vols. (New Brunswick, N.J.: Transaction Publishers, 1991), and Richard Swedberg in *Joseph A. Schumpeter: His Life and Work* (Cambridge, Eng.: Polity Press, 1991) expose how little Schumpeter's perspective allowed him to recognize the threat of Hitler's election in Germany. These biographers find indications of Schumpeter's sympathy for the Nazi party. In this sense, we need to explore whether the apparently value-free procedural democratic theory did not have its origins in a prescriptive intention to support elite control of the socialist tendencies of the late 1920s and 1930s.

14. This definition seeks to incorporate David Held's observation "that the meaning of national democratic decision–making today has to be explored in the context of a complex multinational, mutlilogic international society, and a huge range of actual and nascent regional and global institutions which transcend and mediate national boundaries." Held, "Democracy," 208.

15. See Charles Levinson, *Vodka Cola* (New York: Gordon and Cremones, n.d.).

16. Patricia Morgan, "Radicals Hijack Swiss Idyll," *Sunday Telegraph*, May 2, 1995. The International League against Drug Prohibition was founded in Rome in April 1989. The Radical Party made clear that the league's aims were (1) to legalize drugs and (2) to abolish the UN Single Convention on Narcotic Drugs of 1961, which prohibits members from legalizing drugs. Two members of the league, Guido Jenny and Hans Schultz, have been the Swiss government's legal

consultants on drugs. Patrick Henderson, "Something Rotten in the State of Switzerland," *Salisbury Review*, March 1995, 10.

17. Alexander Stille, *Excellent Cadavers: The Mafia and the Death of the First Italian Republic* (New York: Vintage, 1996), 207.

18. David Moller, "Drugs; Why We Must Stay Tough," *Reader's Digest*, July 1994.

19. Franziska Haller, "Harm Reduction: A Declaration of Surrender in the Face of Human Suffering," paper presented to the Verein Zur Forderung Der Psychologischen Menschenkenntris (hereafter VPM), October 17–20, 1996, 6.

20. Franziska Haller, "The Swiss Drug Situation and Its Impact on Europe and the World," unpublished paper (December 6, 1995), 2.

21. "On November 9, 1995, a group of 94 corporate executives, mostly company presidents and chairmen of the board of directors, presented a paper supporting a very liberal drug policy, including the demand for a major expansion of legal heroin distribution to drug addicts, as a way to research the pros and cons of so-called legal drug trade for the future. [Their paper supports] the official Swiss drug policy of legal distribution of narcotic drugs to drug addicts. They even demand preparation for the implementation of a legalized private drug trade with the means of a 'broadly implemented, geographically scattered, medically prescribed drug distribution.'" Franziska Haller, "Short Explanation of the Swiss Drug Situation and the Position Paper of Some Important Business Leaders," unpublished paper, (September 18, 1997), 1.

22. "Swiss OK Distribution of Heroin," *Daily Progress* (Charlottesville, Va.), September 29, 1997, A4.

23. Annemarie Buchholz-Kaiser, "Swiss Drug Policy: The Present Situation" VPM, April 28, 1992, 7.

24. These marginal groups include remnants of the narcotics trafficking organizations of the former Soviet Union and East European intelligence services. These intelligence services became involved in narcotics trafficking during the cold war and sought, through facilitating drug addiction in the West, to expand crime, unemployment, and internal conflict, thereby promoting a crisis in Western democracies. The chairman of the Drug Aid Cologne Association was the former Stasi agent Wilhem Vollman, who was also a member of the North Rhine-Westfalia Parliament. According to Swiss sources, he was a Stasi agent for twenty years and cultivated relationships with Swiss journalists.

25. *Neue Zücher Zeitung*, November 26, 1998, 72–73.

26. Franziska Haller explores this theory in " Swiss Drug Situation," VPM, March 12, 1996.

27. "VPM Is Troublesome in the Drug Problem," VPM, n.d., 2.

28. ECDP is now scheduled to expand its legalization network to Latin America. In 1997, the mayor of Medellin, Colombia, invited two leading Frankfurt Resolution advocates from Germany to address mayors of major Latin American cities, including Lima, Santiago de Chile, Buenos Aires, and La Paz, along with the police commissioner of Caracas. The U.S. Drug Policy Founda-

tion was involved in the preparations for the Medellin conference. The conference's preliminary objective was to push for the provision of hard drugs to addicts under medical supervision. According to *Der Spiegel*, a "Medellin statement" was designed to attack the U.S. position against drugs and call for treatment of drug addiction. The meeting in Colombia was designed to challenge the U.S. sphere of influence in seeking to extend the legalization network into areas of vital U.S. interest. *Der Spiegel* 36, (1997), 15.

29. Barry R. Weingast, "The Political Foundations of Democracy and the Role of Law," *American Political Science Review* 91, no. 2 (June 1997), 245–63.

CHAPTER 4.

1. Although both British and American interests were involved in the opium trade, a comparison of the relationship of the merchants' interests with their respective governments' illustrates how involved the British government became in protecting the trade. The East India Company, which was initially granted a private monopoly by the British government over production in the Ganges River basin, became a public monopoly in 1773 under Warren Hastings. When private U.S. companies entered the China trade in 1784, they were prohibited from bringing opium from India to China. The American firms (the most important of which was the J and T. H. Perkins and Company) therefore brought Turkish opium directly to China. Later, in the 1830s, Perkins and Company developed a relationship with important English commercial financiers such as the Barings, which allowed it to purchase the drug in London and Gibraltar. In addition, the Americans exploited the interests of British textile manufacturers, who used the Americans to get around the government-protected monopoly that was restricting the sale of their textiles. U.S. vessels were part of the anti-monopoly consortium of British interests that tried to break the government-maintained monopoly on the opium trade in Britain. This particular aspect of British imperialism indicates how close privileged private interests in commerce and finance were to government policy making. Later, the private and government-backed opium traders combined in the opium wars to impose their oligarchic will on China. The standard study on the British opium trade is that of David Edward Owen, *British Opium Policy in China and India* (New Haven, Conn.: Yale University Press, 1934). For an account of the most important New England interests in the opium trade, see Samuel Eliot Morison, *The Maritime History of Massachusetts, 1783–1860* (Boston: Houghton Mifflin, 1921) and Charles Clarkson Stelle, *Americans and the China Opium Trade in the Nineteenth Century* (New York: Arno, 1981). The Dutch and Portuguese were also prominent in the drug trade. The Dutch Trading Company, which was set up to manage the trade, used a number of merchant families to sell opium from the Middle East to the East Indies. See Jan Schmidt, *From Anatolia to Indonesia: Opium Trade and the Dutch Community of Izmir, 1820–1940* (Netherlands: Nederlands Historisch–Archaeologisch Instituut Te Istanbul, 1998).

2. Thomas B. Fowler, "Winning the War on Drugs: Can We Get There from Here?" in *Journal of Social, Political and Economic Studies*, 15, no. 4 (winter 1990), 403–21.

3. Brian Inglis, *The Opium War* (London: Hodder and Stoughton, 1976), 45. The importation of opium into China was prohibited, "under the severest penalties —not only loss of life to the guilty person, but extirpation of his family, and the confiscation of the ship or vessel that imports it, which is immediately burnt. We therefore beg you will positively forbid any of our commanders or others receiving it sending on board for this place —should it happen to be discovered it may be of the utmost consequence to our trade here—and not only to our trade but to our persons. We are here liable to answer for the misdemeanors of any persons who may come as passengers on our ships—also the security merchant of the ship is answerable for the duties on any goods they may bring. Opium brought by them may equally involve us in difficulties, as if brought by the commanders, or any officer belonging to the ships." This meant that the company and the council were involved in deliberate law breaking. Inglis, *Opium War*, 28.

4. Ibid., 52.

5. Maurice Collis, *Foreign Mud: The Opium Imbroglio at Canton in the 1830s and the Anglo-Chinese War* (New York: Norton, 1968), 60.

6. Ibid., 64.

7. Ibid., 79.

8. In 1837, the Chinese emperor had explored the possibility of legalizing the opium traffic at the suggestion of a member of the royal court, who argued that preventing the trading and consumption of narcotics was impossible. The ban on narcotics had not prevented opium from entering the country, nor had it prevented consumption, crime, and blackmail. It was suggested that "If opium exports were legalized, the only sufferers would be the addicts; and the community could well afford to allow them to smoke themselves to death, as the country was already over–populated." But, to the officials in the provinces, the court's proposal to legalize drugs was considered subversive. Opponents of legalizing drugs in the provinces pointed out that when the emperor had sent the army against rebels in 1832 it found that its armed forces had been debilitated by having so many opium smokers in it. The emperor thus agreed with those in the provinces who felt that prohibition should continue. Inglis, *Opium War*, 111–12.

9. Ibid.

10. Hsin-pao Chang, *Commissioner Lin and the Opium War* (New York: Norton, 1964), 35.

11. For more background on this, see Collis, *Foreign Mud*, 184–86, 118.

12. Ibid., 135.

13. Daniel Sneider and Marilyn James, "The World's Oldest Crime Syndicate," *War on Drugs* 2, no. 7 (September 1981), 16–18.

14. Joseph D. Douglass, Jr., *Red Cocaine: The Drugging of America* (Atlanta: Clarion House, 1990), 2.

15. Ibid., 167–69.

16. U.S. Senate, *Hearings before the Subcommittee to Investigate the Administration of the Internal Security Act and Other Internal Security Laws of the Committee on the Judiciary*, March 8, May 13, and March 19, 1955 (Washington, D.C.: Government Printing Office, 1955).

17. Douglass, *Red Cocaine*, 4.

18. Ibid., 8–12.

19. Ibid., 23.

20. Alfred W. McCoy, *The Politics of Heroin: CIA Complicity in the Global Drug Trade* (New York: Lawrence Hill Books, 1991), 195–96.

21. Ibid., 385.

22. Peter Truell and Larry Gurwin, *False Profits: The Inside Story of BCCI, the World's Most Corrupt Financial Empire* (Boston: Houghton Mifflin, 1992), 133, 159–60.

23. Jonathan Beaty and S. C. Gwynne, *The Outlaw Bank: A Wild Ride into the Secret Heart of BCCI* (New York: Random House, 1993), 295.

24. Peter Dale Scott and Jonathan Marshall, *Cocaine Politics: Drugs, Armies and the CIA in Central America* (Berkeley: University of California Press, 1991), 104, 106.

25. McCoy, *Politics of Heroin*, 482.

31. Ibid., 484.

32. Ibid., 385.

CHAPTER 5

1. Henner Hess, "The Traditional Sicilian Mafia: Organized Crime and Repressive Crime," in Robert J. Kelly, ed., *Organized Crime: A Global Perspective* (Totowa, N.J.: Roman and Littlefield, 1986), 127.

2. Pierre Tremblay and Richard Kedzior, "Analyzing the Organization of Crime in Montreal, 1920–80: A Canadian Test Case," in Kelly, ed., *Organized Crime*, 84.

3. Stephen Handelman, "The Russian Mafia," *Foreign Affairs*, March-April 1994, 86.

4. Ibid.

5. Sterling, *Thieves' World*, 99, 49.

6. Ibid.

7. Stephen Handelman, *Comrade Criminal: Russia's New Mafiya* (New Haven, Conn.: Yale University Press, 1995), 110–11.

8. Neela Banerjee, "Russian Organized Crime Goes Global: Gangs Use Skills Honed in Former Police State," *Wall Street Journal*, December 22, 1994, A10.

9. Claire H. Sterling, "Redfellas," *New Republic*, April 11, 1994, 19–20.

10. Caspar Weinberger, "Davos and Russia," *Forbes*, March 28, 1994, 67.

11. "Russia's Mafia," *Economist*, July 9, 1994, 19–20.

12. Sterling, "Redfellas," 19–20.

13. Paul Klebnikov, "Joe Stalin's Heirs," *Forbes*, September 27, 1993, 128.

14. Sterling, *Thieves' World*, 221.

15. Alejandro Ramos, Jenaro Villamil, Victor Batta, José Luis Ramírez, Fernando García, Edgar Hernandez, and Berta Alicia Galindo, "Organized Crime: Transnational Threat," *El Financiero*, special edition, October 9, 1994.

16. Sterling, *Thieves' World*, 76.

17. *El Financiero*, special edition, 48.

18. Ibid.

19. The ex-prime minister Guilio Andreotti, a Christian Democrat, and Socialist Bettino Craxi are the most striking examples of high-level officials who fell in disgrace for their connections with the criminal world. Andreotti, who was prime minister of Italy seven times, has been charged with other crimes besides that of being the political "fixer" in Rome for the Sicilian mafia. He has been directly linked to the murder of Mino Pecorelli, the editor of an Italian tabloid newspaper. Allegedly, Pecorelli was killed on the orders of the mafia as a favor to Andreotti. Robert Graham, "Andreotti Bound over in Slaying of Editor: Already on Trial in Mafia-Links Case," *Washington Times*, November 6, 1995, A17.

20. *The Economist*, March 26, 1994, 66; October 23, 1993, 25.

21. Ibid. The mafia had guaranteed the Christian Democrats more than $3\frac{1}{2}$ million votes in southern Italy.

22. Brian R. Sullivan, "Italian Mafia: A Cautionary Tale," unpublished manuscript prepared for the American Bar Association Conference on International Crime, 8–9.

23. Sterling, *Thieves' World*, 44.

24. Dennis Bloodworth, *The Chinese Looking Glass* (New York: Farrar, Straus and Giroux, 1967).

25. *El Financiero*, special edition, 48.

26. Diane Stormont, "Hong Kong Gangs Are on the Move: Triads Follow Immigrants Abroad," *Washington Times*, November 25, 1994, A22.

27. *El Financiero*, special edition.

28. Ibid.

29. Sterling, *Thieves' World*, 157.

30. Velisarios Kattoulas, "Japan's Yakuza Claim Place among Criminal Elite," *Washington Times*, November 25, 1994, A22.

31. Ibid.

32. Norihiko Shirouzu, "U.S.–Japan Ship Fight Is Being Complicated by Talk of Mob Ties," *Wall Street Journal*, October 21, 1997, A13.

33. Kattoulas, "Japan's Yakuza," A22.

34. Stan Yarbro, "Cocaine Trade Shifts in Colombia," *Christian Science Monitor*, June 3, 1991, 3.

35. "Cali Earns a New Reputation: World's No. 1 cocaine Seller," *New York Times*, May 15, 1991, A8; Douglas Farah, "Rid of Rivals, Flush with Cash," *Washington Post*, June 16, 1994, A27.

36. Douglas Farah, "Cali's Quiet Cartel Becomes Number One," *Washington Post*, October 17, 1990, A18. Miguel and Gilberto Rodríguez Orejuela were arrested in 1995 and lost their power.

37. Ibid.

38. Ibid.

39. Stephen Flynn, "Worldwide Drug Scourge," *Brookings Review*, winter 1993, 10.

40. "DEA Moves against Cali Cocaine Cartel," *Daily Progress* (Charlottesville, Va.), September 2, 1994, A3.

41. Adam Thompson, "Colombian and Russian Drug Groups Link Up," *Financial Times*, March 28–29, 1998, 4.

42. Jamie Dettmer, "A Storm of Drugs and Guns in Colombia," *Washington Times*, October 27, 1997, A17.

43. "Colombia May Get U.S. Aid in Civil War," *Washington Times*, October 13, 1997, A13.

44. The former head of the Gulf cartel, Juan García Abrego, was arrested by the FBI in 1995. Jorge Fernández Menendez, "Un narcodemócrata," *El Financiero*, February 12, 1996, 48.

45. Eduardo Valle, advisor to the former attorney general, in an open letter to the president, (*Proceso* 926, August 1, 1994) and Carlos Marín, "Alerté a Colosio y comenzó a dar pasos para librarse de los narcopolíticos, pero se le adelantaron" (*Proceso* 925, August 15, 1994).

46. Molly Moore, "Drug Lord Goes Home in a Coffin," *Washington Post*, July 12, 1997, A18.

47. Molly Moore, "Dead Drug Lord Settles Up: Mexican Surgeons Found Encased in Cement," *Washington Post*, November 7, 1997, A1. At least three theories are circulating in Mexico linking Amado Carrillo's death to the Palacio kidnapping and charging that Palacio's body replaced Carrillo's in the morgue. The theories are (1) Amado Carrillo staged his own "death" so he could continue his illegal operations without being sought by authorities; (2) he staged his "death" so he could retire and live in peace on his great wealth; and (3) he still lives and is a protected witness for the DEA. All these theories have been rejected by Mexican and American authorities. Amado's brother, Vicente, has apparently emerged on top and has moved much of the Juárez cartel's operation to the Yucatan Peninsula, with Cancun and other tourist centers providing cover for cartel activities. As an interesting side note: In a separate court case in New York, authorities "froze about $26 million in two Citibank accounts reportedly used by Carrillo to launder drug proceeds." Moore, "Dead Drug Lord," A29.

48. Paul Carroll and Dianne Solis, "García Is Enemy in Mexican War on Drugs," *Wall Street Journal*, December 13, 1994, A15.

49. Douglas Farah, "Mercenaries at Work for Mexico's Drug Families," *Washington Post*, October 30, 1997, A25, A27. The Arellano Félix family is made up of seven brothers and four sisters.

50. *El Financiero*, special edition, 51.

51. Ibid.

52. Ibid.

53. William Branigan, "Newly Named Mexican Officials Linked to Drugs," *Washington Post*, January 7, 1989, A1.

54. William Branigan, "DEA Agent's '85 Death Still Entangles Mexicans," *Washington Post*, September 14, 1989, A34.

55. Marjorie Miller, "Mexico's War on Drugs Confronts Enemy Within," *Los Angeles Times*, June 21, 1993, A1.

56. Kate Doyle, "The Militarization of the Drug War in Mexico," *Current History*, February 1993, 85.

57. Hugo Martínez McNaught, "Encargó Amado Carrillo acciones antinarco," *Reforma*, May 25, 1997.

58. On July 23, 1997, ten Russians, led by Russian capo Alexandrovich Zakharov, were expelled from Mexico. This reflects an alliance of Colombian, Mexican, and Russian cartel operations. Miguel Angel Ortega, "Joint venture criminal entre mafias mexicanas y rusas," *El Financiero*, August 3, 1997, 28, and Martín Moreno, "Los mercenarios rusos, expulsados de México," *Epoca*, August 4, 1997, 12.

59. Peter A. Lupsha, "Organized Crime in the United States," in Kelly, ed., *Organized Crime*, 43–44, 51.

60. Hank Messick, *Lansky* (New York: Berkeley Medallion Books, 1971), 83, 242.

61. Ibid.

62. Cleveland was represented by Lou Rothkopf and Moe Dalitz, and the Detroit mob was led by Joe Bernstein's Purple Gang, the operators of the so-called Little Jewish Navy on Lake Erie. Philadelphia's representatives included Nig Rosen and Max "Boo Boo" Hoff. Tom Pendergast, the boss of Kansas City, sent one of his lieutenants, John Lazia. New Jersey's representative was Abner "Longie" Zwillman.

63. Dan E. Modea, *Dark Victory: Ronald Reagan, MCA, and the Mob* (New York: Viking, 1986), 23. In 1931, George Browne, head of Chicago's local union of the International Alliance of Theatrical Stage Employees (IATSE), forged an alliance with Bioff to make sweetheart arrangements with the largest theatre chain in the country.

64. Nick Tosches, "The Man Who Kept the Secrets," *Vanity Fair*, April 1997, 184. When Korshak died on January 20, 1996, the headline of the *New York Times* obituary read, "Dies; Fabled Fixer for the Chicago Mob."

65. Modea, *Dark Victory*, 182.

66. The principal bosses in Las Vegas were Frank Costello, Frank Erickson, Meyer Lansky, Bugsy Siegel, Abner "Longie" Zwillman, Morris "Moe" Dalitz, Jake Guzik, and Tony Accardo. Ronald A. Farrell and Carole Case, *The Black Book and the Mob: The Untold Story of the Control of Nevada's Casinos* (Madison: The University of Wisconsin Press, 1995), 22 .

67. Messick, *Lansky*, 89.

68. Alfred W. McCoy with Cathleen B. Read and Loenard Adams II, "The Mafia Connection," in Peter Park and Wasyl Matveychuk, eds., *Culture and Politics of Drugs* (Dubuque, Iowa: Kendall/Hunt, 1986), 115.

69. Messick, *Lansky*, 136.

70. Tosches, "Man Who Kept Secrets," 192.

71. Farrell and Case, *Black Book*, 26.

72. Konstandinos Kalimtgis, David Goldman, and Jeffrey Steinberg, *Dope, Inc.: Britain's Opium War against the U.S.* (New York: New Benjamin Franklin Publishing House, 1978), 321–35. According to this study, "Resorts International was financed largely with a transfer of funds from the Banque de Credit Internationale of Tibor Rosenbaum and Major Louis Mortimer Bloomfield, and the Investors Overseas Service of Bernie Cornfield and the Rothschild family" 325.

73. Tosches, "Man Who Kept Secrets," 197.

74. Modea, *Dark Victory*, 8.

75. Messick, *Lansky*, 230–31.

76. Lupsha, "Organized Crime"; John L. Smith, *Running Scared: The Life and Treacherous Times of Las Vegas Casino King Steve Wynn* (New York, Barricade Books, 1995), 69; Messick, *Lansky*, 69. In 1933, when Prohibition ended and liquor became legal again, Rosenstiel became a distributor. According to Hank Messick, "Rosentiel's chief rival in the legitimate liquor business was Samuel Bronfman who founded Seagram's. Bronfman became the richest man in Canada by shipping booze to Rum Rows off the East Coast during Prohibition, and was deeply involved with such Lansky allies as Abner 'Longie' Zwillman and the Big Seven. In later years both Rosentiel and Bronfman achieved respectability and their money played important roles in the American economy, but their personal hatred remained." Messick, *Lansky*, 70.

77. Ibid., 19–21.

78. Farrell and Case, *Black Book*, 24.

79. Ibid., xi.

80. Modea, *Dark Victory*, 118.

81. Farrell and Case, *Black Book*, 37.

82. "The threat of organized crime is seen as emanating from Italians. So pervasive is this belief that, when Jews are identified with organized crime, they are seen as 'fronting' for Italians. Even when circumstances suggest that Jews control casinos and some Italians may be working for them, the evidence is sometimes twisted to fit with the more popular belief." Ibid., 37–38.

83. Smith, *Running Scared*, 143, 147.

84. Ibid., 114.

85. For a detailed summary of this insider operation, see James B. Stewart, *Den of Thieves* (New York: Touchstone, 1991), 213–14.

86. Smith, *Running Scared*, 204. "The casino companies to benefit from Milken's junk bonds make up a Las Vegas Who's Who: Bally's Caesars Palace, Circus Circus, Harrah's, Holiday Inn, Sahara Resorts, Sands, Showboat, Riviera, and Tropicana." Ibid., 192.

87. Gary Weiss, "The Mob on Wall Street," *Business Week*, December 16, 1996, 94.

88. Ferrell and Case, *Black Book*, 40. Rosselli had been Al Capone's first operative in Hollywood.

89. Ramos, et al., "Organized Crime."

90. Alan A. Block, "A Modern Marriage of Convenience: A Collaboration between Organized Crime and U.S. Intelligence," Kelly, ed., *Organized Crime*, 72–73.

91. Ibid., 58–77.

92. McCoy, "Politics of Heroin," 31–45.

93. Sullivan, "Italian Mafia," 9.

94. McCoy, "Politics of Heroin," 15.

95. Sterling, *Thieves' World*, 22.

96. Ramos, et al., "Organized Crime."

CHAPTER 6

1. The July 1944 Bretton Woods Agreement permitted governments under Article 6-3 to use exchange controls to curtail capital movements. In addition, the agreement under Article 8-2b permitted governments to cooperate in controlling capital movements. The two leading theorists of the agreement were John Maynard Keynes and Harry Dexter White. They sought a restrictive regime with respect to international capital movements. The participants at Bretton Woods also passed a resolution calling for the liquidation of the Bank for International Settlements (BIS) at "the earliest possible moment." Nonetheless, the decision to liquidate the BIS was not enforced, and in November 1946 the European Central Bankers resumed the monthly meetings that had been suspended in 1939. From the beginning, the U.S. financial community opposed capital controls, as they would interfere with New York's position as the principal international financial center after World War II. American interests, supported by the liberal ideologists William Ropke and Friedrich Hayek, influenced the intellectual and political climate to support the globalization of the international financial markets under the BIS regime. One of the best accounts of this development is found in Eric Helleiner's *States and the Reemergence of Global Finance: From Bretton Woods to the 1990s* (Ithaca, N.Y.: Cornell University Press, 1994).

2. Ron Chernow, *The House of Morgan: An American Banking Dynasty and the Rise of Modern Finance* (New York: Simon and Schuster, 1990), 375.

3. IMF Survey, published by the International Monetary Fund, July 29, 1996, 246.

4. Ibid.; *The Economist*, "Money-Launderers on the Line," June 25, 1994, 81.

5. House Committee on Banking, Finance, and Urban Affairs, *Federal Governments Response to Money Laundering: Hearings before the House Committee on Banking, Finance, and Urban Affairs*, May 25–26, 1993, 26.

6. See Douglass Farah, "Mexican Banks Laundered Drug Money, U.S. Charges," *Washington Post*, May 19, 1998, A1, A17; and Don Van Natta, Jr., "U.S. Indicts 26 Mexican Bankers in Laundering of Drug Funds," *New York Times*, May 19, 1998, A6. Mexico's chief bank regulator, Eduardo Fernández García, complained to Alan Greenspan, the chairman of the U.S. Federal Reserve, that Mexico had not been informed of the undercover operation. Since its beginning in November 1995 the undercover operation was kept secret from the Mexican government for fear of leaks and cartel penetration of the government. As a result of the sting there was a sharp deterioration in U.S.–Mexican relations.

7. Rachel Ehrenfeld, *Evil Money: Encounters along the Money Trail* (New York: Harper Business, 1992), 5–10.

8. Ibid., 13.

9. Ibid., 43. Since the 1970s, U.S. banks are required to file reports on all cash transactions larger than $10,000. Since 1986, these Cash Transaction Reports (CTRs) have been required to be filed with the Internal Revenue Service (IRS) under the Bank Secrecy Act. U.S. banks that do not comply face penalties.

10. Ibid., 53.

11. Larry Gurwin, *The Calvi Affair: Death of a Banker* (London: MacMillan, 1983), 14.

12. William Whalen, *Christianity and American Freemasonry* (San Francisco: Ignatius Press, 1958), 179–80.

13. "Conociose en Italia una lista de miembros de una logia masónica: Figuran entre otros argentinos López Rega, Lastiri, Massera, Suárez Masón y de la Plaza," *La Prensa* (Buenos Aires), May 22, 1981, 2.

14. Although the official cause of Calvi's death was listed as suicide, the actual circumstances surrounding it remain a mystery. Shortly before his death, Calvi was seen in the company of people linked to the mafia and Italian intelligence agencies. Calvi's family believes he was prepared to tell all he knew of his financial, political, and underworld connections and claims he was murdered. In 1992, supporting evidence for the murder thesis came from Juerg Heer, a senior executive and credit manager at the private Rothschild Bank AG in Zurich, who worked closely with the bank's chairman, Baron Elie de Rothschild. After being charged for taking kickbacks, Heer told investigators that he had helped Baron Rothschild concoct front companies for Italian interests that wished to avoid taxes and that he had "personally handed over a suitcase stuffed with what he later was told was $5 million for the killers of Roberto Calvi." Peter Gumbel, "A Swiss Bank Squirms as Officer It's Suing Tells of Sleazy Deals: He Says Baron Who Headed Rothschild Bank AG Hid the Ownership of Assets," *Wall Street Journal*, October 11, 1992, A1.

15. Beaty and Gwynne, *Outlaw Bank*, 135.

16. Ibid., xxiv. Under a "Ponzi scheme," a bank illegally repays old depositors from new deposits. Such a scheme is sustainable only as long as deposits continue to double or increase beyond the demand of the old depositors.

17. Ibid., 136.

18. The first Eurodollars came into being after World War II when the Soviet Union deposited its dollars in Paris and London. With Eurodollars came "Euromarkets," unregulated overseas markets, or markets that U.S. banks could use to avoid domestic regulations. Using the 1919 Edge Act, which allowed them to take equity stakes in foreign banks if the country did not allow U.S. branches there, American banks began to finance overseas businesses through the Euromarket. U.S. involvement became substantial after the middle of 1963 when President Kennedy proposed an Interest Equalization Tax to check U.S. capital outflows.

19. Beaty and Gwynne, *Outlaw Bank*, 151–52.

20. For more information on this, see Christopher Byron, "Body of Evidence," *New York* 27 (January 24, 1994), 14–15; and James Ring Adams, "Closing the BCCI Curtain," *American Spectator*, September 1994.

21. Beaty and Gwynne, *Outlaw Bank*, 266.

22. Robert E. Powis, *The Money Launderers: Lessons from the Drug Wars—How Billions of Illegal Dollars Are Washed through Banks and Businesses* (Chicago: Probus, 1992), 237.

23. Jagannath Dubashi, "The Bank That Knows Too Much," *Financial World*, November 29, 1988, 32–33. Juerg Heer of the Rothschild Bank reported that one of the general managers of the bank, Alfred Hartmann, constructed front companies "to siphon some BCCI funds out of Nigeria." Heer further tied the Rothschild Bank to BCCI, claiming that Hartmann was the chairman of the Swiss unit of BCCI. Heer's charges connected a major transnational financial enterprise to BCCI's illegal operations and suggested that money-laundering operations are far more pervasive among legitimate banks than had been discovered thus far. Gumbel, "Swiss Bank Squirms," A6.

24. *United States v. First National Bank of Boston*, filed in Clerk's Office, United States District Court, District of Massachusetts, February 7, 1985.

25. Most of the money was shipped to three Swiss banks: Credit Suisse of Zurich, Swiss Bank Corp. of Basel, and Union Bank of Switzerland in Zurich. Other banks involved with lesser amounts included the Bank of Boston's own branch in Luxembourg, Barclays Bank International, and the Canadian Imperial Bank, among others.

26. John Wong and William F. Doherty, "Bank of Boston Guilty in Cash-Transfer Case," *Boston Globe*, February 8, 1985, 1, 70. This case may have contributed to opposition in Congress to President Clinton's 1997 appointment of Governor Weld as U.S. ambassador to Mexico because it raised doubts about his commitment to combating money laundering.

27. Anthony DePalma with Peter Truell, "A Mexican Mover and Shaker and How His Millions Moved," *New York Times*, June 5, 1996, A12. Banco Cremi SA was one of two banks owned by Carlos Cabal Peniche, who in late 1994 made illegal contributions to the PRI party in Mexico, using his banks in an elaborate self-lending scheme that involved several hundred million dollars. Cabal Peniche later became a fugitive from Mexican justice.

28. "Raul Salinas May Be Tied to Huge Fund," *Wall Street Journal*, June 7, 1996, A9.

29. DePalma, "Mexican Mover and Shaker," A12.

30. *Money Laundering Alert*, April 1996.

31. Laurie Hays, "Citibank 'Cop' Was Kept Off Salinas Probe," *Wall Street Journal*, June 11 1996, A6.

32. Robert Fiske had previously represented former defense secretary Clark Clifford and Washington lawyer Robert Altman in the BCCI case and had served as independent counsel for the U.S. government in the 1994 investigation of the Whitewater Development Corp. investments. Laurie Hays, "Citibank Hires a Noted Defense Lawyer as Salinas Inquiry Appears to Deepen," *Wall Street Journal*, July 30, 1996; Kathleen Day, "Citibank Faulted for Mexican Transactions," *Washington Post*, December 4, 1998, A1, A24; Tim Golden, "U.S. Says Citibank Bent Rules for Salinas Deposit," *International Herald Tribune*, December 5–6, 1998, 1.

33. Christopher Whalen, "The G3 Money Launderers: How Russia, Mexico and, of All Countries, Israel Are Cleaning Up in a Dirty Business," *International Economy*, May/June 1996, 55.

34. According to the definition of an anarchical political system, the units of that system are functionally undifferentiated, distinguished primarily by their greater or lesser abilities to perform similar tasks. If organized criminal activity with respect to narcotics raises such abilities of the state, then it can be expected that more and more states will forge ties with criminal organizations.

CHAPTER 7

1. Handelman, *Comrade Criminal*, 113.

2. Ibid., 102.

3. Ibid., 70.

4. Ibid., 56.

5. Ibid., 195.

6. Geoffry York, "Majority of Russia's Rich Once Were Top Communists," *Washington Times*, September 24, 1994, A9.

7. Ibid.

8. Sterling, *Thieves' World*, 93.

9. Ibid.

10. *El Financiero*, special edition.

11. Sterling, *Thieves' World*, 99.

12. Joseph R. Blasi, Maya Kroumova, and Douglas Kruse, *Kremlin Capitalism* (Ithaca, N.Y.: Cornell University Press, 1997), 171.

13. Michelle Celarier, "Gangster Economics," *Global Finance* 7 (September 1993), 48–54.

14. Chrystia Freeland, John Thornhill, and Andrew Gowers, "Moscow's Group of Seven," *Financial Times*, November 1, 1996, 15.

15. *Washington Post*, November 6, 1997, A25.

16. Handelman, *Comrade Criminal*, 202.

17. Ibid., 285.

18. See Alfred Kokh, *The Selling of the Soviet Empire: Politics and Economics of Russia's Privatization—Revelations of the Principal Insider* (New York: S.P.I. Books, 1998).

19. The literature on the Andean region's drug problem is extensive. Much of the Spanish language books on Peru and Bolivia focus on peasants' dependence on the crop and the degree to which the problem is driven by demand rather than by supply. A good source for the Peruvian perspective is the book edited by D. García Sayán, *Coca, Cocaina y Narcotráfico: Laberinto en los Andes* (Lima: Comisión Andina de Juristas, 1989). The role of insurgents is described there as developing through the protection of peasant growers. Some of this literature—for example, the writings of Raúl Barrios Morón, *Bolivia y Estados Unidos: Democracia, Derechos Humanos y Narcotráfico* (La Paz: FIACSO, 1989)—does deal with corruption at the highest levels of the government but focuses exclusively on the García Meza rule between 1980 and 1982. To build an accurate picture of the corruption problem, a broad view of periodicals is essential.

20. Scott and Marshall, *Cocaine Politics*, 83–84.

21. Rensselaer W. Lee III, *The White Labyrinth: Cocaine and Political Power* (New Brunswick, N.J.: Transaction Publishers, 1990), 106.

22. U.S. House, *Hearing before the Committee on Banking, Finance, and Urban Affairs*, 102nd Cong., 1st sess., Part 1, September 11, 1991, 986.

23. Truell and Gurwin, *False Profits*, 214.

24. Cynthia McClintock, "Opportunities and Constraints to Source Reduction of Coca: The Peruvian Socio-Political Context," U.S. House, Office of Technology Assessment, H3-495.0 (Washington, D.C.: Government Printing Office, 1992), 32.

25. Simon Strong, "Peru Is Losing More Than the Drug War," *New York Times*, February 17, 1992, A17.

26. Coletta Youngers, *Key Congressional Concerns Regarding Peru* (Washington, D.C.: Washington Office on Latin America, 1992), 32.

27. U.S. House, *Joint Hearing of the Committee on Foreign Affairs: The Situation in Peru and the Future of the War on Drugs*, 102d Cong., 2nd sess., (Washington, D.C.: Government Printing Office, 1992), 62.

28. Enrique Obando, "Fujimori and the Military: A Marriage of Convenience," *NACLA* 30, no. 1 (July/August 1996), 35.

29. Ibid.

30. Peter Andreas, "Profits, Poverty, and Illegality: The Logic of Drug Corruption," *NACLA* 27, no. 3, (November/Decemter 1993), 26.

31. Manuel Castillo Ochoa, "Fujimori and the Business Class: A Prickly Partnership," *NACLA* 30, no. 1 (July/August 1996), 27.

32. John Simpson, *In the Forests of the Night* (New York: Random House, 1993), 186. Additional material on this subject is provided by Joseph A. Gagliano,

Coca Production in Peru: The Historical Debate (Tucson: University of Arizona Press, 1994); Edmundo Morales, *Cocaine: White Gold Rush in Peru* (Tucson: University of Arizona Press, 1989); and Alvaro Vargas Llosa, *The Madness of Things Peruvian: Democracy under Seige* (New Brunswick, N.J.: Transaction Publishers, 1994).

33. Kevin Healy, "Recent Literature on Drugs in Bolivia," in Bruce M. Bagley and William O. Walker III, eds., *Drug Trafficking in the Americas* (New Brunswick, N.J.: Transaction Publishers, 1994), 205.

34. U.S. Department of State, Bureau of International Narcotics Matters, *International Narcotics Control Strategy Report*, Washington, D.C.: Government Printing Office, 1993.

35. There is considerable literature on the Bolivian problem. Barrios Morón in his *Bolivia y Estados Unidos* (1989) makes the case for the fusion of the state and narcotics trafficking in Bolivia. The Latin American Bureau (LAB) in London made an extensive study of the state-military connection in the García Meza regime and tied the military to the previous regime of General Banzer and his family as well as to the Argentine military and to fascists. Latin American Bureau, *Narcotráfico y Política: Militarismo y Mafia en Bolivia* (Madrid: Iepala, 1982).

36. Alain Labrousse, "Dependence on Drugs: Unemployment, Migration and an Alternative Path to Development in Bolivia," *International Labor Review* 129, no. 3 (1990), 335.

37. Andreas, "Profits, Poverty and Illegality," 27.

38. Melvin Burke, "Bolivia: The Politics of Cocaine," *Current History*, February 1991, 66.

39. Andreas, "Profits, Poverty and Illegality," 28.

40. Chris Philipsborn, "Cocaine Squeeze," *New Statesman and Society*, February 12, 1993, 10–11.

41. "Rico Toro Faces Extradition to U.S.," *Latin American Regional Reports: Andean Group*, 9 March 1995.

42. *FBIS: Latin America*, 2 March 1995, 32.

43. Ibid., 40.

44. See Lee, *White Labyrinth*, 129.

45. A representative of the CAPHL attended the George Washington University conference, "The War on Drugs: Addicted to Failure," in June 1998.

46. James Brooke, "Venezuelans Secretly Support Army Coup Plotters," *New York Times*, February 9, 1992, 19.

47. Thor Halvorssen, "The Price of Vigilance in Venezuela's Banking Community," *Wall Street Journal*, March 4, 1994, A9.

48. Gaeton Fonzi, "The Troublemaker," *Pennsylvania Gazette*, November 1994, 23.

49. Halvorssen, "Price of Vigilence," A9.

50. Fonzi, "Troublemaker," 23.

51. José de Córdoba, "Venezuelan Bankers Abroad Aren't Loved But They're Wanted," *Wall Street Journal*, July 31, 1996, A1.

52. Ibid., A10, A1.

CHAPTER 8

1. Farah, "Mercenaries at Work," *Washington Post*, October 30, 1997, A25.

2. Established in March 1929 in Queretaro, the city where the Constitution of 1917 was written, the PRI was originally called the National Revolutionary Party (Partido Nacional Revolucionario, or PNR). From 1937 to 1945, it was called the Party of the Mexican Revolution (Partido de la Revolución Maxicana, or PRM) and since then, the Institutional Revolutionary Party (Partido Revolucionario Institucional, or PRI).

3. Theodore C. Sorensen, *Las Perspectivas para Unas Elecciones Libres, Limpias y Honestas en México: Un Informe ante El Consejo Coordinador Empresarial*, August 15, 1994, 51.

4. Ricardo H. Andonaegui, "Culpa El Buho al cartel del Golfo del homicidio de Colosio," *El Dia*, September 5, 1994.

5. *Huellas* 98 (August 29, 1994), 13.

6. José Carreno, "Solo las autoridades federales pudieron perpetrar el asesinato de LDC," *Universal*, August 26, 1994.

7. Tod Robberson, "Probe in Mexico Raises New Round of Questions," *Washington Post*, February 26, 1995, A22.

8. For an excellent account of these charges, see Tim Golden, "Mexico Inquiry into Candidate's Killing Falters: Conspiracy Case Far from Proved," *New York Times*, May 21, 1994, 3.

9. "Second Gunman Is Arrested in Assassination in Mexico," *New York Times*, February 26, 1995, p.8.

10. David C. Jordan, *Revolutionary Cuba and the End of the Cold War* (Lanham, Md.: University Press of America, 1993), 193–94.

11. Eduardo Valle testimony before U.S. Senate, August 1995.

12. *New York Times*, February 26, 1995, A8.

13. Dolia Estevez, "'México, Blanco de las Mafias; Alianza Mundial Para Subvertir el Orden', Dice Brian Crozier," *El Financiero*, September 21, 1994.

14. Eduardo Valle, *El Segundo Disparo: La Narcodemocracia Mexicana* (Mexico, D.F.: Editoria Oceano de Mexico, 1995), and Juan José Coello, "Vivimos narcodemocracia," *Reforma*, May 11, 1994.

15. Peter A. Lupsha, "Drug Lords and Narco-Corruption: The Players Change but the Game Continues," in Alfred W. McCoy and Alan A. Block, eds., *War on Drugs: Studies in the Failure of U.S. Narcotics Policy* (San Francisco: Westview Press, 1992), 185.

16. Ibid.

17. José de Córdoba, "Date in L.A. Keeps Mexican Governor from Visiting U.S.," *Wall Street Journal*, March 5, 1997, A8.

18. Lupsha, "Drug Lords," 186.

19. Carlos Puig, "'No afirmo nada: solo pido que se investigue' . . . y Eduardo Valle Da Nombres y Mas Nombres," *Proceso* 931 (September 5, 1994), 30.

20. Christopher Whalen, "Mexico: The Narco System," *Dinero* (Colombia), English trans., *List Mexico 2000*, November, 29, 1995.

21. Tim Golden, "Tons of Cocaine Reaching Mexico in Old Jets," *New York Times*, January 10, 1995, A1, A8.

22. *Proceso* 928, 21.

23. Carlos Ramírez, "Indicador Politico," *El Financiero*, September 9, 1994.

24. Anne Marie Mergier, "Ofensiva de Moussavi: 'IBM me pidió llegar a un arreglo, Caso obstaculizó a la justicia y la Contraloria lo avaló,'" *Proceso* 857 (April 5, 1993), 6–15. A comparison of Moussavi's map and the Seneam map is found on page 21 in another article by Mergier, "Moussavi acusa: 'Andrés Caso fue objeto de una acusación muy seria, se pedía su encarcelamiento . . . pero todo quedó enterrado'," *Proceso* 859 (April 19, 1993), 18–21. Additional accounts of the Moussavi affair can be found in *Proceso* 858, 863, 867, and 868.

25. Jordan, *Revolutionary Cuba*, 194.

26. Valle, *El Segundo Disparo*, 20.

27. Rodolfo Rojas-Zea, "Narcotráfico, la Multinacional Mas Importante del Crímen," *El Financiero*, May 15, 1994, 18.

28. Morris, *Corruption and Politics*, 99.

29. Puig, "No afirmo." Some economic analysts questioned Cabal Peniche's financial ability to buy two Mexican banks and two American food companies for an estimated $2 billion. According to the Mexican secreetary of finance, there were gross irregularities in the Cremi-Union Financial group, including

- Illicit operations in extending credit to businesses lacking sufficient funds.
- Self-lending by Carlos Cabal Peniche, president of the executive board, through different people.
- Utilization of bank resources to make acquisitions worth over $1 billion. Among the companies bought were Del Monte Fresh Produce, Del Monte Cans, and the Cremi Financial Group.

Seven executives from Banco Union and five from Arrendadora Pragma were implicated in the fraud against these businesses and were detained. Those detained were high-level directors and managers, including the president of administration of Mexican commerce and industry of Arrendadora Pragma. They were charged with renewal of credit to people or firms in a known state of insolvency and alteration of accounting books to distort the true nature of assets, liabilities, and results of the credit institution. Tizoc Arista, "Quienes son los políticos cómplices de Cabal y que aun lo protegen," *Quehacer Político* 679 (September 12, 1994), 10.

30. Rosa Maria Olgun Islas, "Carlos Cabal: ascenso de vertigo, caida de rayo," *Punto*, September 12, 1994, 13; Jacinto R. Munguia, "La negligencia oficial facilitó los autoprestamos" and "El escándalo Cabal descubre a notables exfuncionarios: De la Madrid, su hijo y Rovirosa niegan ser socios del prófugo," *Punto*, September 12, 1994, 14; Arista, "Quienes son los políticos," 6–12; Jose Silva M., "Patrones tabasquenos califican como una tragedia la caida de Cabal Peniche," 12–15; Carlos Alva Bri, "El fraude-contubernia Banpesca que cometieron Ojeda, Cabal y De la Madrid C.," 16–20—all in *Quehacer Político* 679 (September 12, 1994).

31. Carlos Ramírez, "El otro choque de trenes," *El Financiero*, September 9, 1994.

32. Maribel González, "Planearon políticos crímen de Colosio," *Reforma*, August 26, 1994, 11A.

33. Dianne Solis, "A Key Leader in Mexico's PRI Is Assassinated," *Wall Street Journal*, September 29, 1994, A9.

34. Juan Barrera Barrera, "Temor y Sospecha Asedian Hasta Insurgentes Norte," *Punto*, October 10, 1994, 15.

35. Rosa Maria Olgun Islas, "Crímenes en serio para controlar congreso y PRI," *Punto*, October 17, 1994, 5.

36. Dora Elena Cortes, "Es Muñóz Rocha agente del grupo político de Hank González?" *El Universal*, October 10, 1994.

37. Carlos Marín, "No se quiere reconocer una descomposición generalizada del aparato que se comprometió con el tráfico de drogas," *Proceso* 937 (October 17, 1994), 26.

38. *Universal*, October 5, 1994.

39. Muñóz Rocha's body was reportedly found buried on Raul Salinas's property, though this allegation was later denied. *Newsweek*, February 22, 1997.

40. *La Carpeta Púrpura* 174 (October 28, 1994), 9.

41. Peter Fritsch and José de Córdoba, "Mexican Ex-Official's 'Family Fortune' Was Drug Payoffs, U.S. Alleges at Trial," *Wall Street Journal*, March 11, 1997, A18.

42. Craig Torres, Joel Millman, and Dianne Solis, "Raúl's World: Cash, Connections—and Corruption?: Salinas Probe Touches Mexico's Top Businessmen, Some with U.S. Partners," *Wall Street Journal*, August 7, 1996, A8. In October 1998 Swiss authorities accused Raúl Salinas of receiving $500 million in payoffs from Colombian and Mexican drug cartesl and seized $114 million deposited in Swiss banks. The investigator's report concluded that Salinas "took control of practically all drug shipments transiting Mexico" after his brother was elected president. He received payments from the heads of both the Cali and Medellin cartels and transferred this money through numerous accounts in America, Switzerland, and other countries, including an additional $23 million uncovered in a Swiss bank branch in London. According to Swiss officials, the 230-page report will not be made public. Salinas's lawyer said the decision will be appealed to the Swiss court. Anne Swardson, "Swiss Call Salinas a Drug Profiteer, Seize Bank Funds," *Washington Post*, October 21, 1998, A1, A22.

43. Douglas Farah, "Mexican Control of U.S. Cocaine Market Grows," Washington Post, August 5, 1997, A11.

44. A contrary position is maintained by Jorge Castaneda and Robert Pastor in Limits to Friendship. They argue that it is the United States, not Mexico that has a drug problem and that the United States should end its antidrug efforts in Latin America and concentrate on domestic demand. See Jorge G. Castaneda and Robert A. Pastor, *Limits to Friendship: the United States and Mexico* (New York: Knopf, 1988), 253. The Carnegie Endowment for International Peace funded Castaneda's work for this book and a Fulbright Fellowship supported Pastor's work.

CHAPTER 9

1. Most of the Spanish literature on the Colombian drug problem has focused on the size of the drug industry and its impact on the nation's economy. Some major authors are Salomón Kalmanovitz, *Economía y nación: una breve historia de Colombia* (Bogotá: Tercer mundo Editores, 1994); A. Reyes, "La violencia y la expansion territorial del narcotrafico" in Carlos G. Arrieta, et al. eds., Narcotrafico en Colombia (Bogota: Coediciones Tercer Mundo-Ediciones Uniandes, 1991). This literature argues that the drug trade has harmed the Colombian economy. Works by Mario Arango argue the opposite. See his *Impacto del Narcotrafico en Antioquia*, 3d ed. (Medellin: Arango, 1988), and his work with Jorge Child, *Narcotrafico: Imperio de la Cocaina* (Mexico, D.F.: Editorial Diana, 1987). All these writers, irrespective of where they stand on the costs or benefits to Colombian society of the impact of drugs, agree that production and distribution of drugs has benefited from the weakening of the state.

2. Lee, *White Labyrinth*, 131.

3. Ana Carrigan, "An Unlikely Hero: Valdivieso's Crusade against Drug Corruption," *NACLA* 30, no. 1 (July/August 1996), 8.

4. David Marcus, "Drug Cartel, Lawyers Feel Heat Rising," *Dallas Morning News*, June 10, 1995, A2.

5. *Washington Post*, February 25, 1980, A18.

6. Carrigan, "Unlikely Hero," 8.

7. Ibid.

8. David van Biema, "Sweet, Sweet Surrender: A Cali Cartel Chief Proposes to Give Up on Conditions So Lenient That They May Strain U.S.–Colombian Relations," *Time*, November 7, 1994, 48.

9. Douglas Farah, "U.S. Weighs Response to Clearing of Colombian Leader: Samper, Absolved of Drug Connection, Calls on Washington to Show 'Mutual Respect,'" *Washington Post*, June 14, 1996, A 17.

10. *Corruption and Drugs in Colombia: Democracy at Risk*, staff report to the U.S. Senate Committee on Foreign Relations (Washington, D.C.: Government Printing Office, February 1996), 9.

11. Carrigan, "Unlikely Hero," 6.

12. Douglas Farah, "U.S. Aid to Colombian Military," *Washington Post*, December 27, 1998, A28.

13. van Biema, "Sweet, Sweet Surrender," 47.

14. Yarbro, "Cocaine Trade Shifts," 3.

15. Douglas Farah, "Mercenaries at Work," A27.

16. "Cali Earns a New Reputation," *New York Times*, May 15, 1991, A8.

17. Farah, "Rid of Rivals, ," A27.

18. Farah, "Cali's Quiet Cartel," A18.

19. Dolia Estevez, "Unida y sin Obstaculos se Prepara la Mafia a Expandir y Afianzar su Control Sobre el Mundo," *El Financiero*, September 6, 1994, 32.

20. Farah, "Cali's Quiet Cartel," A18.

21. Ibid.

22. Dudley Althaus, "Drug-Trade Shift to Mexico Stirs Worry," *Washington Times*, November 11, 1997, A16.

23. "The Military-Drug Links in Colombia," *Latin American Weekly Report*, June 23, 1988, 4.

24. *Corruption and Drugs*, U.S. Senate Foreign Relations Committee staff report, February 1996, 11.

25. Peeler, "Elite Settlements," 81.

26. *Corruption and Drugs*, U.S. Senate Foreign Relations Committee, staff report, February 1996, 7.

27. Quoted by Marcus, "Drug Cartel," 1A.

28. William J. Olson, testimony before the U.S. Senate Foreign Relations Subcommittee on the Western Hemisphere, April 4, 1995, 4.

29. *Corruption and Drugs*, U.S. Senate Foreign Relations Committee staff report, February 1996, 7.

30. Stephen H. Greene, "DEA's Role in Attacking Narcotics Trafficking in the Western Hemisphere," a statement before the U.S. Senate Foreign Relations Subcommittee on the Western Hemisphere, April 4, 1995, 3.

31. van Biema, "Sweet, Sweet Surrender," 48.

32. The territories under insurgent control border on Ecuador, which is now a major transshipment point for Colombian cocaine and heroin and a major supplier of precursor chemicals necessary to transform the raw material into a consumer product. Much of the contraband traffic takes place in eastern Ecuador, and since the signing of the Acta Presidencial de Brasilia on October 26, 1998, the Peruvian-Ecuadorian border has also been demilitarized. The act made both sides of the frontier an ecological protection zone, thus creating an enormous area where drug trafficking proceeds easily between Ecuador, Peru, and Colombia—as well as between Pacific and Atlantic ports—without much military interference from the three states. Douglas Farah, "Drug Traffickers Move into Ecuador: Colombian Contraband Taken to Pacific Ports," *Washington Post*, April 26, 1998, A24; Laura Brooks, "For Colombian Town, a Hand-over to Fear: Rebels to Take Formal Control of Areas Where They Already Wield Fierce

Power," *Washington Post*, September 29, 1998, A26. It should be noted that a policy split on Colombia exists in Washington. The former U.S. ambassador to Colombia, Myles Frechette, has argued that evidence of a link between FARC/ELN and the drug trade was weak. Bernard Aronson, the assistant secretary of state for Latin America during the Bush administration, argued in a *Washington Post* op ed piece of May 21, 1998, that war should not be waged against the FARC and the ELN but that the United States should test the insurgents' offer to cooperate in eradicating the coca fields under their protection. Both the head of the U.S. Southern Command, Gen. Charles Wilhelm, and the U.S. drug czar, Gen. Barry McCaffrey, have maintained that the FARC/ELN insurgency is intimately connected to the drug trade. Rens Lee, the author of several books on the narcotics problem in the Andean region, responded to Aronson in the *Washington Post* on June 11, 1998, arguing that the guerrilla organizations have little incentive to demobilize on the basis of their $1 billion annual earnings and that any offer to help set up alternative crops should be met with skepticism.

CHAPTER 10

1. Huntington, *Clash of Civilizations?* 22.

2. This book discusses not the scientific merits of Darwin's theory but its implications for political culture and belief systems.

3. Darwin's theory of evolution led to a famous debate in 1860 between Huxley and Bishop Samuel Wilberforce at the British Association for the Advancement of Science. Huxley argued for evolution, saying humans descended from apes, and Wilberforce argued for creation, saying humans descended from Adam and Eve.

4. Ronald W. Clark, *The Huxleys* (London: Heinemann, 1968), 348.

5. Ibid., 348–49.

6. Ibid., 173.

7. H. G. Wells, *The Open Conspiracy* (London: Doubleday, Doran, 1928), 142–43.

8. W. Warren Wagar, *H. G. Wells and the World State* (New Haven, Conn.: Yale University Press, 1961), 6–7.

9. Clark, *Huxleys*, 332.

10. Ibid., 333.

11. Aldous Huxley, *Brave New World Revisited* (New York: Harper & Row, 1965), 2.

12. Ibid., 56.

13. Timothy Leary, *Changing My Mind, among Others: Lifetime Writings, Selected and Introduced by the Author* (Englewood Cliffs, N.J.: Prentice-Hall, 1982), 141, 142.

14. Ibid., 173. It was at Harvard that Leary met Aldous Huxley.

15. Ibid., 174–75. Leary died of prostate cancer in 1996.

16. John Marks, "Drugs in the Cold War: In Search of Chemical Intelligence—Mushrooms to Counterculture," in Park and Matveychuk, eds., *Culture and Politics*, 135.

17. Martin A. Lee and Bruce Shlain, *Acid Dreams: The CIA, LSD, and the Sixties Rebellion* (New York: Grove Press, 1985), xix.

18. Robert G. Pielke, *You Say You Want a Revolution: Rock Music in American Culture* (Chicago: Nelson-Hall, 1986), 35.

19. Carl A. Raschke, *Painted Black: From Drug Killings to Heavy Metal: The Alarming True Story of How Satanism Is Terrorizing Our Communities* (San Francisco: Harper & Row, 1990).

20. Allan David Bloom, *The Closing Of The American Mind: How Higher Education Has Failed Democracy and Impoverished the Souls of Today's Students* (New York: Simon and Schuster, 1987).

21. Pielke, *You Say You Want a Revolution*.

22. Karen Schoemer, "Rockers, Models, and the New Allure of Heroin," *Newsweek*, August 26, 1996, 53. Many bands have been linked to heroin by a band member's use, arrest, or recovery, including Nirvana, Hole, Smashing Pumpkins, Everclear, Blind Melon, Skinny Puppy, 7 Year Bitch, Red Hot Chili Peppers, Stone Temple Pilots, the Breeders, Alice in Chains, Sublime, Sex Pistols, Porno for Pyros, and Depeche Mode. For additional comments on this, see Gabriel G. Nahas, *Cocaine: The Great White Plague* (Middlebury, Vt.: Paul S. Eriksson, 1989), 96–97.

23. Schoemer, "Rockers."

24. Roger Catlin, "Heroin's Grip on Music World is Nothing New," *Daily Progress* (Charlottesville, Va.), August 22, 1996, D4.

25. As quoted in *Harpers*, "Targeting the Stoned Cyberpunk," December 1994, 24.

26. *Lemon v. Kurtzman*, 403 U.S. 602 (1970), 622.

27. Robert Sweet, "The War On Drugs Is Lost," *National Review*, February 12, 1996, cover story.

28. Edward J. Tully and Marguerite A. Bennett, "Pro-Legalization Arguments Reviewed and Rejected," in Rod L. Evans and Irwin M. Berent, eds., *Drug Legalization: For and Against* (La Salle, Ill.: Open Court, 1992), 65.

29. Sweet, " War on Drugs," 44.

30. Ibid.

31. Merrill A. Smith, "The Drug Problem: Is There an Answer?," on Evans and Berent, eds., *Drug Legalization*, 83.

32. Lee, *White Labyrinth*, 240.

33. Nahas, *Cocaine*, 107.

34. Bernard Weinraub, "David Geffen: Still Hungry," *New York Times Magazine*, May 2, 1994, 28.

35. Arnold S. Trebach, comments at the 8th Annual Conference of the Drug Policy Foundation, Washington, D.C., November 17, 1994.

36. Ibid.

37. The ACLU seeks the legalization of marijuana but has not taken a stance with respect to other drugs.

38. Keith Stroup, founder of NORML, was connected to the Playboy Foundation through Bob Gutwillig who, as a Playboy vice president, channeled money to Tom Forcade of the Yippies, who in turn funneled money to *High Times*, "the unofficial voice of America's heroin, cocaine, and marijuana dealers." In the 1960s Timothy Leary was a frequent contributor to *Playboy*, which first promoted drug legalization in the mid-1970s. Jeffrey Steinberg, "Opening the Playboy File," *War on Drugs* 2, no. 6, (July 1981), 15–16.

39. *Wall Street Journal*, December 14, 1994, A16.

40. David Boaz, "The Legalization of Drugs," *Vital Speeches of the Day*, May 15, 1988, 685.

41. Steven B. Duke and Albert C. Gross, *America's Longest War: Rethinking our Tragic Crusade Against Drugs* (New York: Putnam, 1993), 157–58.

42. Ethan A. Nadelmann, "Global Prohibition Regimes: The Evolution of Norms in International Society," *International Organization* 44 (August 1990), 479–526.

43. Mathea Falco, "Foreign Drugs, Foreign Wars," *Daedalus*, summer 1992, 10.

44. Joseph J. Romm, *Defining National Security* (New York: Council on Foreign Relations, 1993), 14.

45. "Five Hundred Drug Geniuses," *Wall Street Journal*, June 10, 1998, A18. "We hope all these sophisticated folks won't feel their judgment is being too terribly offended if we say quite bluntly: They have just been enlisted in Mr. Soros's legalization crusade," the *Wall Street Journal* editorialized. The signers were "rounded up by an outfit bankrolled by financier George Soros, the man who underwrote the successful California effort to legalize 'medical marijuana.'"

46. "Use of Drugs by Teenagers Getting Worse," *Washington Post*, December 13, 1994, A17.

47. The National Household Survey on Drug Abuse, as reported in Suro, "Teens' Use of Drugs," A1, and Joyce Price, "Drug Use By Teens Doubles in 3 Years," *Washington Times*, August 21, 1996, A1.

48. Robert Suro, "Dip in Teen Drug Useis Hailed as Hopeful by Federal Officials," *Washington Post*, August 7, 1997, A10.

49. Bureau of Justice Statistics, *Drugs and Crime Facts, 1991* (Washington, D.C.: Government Printing Office, 1992).

50. Bureau of Justice Statistics, *Correctional Populations in the United States, 1991* (Washington, D.C.: Government Printing Office, 1993), 35.

51. Ibid., 5–6.

52. *Sourcebook of Criminal Justice Statistics, 1992*, 627. These data show that the rate of those committing offenses under the influence was almost double the rate (17.1 percent) of offenses committed in order to buy drugs. Prisoners were under the influence of drugs at the time of offense for 28.2 percent of violent

offenses, 35.4 percent of property offenses, 36.9 percent of drug offenses, and 18 percent of public order offenses. The rate for women was even higher, with 36.3 percent of the prisoners having been under the influence of drugs at the time of the offense. Data for women are from the *Sourcebook of Criminal Justice Statistics, 1993*, 622.

53. Roberto Suro, "Study Finds Decline in Teen Substance Abuse," *Washington Post*, December 19, 1998, A3.

54. William A. Donohue, *Twilight of Liberty: the Legacy of the ACLU* (New Brunswick, N.J.: Transaction Publishers, 1994), 255.

55. There has always been a role for the medicinal use of drugs. Morphine, developed from opium as a painkiller , minimizes opium's addictive qualities. The objective of medically prescribed drugs has been to maximize therapeutic effects while minimizing addictive side effects. The claim that cannabis serves as a genuine medicine can be made only to the degree that the pharmaceutical industry has determined its beneficial effects, synthesized the appropriate chemicals, and identified the conditions for which it is an appropriate remedy— all after extensive clinical trials. As the situation now stands, those who recommend the medical use of cannabis do so without knowing the quality of the plant, the appropriate dose for any disease, or the clinically determined side effects for various populations for which it may be an appropriate remedy. Advocates of using cannabis for various illnesses cannot point to any clinically controlled studies or any scientific standard for measuring plant quality, nor can they identify the populations for which the drug might be dangerous. Finally, no studies have yet been made to show that medicines derived from cannabis are better than other clinically approved medicines.

56. For a further discussion of the debate over drug legalization, see Evans and Berent, eds., *Drug Legalization*.

57. Huxley, *Brave New World Revisited*, 60.

58. Ibid., 60–61.

59. Leszek Kolakowski, *Main Currents of Marxism: The Breakdown*, vol. 3 (New York: Oxford University Press, 1978), 49.

CHAPTER 11

1. Bruce Russett, *Grasping the Democratic Peace: Principles for a Post–Cold War World* (Princeton, N.J.: Princeton University Press, 1993), 4; James Lee Ray, *Democracy and International Conflict* (Columbia: University of South Carolina Press, 1995); Rudolph J. Rummel, "Libertarianism and International Violence," *Journal of Conflict Resolution* 27, no. 1 (March 1983), 21–71; Stewart A. Bremer, "Dangerous Dyads: Interstate War, 1816–1965," *Journal of Conflict Resolution* 36, no. 2 (June 1992), 309–341.

2. Russett, *Grasping the Democratic Peace*, 11.

3. Ibid., 14.

4. Ibid., 31.

5. Ibid., 13–14.

6. Sun Tzu, *The Art of War* (New York: Oxford University Press, 1978), 77. "For to win one hundred victories in one hundred battles is not the acme of skill. To subdue the enemy without fighting is the acme of skill."

7. Carl von Clausewitz, *On War*, ed. and trans. by Michael Howard and Peter Paret (Princeton, N.J.: Princeton University Press, 1976), 87. According to von Clausewitz, "War is simply a continuation of political intercourse, with the addition of other means" 605.

8. Antonio Gramsci, *Selections from the Prison Notebooks*, ed. and trans. by Quintin Hoare and Geoffrey Nowell Smith (New York: International Publishers, 1992), 185. Gramsci's political strategy was to build up alternative social foundations to a predominant hegemony, which would then be replaced by a counterhegemony, with force being used only at the appropriate time to usher in the alternative order.

9. Russett, *Grasping the Democratic Peace*, ix.

10. Anthony Lake, "The Reach of Democracy: Tying Power to Diplomacy," *New York Times*, September 23, 1994, A35.

11. Mansfield and Snyder, "Democratization," 5–38.

12. Ibid., 17.

13. Ibid., 19–20.

14. Ibid., 22, 25.

15. Office of National Drug Control Policy (ONDCP), "United States and Mexico Counterdrug Cooperation," *Report to Congress*, vol. 1, September 1997, 1–43.

16. Anthony D. Smith, *The Ethnic Revival in the Modern World* (Cambridge: Cambridge University Press, 1981). See especially chapters 7 and 10.

17. A useful treatment of the rising indigenous movements in Latin America can be found in the NACLA *Report on the Americas* 29, no. 5 (March/April 1996).

18. John Ruggie introduced the idea of international regimes in 1975. He defined the international regime as "a set of mutual expectations, rules and regulations, plans, organizational energies and financial commitments, which have been accepted by a group of states." John Ruggie, "International Responses to Technology: Concepts and Trends," *International Organization* 29, no. 3, 570. A number of political scientists came up with a collective definition of international regimes as "sets of implicit or explicit principles, norms, rules and decision-making procedures around which actors' expectations converge in a given area of international relations." *Principles* they define as "beliefs of fact, causation, and rectitude," *norms* as "standards of behavior . . . in terms of rights and obligations," *rules* as "specific prescriptions or proscriptions for action," and *decision-making procedures* as "prevailing practices for making and implementing collective choice." Stephen D. Krasner, "Structural Causes and Regime Consequences: Regimes as Intervening Variables," in Stephen Krasner, ed., *International Regimes* (Ithaca, N.Y.: Cornell University Press, 1983), 2.

19. Quoted in Helleiner, *States and Global Finance*, 200.

20. Once a regime has been established, as the international monetary regime has been, it is generally considered that the marginal cost for adding new issue areas to it is lower than it would be to add issues without a preexisting regime. It is therefore considered normal to "nest" specific new agreements within regimes. For a discussion of nesting, see Robert O. Keohane, *After Hegemony: Cooperation and Discord in the World Political Economy* (Princeton, N.J.: Princeton University Press, 1984), 90–91.

21. See Barry Eichengreen, "Hegemonic Stability Theories of the International Monetary System," in *Can Nations Agree? Issues in International Economic Cooperation* (Washington, D.C.: Brookings Institution, 1989), 298. This article is also reprinted in Jeffry A. Frieden and David A. Lake, *International Political Economy: Perspective on Global Power and Wealth*, 3d ed., (New York: St. Martin's Press, 1995), 230–54.

22. Keohane, *After Hegemony*, 9. For readers primarily interested in the theoretical debates in international relations rather than in diagnostic issues, this study suggests that a dominant state's interest in cooperation, for domestic and international regime reasons, should and can prevail over structural anarchy and transnational capitalist interests. It does not suggest that such a result is inevitable, only that if accountable government is desired, then a realistic international relations theory will understand states as fragmented rather than as unified and rational, actors and capital as potentially either sustaining or undermining state autonomy. An accountable international regime will regulate capital flows that undermine an accountable domestic state's regime. Drug politics is a test for an institutionalist realist approach to international politics. If anocracies and speculative capital interests prevail, then pessimistic realist predictions will unfortunately be normative and diagnostic.

23. David A. Andelman, "The Drug Money Maze," *Foreign Affairs* 73, no. 4 (July-August 1994), 106.

24. Ibid.

25. Andrea M. Grilli, "Preventing Billions from Being Washed Offshore: A Growing Approach to Stopping International Drug Trafficking," *Syracuse Journal of International Law and Commerce* 1465, 65–88.

26. Office of National Drug Control Policy (ONDCP), "Enhanced Multilateral Drug Control Cooperation," *Report to Congress*, vol. 1, September 1997, 1–18.

27. John LaWare, testimony before the U.S. House Committee on Banking, Finance, and Urban Affairs, May 26, 1993, *Federal Reserve Bulletin*, July 1993, 689–94.

28. Mark Arend, "Money Laundering Law Is (So Far) Mostly a Blessing," *ABA Banking Journal*, February 1993, 69–71.

29. John LaWare, testimony before the U.S. House Committee on Banking, Finance, and Urban Affairs, Subcommittee on International Development, Finance, Trade and Monetary Policy, November 9, 1993, 19–22.

30. For a discussion of the dilemmas facing states in the globalizing economy, see Peter Evans, "The Eclipse of the State? Reflections on Stateness in an Era of Globalization," World Politics 50, no. 1 (October 1997), 62–87.

CHAPTER 12

1. *Washington Post,* June 8, 1997, A18.

2. Inglis, *Opium War,* 35.

3. Jimmie L. Reeves and Richard Campbell, *Cracked Coverage* (Durham, N.C.: Duke University Press, 1994).

4. *Ways to a Drug-Free Society and Physiopathology of Illicit Drugs,* (Zurich: VPM, 1991).

SELECTED BIBLIOGRAPHY

BOOKS

Bagley, Bruce Michael, and William O. Walker III, eds. *Drug Trafficking in the Americas*. New Brunswick, N.J.: Transaction Publishers, 1994.

Beaty, Jonathan, and S. C. Gwynne. *The Outlaw Bank: A Wild Ride into the Secret Heart of BCCI*. New York: Random House, 1993.

Bork, Robert H. *The Tempting of America: The Political Seduction of the Law*. New York: The Free Press, 1990.

Brown, Michael E., ed. *Ethnic Conflict and International Security*. Princeton, N.J.: Princeton University Press, 1993.

Castaneda, Jorge G., and Robert A. Pastor. *Limits to Friendship: The United States and Mexico*. New York: Knopf, 1988.

Chang, Hsin-pao. *Commissioner Lin and the Opium War*. New York: Norton, 1964.

Clark, Ronald W. *The Huxleys*. London: Heinemann, 1968.

Clausewitz, Carl von. *On War*. Edited and translated by Michael Howard and Peter Paret. Princeton, N.J.: Princeton University Press, 1976.

Collis, Maurice. *Foreign Mud: The Opium Imbroglio at Canton in the 1830s and the Anglo-Chinese War*. New York: Norton,

Dahl, Robert A. *Polyarchy: Participation and Opposition*. New Haven, Conn.: Yale University Press, 1971.

Donohue, William A. *Twilight of Liberty: The Legacy of the ACLU*. New Brunswick, N.J.: Transaction Publishers 1994.

Douglass, Joseph D., Jr. *Red Cocaine: The Drugging of America*. Atlanta: Clarion House, 1990.

Duke, Steven B., and Albert C. Gross. *America's Longest War: Rethinking Our Tragic Crusade Against Drugs*. New York: Putnam, 1993.

269

Ehrenfeld, Rachel. *Evil Money: Encounters along the Money Trail.* New York: Harper Business, 1992.

Evans, Rod L., and Irwin M. Berent, eds. *Drug Legalization: For and Against.* La Salle, Ill.: Open Court, 1992.

Gottlieb, Gidon. *Nation against State.* New York: Council on Foreign Relations Press, 1993 .

Gramsci, Antonio. *Selections from the Prison Notebooks.* Edited and translated by Quintin Hoare and Geoffrey Nowell Smith. New York: International Publishers, 1992.

Gurwin, Larry. *The Calvi Affair: Death of a Banker.* London: Macmillan Company, 1983.

Handelman, Stephen. *Comrade Criminal: Russia's New Mafiya.* New Haven, Conn.: Yale University Press, 1995.

Hereth, Michael. *Alexis de Tocqueville: Threats to Freedom in Democracy.* Durham, N.C.: Duke University Press, 1986.

Higley, John, and Richard Gunther, eds. *Elites and Democratic Consolidation in Latin America and Southern Europe.* Cambridge: Cambridge University Press, 1992.

Huntington, Samuel P. *The Third Wave.* Norman: University of Oklahoma Press, 1991.

―――. *The Clash of Civilizations?* New York: Foreign Affairs Reader, 1993.

Jordan, David C. *Revolutionary Cuba and the End of the Cold War.* Lanham, Md.: University Press of America, 1993.

Kelly, Robert J., ed. *Organized Crime: A Global Perspective.* Totowa, N.J.: Roman and Littlefield, 1986.

Kolakowski, Leszek. *Main Currents of Marxism: The Breakdown.* Vol. 3. New York: Oxford University Press, 1978.

Leary, Timothy. *Changing My Mind, among Others: Lifetime Writings, Selected and Introduced by the Author.* Englewood Cliffs, N.J.: Prentice-Hall, 1982.

Lee, Rensselaer W., III. *The White Labyrinth: Cocaine and Political Power.* New Brunswick, N.J.: Transaction Publishers, 1991.

Machiavelli, Niccolo. *The Discourses.* New York: Modern Library, 1950.

Mainwaring, Scott, Guillermo O'Donnell, and Samuel J. Valenzuela, eds. *Issues in Democratic Consolidation: The New South American Democracies in Comparative Perspective.* Notre Dame, Ind.: University of Notre Dame Press, 1992.

McCoy, Alfred W. *The Politics of Heroin: CIA Complicity in the Global Drug Trade.* New York: Lawrence Hill Books, 1991.

McCoy, Alfred W., and Alan A. Block, eds. *War on Drugs: Studies in the Failure of U.S. Narcotics Policy.* San Francisco: Westview Press, 1992.

Morris, Stephen D. *Corruption and Politics in Contemporary Mexico.* Tuscaloosa: University of Alabama Press, 1991.

Mosca, Gaetano. *The Ruling Class.* New York: McGraw-Hill, 1939.

Pielke, Robert G. *You Say You Want a Revolution: Rock Music in American Culture.* Chicago: Nelson-Hall, 1986.

Powis, Robert E. *The Money Launderers: Lessons from the Drug Wars—How Billions of Illegal Dollars Are Washed through Banks and Businesses.* Chicago: Probus, 1992.

Romm, Joseph J. *Defining National Security.* New York: Council on Foreign Relations, 1993.

Russett, Bruce. *Grasping the Democratic Peace: Principles for a Post–Cold War World.* Princeton, N.J.: Princeton University Press, 1993.

Sandoz, Ellis, ed. *Political Sermons of the American Founding Era: 1730–1805.* Indianapolis: Liberty Press, 1991.

Schumpeter, Joseph. *Capitalism, Socialism and Democracy.* Harper & Brothers. 1947.

Scott, Peter Dale, and Jonathan Marshall. *Cocaine Politics: Drugs, Armies and the CIA in Central America.* Berkeley: University of California Press, 1991.

Sorensen, Theodore C. *Las Perspectivas para unas Elecciones Libres, Limpias y Honestas en Mexico: Un Informe ante El Consejo Coordinador Empresarial,* August 15, 1994.

Sterling, Claire H. *Thieves' World.* New York: Simon & Schuster, 1994.

Sun Tzu, *The Art of War.* New York: Oxford University Press, 1978.

Tocqueville, Alexis de. *Democracy in America.* Vols. 1 and 2. New York: Vintage, 1972.

Truell, Peter, and Larry Gurwin. *False Profits: The Inside Story of BCCI, the World's Most Corrupt Financial Empire.* Boston: Houghton Mifflin, 1992.

Valle, Eduardo. *El Segundo Disparo: La Narcodemocracia Mexicana.* Mexico, D.F.: Editoria Oceano de Mexico, 1995.

Waldo, Dwight. *Political Science in America.* Paris: Unesco, 1956

Wells, H. G., *The Open Conspiracy,* London: Doubleday, Doran, 1928.

ARTICLES

Alva Bri, Carlos, "El fraude-contubernia Banpesca que cometieron Ojeda, Cabal y De la Madrid C." *Quehacer Politico* 679 (September 12, 1994).

Andelman, David A. "The Drug Money Maze." *Foreign Affairs* 73, no. 4, (July-August 1994).

Andonaegui, Ricardo H. "Culpa El Buho al cartel del Golfo del homicidio de Colosio." *El Dia,* September 5, 1994.

Arend, Mark. "Money Laundering Law Is (So Far) Mostly a Blessing." *ABA Banking Journal,* February 1993.

Arista, Tizoc. "Quienes son los políticos complices de Cabal y que aun lo protegen." *Quehacer Politico* 679 (September 12, 1994).

Banerjee, Neela. "Russian Organized Crime Goes Global: Gangs Use Skills Honed in Former Police State." *Wall Street Journal,* December 22, 1994.

Barrera Barrera, Juan. "Temor y Sospecha Asedian Hasta Insurgentes del Norte." *Punto*, October 10, 1994.

Biema, David van. "Sweet, Sweet Surrender: A Cali Cartel Chief Proposes to Give Up on Conditions So Lenient That They May Strain U.S.-Colombian Relations." *Time*, November 7, 1994.

Boaz, David. "The Legalization of Drugs", *Vital Speeches of the Day*, May 15, 1988.

Branigan, William. "Newly Named Mexican Officials Linked to Drugs." *Washington Post*, January 7, 1989.

———. "DEA Agent's '85 Death Still Entangles Mexicans." *Washington Post*, September 14, 1989.

Brooke, James. "Venezuelans Secretly Support Army Coup Plotters." *New York Times*, February 9, 1992.

Burke, Melvin. "Bolivia: The Politics of Cocaine." *Current History*, February 1991.

Carreno, Jose. "Solo las autoridades federales pudieron perpetrar el asesinato de LDC." *El Universal*, August 26, 1994.

Carroll, Paul, and Diane Solis. "Garcia is Enemy in Mexican War on Drugs." *Wall Street Journal*, December 13, 1994.

Celarier, Michelle. "Gangster Economics." *Global Finance*, September 1993, Vol. 7.

Coello, Juan José. "Vivimos narco-democracia." *Reforma*, May 11, 1994.

Cortes, Dora Elena. "Es Muñóz Rocha agente del grupo político de Hank González?" *El Universal*, October 10, 1994.

Doyle, Kate. "The Militarization of the Drug War in Mexico." *Current History*, February 1993.

Dubashi, Jagannath. "The Bank That Knows Too Much." *Financial World*, November 29, 1988.

Estevez, Dolia. "Unida y sin Obstáculos se Prepara la Mafia a Expandir y Afianzar su Control Sobre el Mundo." *El Financiero*, September 6, 1994.

———. "'México, Blanco de las Mafias; Alianza Mundial Para Subvertir el Orden', Dice Brian Crozier." *El Financiero*, September 21, 1994.

Falco, Mathea. "Foreign Drugs, Foreign Wars." *Daedalus*, summer 1992.

Farah, Douglas. "Cali's Quiet Cartel Becomes Number One." *Washington Post*, October 17, 1990.

———. "Rid of Rivals, Flush with Cash." *Washington Post*, June 16, 1994.

Fernández Menendez, Jorge. "Un narcodemócrata." *El Financiero*, Feb. 12, 1996.

Flynn, Stephen. "Worldwide Drug Scourge." *Brookings Review*, winter 1993.

Fowler, Thomas B. "Winning the War on Drugs: Can We Get There from Here?" *Journal of Social, Political and Economic Studies* 15, no. 4 (winter 1990).

González, Maribel. "Planearon políticos crimen de Colosio." *Reforma*, August 26, 1994.

Graham, Robert. "Andreotti Bound Over in Slaying of Editor: Already on Trial in Mafia-Links Case." *Washington Times*, November 6, 1995.

Grilli, Andrea M. "Preventing Billions from Being Washed Offshore: A Growing Approach to Stopping International Drug Trafficking." *Syracuse Journal of International Law and Commerce* 1465.

Gurr, Ted Robert. "Persistence and Change in Political Systems, 1800–1971." *American Political Science Review* 68, no. 4, December 1974.

Handelman, Stephen. "The Russian Mafia." *Foreign Affairs*, March-April 1994.

Johnston Hernández, Beatriz. "Del expediente de un juicio en Texas: Como subprocurador, Coello Trejo recibió 'mas de un millón de dólares' de García Abrego." *Proceso* 934 (September 26, 1994).

Kattoulas, Velisarios. "Japan's Yakuza Claim Place Among Criminal Elite." *Washington Times*, November 25, 1994.

Klebnikov, Paul. "Joe Stalin's Heirs." *Forbes*, September 27, 1993.

Kurth, James. "The Real Clash." *National Interest* 37 (fall 1994).

Labrousse, Alain. "Dependence on Drugs: Unemployment, Migration and an Alternative Path to Development in Bolivia." *International Labor Review* 129, no. 3, (1990).

Lake, Anthony. "The Reach of Democracy: Tying Power to Diplomacy." *New York Times*, September 23, 1994.

Mansfield, Edward D., and Jack Snyder. "Democratization and the Danger of War." *International Security* 20, no. 1 (summer 1995).

Marcus, David. "Drug Cartel, Lawyers Feel Heat Rising." *Dallas Morning News*, June 10, 1995.

Marin, Carlos. "No se quiere reconocer una descomposición generalizada del aparato que se comprometió con el tráfico de drogas." *Proceso* 937 (October 17, 1994).

Meloni, Robert S. "Secret Meetings in Arkansas." *Wall Street Journal*, May 13, 1994.

Mergier, Anne Marie. "Ofensiva de Moussavi: 'IBM me pidió llegar a un arreglo, Caso obstaculizó a la justicia y la Contraloria lo avaló.'" *Proceso* 857 (April 5, 1993).

———. "Moussavi acusa: 'Andres Caso fue objeto de una acusación muy seria, se pedía su encarcelamiento . . . pero todo quedó enterrado.'" *Proceso* 859 (April 19, 1993).

Miller, Marjorie. "Mexico's War on Drugs Confronts Enemy Within." *Los Angeles Times*, June 21, 1993.

Munguia, Jacinto R. "La negligencia oficial facilitó los autoprestamos" and "El escandalo Cabal descubre a notables exfuncionarios: De la Madrid, su hijo y Rovirosa niegan ser socios del profugo." *Punto*, September 12, 1994.

Olgun Islas, Rosa Maria. "Carlos Cabal: ascenso de vertigo, caida de rayo." *Punto*, September 12, 1994.

———. "Crímenes en serio para controlar congreso y PRI." *Punto*, October 17, 1994.

Philipsborn, Chris. "Cocaine Squeeze." *New Statesman and Society*, February 12, 1993.

Puig, Carlos. "'No afirmo nada: solo pido que se investigue' . . . y Eduardo Valle Da Nombres y Mas Nombres." *Proceso* 931 (September 5, 1994).

Ramírez, Carlos. "Indicador Político." *El Financiero*, September 9, 1994.

———. "El otro choque de trenes." *El Financiero*, September 9, 1994.

Ramos, Alejandro, Jenaro Villamil, Victor Batta, Jose Luis Ramírez, Fernando García, Edgar Hernández, and Berta Alicia Galindo. "Organized Crime: Transnational Threat." *El Financiero* (special edition), October 9, 1994.

Rojas-Zea, Rodolfo. "Narcotráfico, la Multinacional Mas Importante del Crímen." *El Financiero*, May 15, 1994.

Silva M., José. "Patrones tabasquenos califican como una tragedia la caida de Cabal Peniche." *Quehacer Politico* 679 (September 12, 1994).

Solis, Dianne. "A Key Leader in Mexico's PRI is Assassinated." *Wall Street Journal*, September 29, 1994.

Sterling, Claire. "Redfellas." *New Republic*, April 11, 1994.

Stormont, Diane. "Hong Kong Gangs Are on the Move: Triads Follow Immigrants Abroad." *Washington Times*, November 25, 1994.

Strong, Simon. "Peru Is Losing More than the Drug War." *New York Times*, February 17, 1992.

Sweet, Robert W. "The War on Drugs Is Lost." *National Review* 48, no. 2 (February 12, 1996).

Valle, Eduardo. "Carlos Marin, 'Alerté a Colosio y comenzó a dar pasos para librarse de los narcopolíticos, pero se le adelantaron.'" *Proceso* 925 (August 15, 1994).

Weinberger, Casper. "Davos and Russia." *Forbes*, March 28, 1994.

Weinraub, Bernard. "David Geffen: Still Hungry." *New York Times Magazine*, May 2, 1994.

Whalen, Christopher. "Mexico: The Narco System." *Dinero* (Colombia). English trans., *List Mexico 2000*, November, 29, 1995.

Yarbro, Stan. "Cocaine Trade Shifts in Colombia." *Christian Science Monitor*, June 30, 1991.

York, Geoffry. "Majority of Russia's Rich Once Were Top Communists." *Washington Times*, September 24, 1994.

NEWSPAPERS AND PERIODICALS

ABA Banking Journal
America and the World
American Political Science Review
Brookings Review
Carpeta Purpura, La (Mexico City)
Christian Science Monitor
Current History
Daedalus
Dallas Morning News
Defining National Security
Dia, El (Mexico City)

Diario Las Americas
Dinero
Economist
Excelsior (Mexico City)
FBIS: Latin America
Financial World
Financiero, El (Mexico City)
Forbes
Foreign Affairs
Global Finance
Huellas (Mexico City)
International Labor Review
International Security
Jornada, La (Mexico City)
Journal of Social, Political and Economic Studies
Latin American Regional Reports
Latin American Weekly Report
List Mexico 2000
Los Angeles Times
Managing Auditing Journal
National Interest
National Review
New Republic
New Statesman and Society
New York Times
New York Times Magazine
Proceso (Mexico City)
Punto (Mexico City)
Quehacer Politico (Mexico City)
Reforma (Mexico City)
Sunday Telegraph (London)
Syracuse Journal of International Law and Commerce
Time
Universal, El (Mexico City)
Wall Street Journal
Washington Post
Washington Times

GOVERNMENT DOCUMENTS AND CONGRESSIONAL TESTIMONIES

Bureau of Justice Statistics. *Correctional Population of the United States, 1991.* Washington, D.C.: Government Printing Office, 1993.

Bureau of Justice Statistics. *Drugs and Crime Facts, 1991.* Washington, D.C. : Government Printing Office, 1992.

Congressional Record, U.S. Senate, March 10, 1989.

Corruption and Drugs in Colombia: Democracy at Risk. Staff Report to the U.S. Senate Committee on Foreign Relations. Washington, D.C.: U.S. Government Printing Office, February 1996.

Greene, Stephen H. "DEA's Role in Attacking Narcotics Trafficking in the Western Hemisphere." Statement before the U.S. Senate Foreign Relations Subcommittee on the Western Hemisphere. April 4, 1995.

House Committee on Banking, Finance, and Urban Affairs. *Federal Governments Response to Money Laundering: Hearings before the House Committee on Banking, Finance, and Urban Affairs.* May 25–26, 1993.

———. *Hearing before the Committee on Banking, Finance and Urban Affairs,* 102d Cong., 1st sess., Part 1, September 11, 1991.

———. *Hearing before the Committee on Banking, Finance, and Urban Affairs,* May 26, 1993. *Federal Reserve Bulletin,* July 1993.

LaWare, John P. Testimony before the Subcommittee on International Development, Finance, Trade, and Monetary Policy of the U.S. Committee on Banking, Finance and Urban Affairs, November 9, 1993.

McClintock, Cynthia. "Opportunities and Constraints to Source Reduction of Coca: The Peruvian Socio-Political Context." U.S. House, Office of Technology Assessment, H3-495.0, Washington, D.C.: Government Printing Office, 1992.

Olson, William J. Testimony before the U.S. Senate Foreign Relations Subcommittee on the Western Hemisphere, April 4, 1995.

Sourcebook of Criminal Justice Statistics, 1992.

Sourcebook of Criminal Justice Statistics, 1993.

U.S. Department of State. Bureau of International Narcotics Matters. *International Narcotics Control Strategy Report.* Washington, D.C.: Government Printing Office, 1993.

U.S. House. *Joint Hearing of the Committee on Foreign Affairs: The Situation in Peru and the Future of the War on Drugs,* 102d Cong., 2d sess. Washington, D.C.: Government Printing Office, 1992.

Youngers, Coletta. *Key Congressional Concerns regarding Peru.* Washington, D.C.: Washington Office on Latin America, 1992.

Supreme Court Cases

Lemon v. Kurtzman, 403 U.S. 602 (1970).

Stone v. Graham, 449 U.S. 30 (1980).

Wallace v. Jaffree, 472 U.S. 38 (1985).

ACLU v. Allegheny County 492 U.S. 573 (1989).

INDEX

Abedi, Agha Hassan, 109, 110, 111
Aburto Martínez, Mario, 146, 147, 148
Accountability, 19, 28, 38, 39, 42, 46, 214;
  in anocracies, 24, 119; corruption and,
  28–29, 35; in democracies, 21–23, 28, 37,
  38, 46–49, 74, 224; in mixed regime, 46;
  narcostatization and, 22, 28, 51, 52, 141;
  religion and, 43
ACT-UP, 187
Adonis, Joe, 89
Afghanistan war, 66, 67, 97, 110
Aguilar Guajardo, Rafael, 86
Aguilar Trevino, Daniel, 154
AIDS, 186, 192
Alaska, 188
Alcide Beltrones, Roberto, 147, 148
Aldana Ibarra, Miguel, 86
Allen, Paul, 182
Almond, Gabriel, 40
Altman, Robert, 254n.32
Alvarez del Castillo, Enrique, 86–87
American Banking Holding Company, 110
American Civil Liberties Union (ACLU),
  183, 187
American Express, 105
American Federation of Musicians (AFM),
  89
American Indians, 105, 176
America's Longest War (Duke and Gross),
  188
Amphetamines, 227, 228
Anarchy, international, 11, 12
Andean Commission of Jurists (CAJ), 132,
  137

Andean Drug Summit (1990), 129
Andelman, David A., 207, 208
Andreas, Peter, 13–14, 130–31, 134
Andreotti, Guilio, 247n.19
Angel dust (phencyclidine; PCP), 227
Angiulo crime family, 112
Annucio-Wylie Anti-Money-Laundering
  Act (1992), 210–12
Anocracies, 9, 21, 22, 24, 39, 119–20, 141,
  174, 193, 196–99, 225–26; Colombia, 158,
  170; Mexico, 143–45, 157; Peru, 132;
  Russia, 120, 126
Anocratization process, 21–22, 119–20,
  167–69, 197, 240n.2
Anslinger, Harry J., 91
Antielitist theory, 26
Apollo Group, 49
Aréllano Félix family, 85, 86, 203
Arévalo Gardoqui, Juan, 86
Argentina, 65, 109
Arizona, 81, 188
Arkansas, 89, 98
Armella, Pedro Aspe, 152
Arms dealing, 66, 75, 76, 84, 98, 110, 111,
  126, 128
Aronson, Bernard, 262n.32
Aruba, 78, 98, 103, 165
Arvey, James, 92
Asian criminal syndicates, 79–82
Atlantic City, New Jersey, 89, 93–94
Authoritarian elites, 43–44, 72, 73, 124,
  126; Peruvian, 131
Authoritarian regimes, 6, 9, 26, 27, 119–20,
  157